THE OCHRE PEOPLE

THE
OCHRE

Scenes from a South African Life

PEOPLE

by NONI JABAVU

ST MARTIN'S PRESS   NEW YORK

First published in the United States of America 1963
Copyright © 1963 by Noni Jabavu
All rights reserved
Library of Congress Catalog Card Number: 63-18766
Manufactured in the United States of America
Published in Great Britain by John Murray, 1963

For Roger

Contents

Acknowledgements

Some writers are comparatively self-contained and can work without constant support from their friends. I must confess that I am not one of them, and am immeasurably indebted to a number of people for crucial help given in individual and imaginative ways:

My husband Michael Cadbury Crosfield; Mr. Peregrine Worsthorne; my kin in South Africa Mrs. Z. K. Matthews and Mrs. Frank Lebentlele who checked facts and references; Lady (Montagu) Norman; her brother-in-law Mr. R. C. Norman; Mr. James Cameron; Mr. Robert Graves; Baroness Ravensdale of Kedleston; Mr. Burnet Webster; Mr. Simon Watson-Taylor; Viscount Dunluce and his parents the Earl and Countess of Antrim.

And as always, my publishers Mrs. Osyth Leeston and Mr. John Grey Murray to both of whom I am most deeply and affectionately grateful for unfailing encouragement, assistance and understanding throughout the writing of this book.

N.J.

Author's Note

May I have a word surreptitiously with Xhosa-speaking readers – *'bite their ear'*, as we say?

The present Orthography of the language came into general use after I had learnt its predecessor and I have never become reconciled to it. I dislike the appearance of symbols like 'th' for aspirated 't'; marks for tone pitch; double vowels in plural noun-prefixes, verb tenses, demonstratives, ideophones, and so on.

This is the reason why, where I have written out a Xhosa sentence, my spelling is erratic. I am among those who, *'eating with the old-fashioned spoon'*, believe that for languages so 'dominantly vocalic in character' as Professor G. P. Lestrade described the group to which Xhosa belongs, nothing short of a new script should be devised. The roman is not suitable, and will always make for troublesome – and ugly – reading or writing.

And may I ask English-speaking readers also to forgive me in their turn? For I have here and there unconsciously inflected a word according to Xhosa rules in trying to convey a non-English thought. When my publishers' reader pointed out that it was an invented construction, I decided to risk letting it remain because it seemed to me that the 'new' word came closer to the meaning I hoped to render than the one which would have been grammatically correct.

Part One

MIDDLEDRIFT

1

OUR house at Middledrift bustled with activity. Women servants hurried, cleaning, polishing floors, door-knobs, dusting.

I sauntered out into the garden and round into the 'yard' as the space at the back is called, by the rain-water tanks and kitchen door, and saw MaDhlamini, one of the women, hard at work. She had just come out of the house carrying mats from bedrooms, about to shake and air them in the back-yard.

Rays of sunlight slanted on the patches of bare ground and yellowed grass on which she trod. They swept over the surrounding countryside which was still covered with dew and shone on it so that the drops flashed and glittered in brilliant colours like strewn diamonds; but where she walked her footmarks put them out, and left dull patches.

The sun lit up her brown cheeks. She trotted quickly, like a stout pony, held the mats away from her body, and her bulky, old-world type of dress buffeted against her bare heels and ankles. Like all women of her class she wore several cotton petticoats under her skirt. As she moved they swung from her thick waist and fleshy hips and gave her the look of quite another sort of plebeian woman, that of the English working women Hogarth liked to portray – large bosom, brawny arms, elbows akimbo.

As I came from one end of the yard I saw a man walking along the path beyond our fence. When he caught sight of her he stopped for a moment and watched her, his head on one side, then said in an exploratory tone of voice, 'How busy you seem to be, sister-of-ours!' His bearded face broke into an expectant smile: he was inviting her to tell him what was going on in the professor's household. She was glad to respond.

'Oh indeed – busy, *busy!* We have visitors, we have been arrived-upon!' They spoke in our language, Xhosa, the voices raised in tones of exclamation; to talk, exchange news was a pleasure.

3

'The maternal uncle of the children has come from *emaXho-seni*!' She had dumped the mats on a wooden bench, shaken one with vigour while she talked, and now took up another.

'Is that a fact? Gambu is here from the Transkei?' . . . Everyone in the region knew that my father's first people-in-law, the Makiwane family, were of the Gambu clan. I had many maternal 'uncles', two of them my mother's surviving real brothers. Others were her cousins or second cousins, but all regarded as close relations because of the extended family system. But the man would know that our servant meant my mother's eldest brother, not having qualified 'the maternal uncle' as she would have done for a lesser one. The stranger would also know that although my father had remarried the year before, she did not mean the second set of in-laws; there were no children of this marriage, so she meant my sister and me.

'That is the fact.' She smiled, and now stopped shaking a mat to point at an old black American saloon motor car outside the garage at the top end of the yard. Small boys from the village had come to wash it down. They were on their way to primary school, a white-washed building on the bend of the hill where our house stood. Their little pile of dog-eared textbooks were childishly balanced on a stone by the clump of red hot poker flowers growing beside the fence.

'There's the wagon that brought him,' she cried. 'Do you see the number plate, "CCY"? the town of Umtata, in the Transkei!'

The man turned and looked at the motor car and exclaimed. She continued: 'And we have been arrived-upon from overseas as well. The eldest daughter of the house is home.'

'Ye-s? I have heard it said-so,' he said, encouraging her by that interrogatory, expectant tone and shifting his position so as to stand and listen more comfortably.

'And here she comes, the calf of here-at-home,' and pointed towards me, 'Our MaJili, *u*Nontando whom her English marriage-people overseas call "Noni".'

I had not in fact flown from England this time but from East Africa. But since I normally lived in London, ordinary people thought only of that.

4

The man looked at me and gave a great exclamation. The sun was getting stronger. While I was being looked at by them both, I felt it warming the back of my neck, my arms, and noticed how it lit the different shades of brown of their complexions. The passer-by narrowed his eyes under the brim of his battered Stetson hat and scrutinized me. He clapped his bony hands together in delight, exclaimed again louder than ever.

'*What!* Do you say so? From across the sea? Oh I beg you sister, greet her for me, greet her!'

I smiled, said nothing; it was not expected of me. I only halted in my tracks to acknowledge the welcome. I saw the young motor car cleaners too, stop what they were doing to watch the exchange between their elders, chamois leather cloths in air.

'Tell her that the village welcomes her; a person who is *much-prized*, being child of our professor. I share his joy in this arrival! Yours too, sister – whose clan name, by the way, eludes me . . . indeed, to be truthful I do not think I actually know it?'

'Dhlamini,' she helped him on the instant.

'Aha, *your* joy too, I say then, Dhlamini-the-beautiful!' He sang out the stylized phrase like music and waved his hand, which made me notice his frayed sleeve – a gesture that was chivalrous and, to me, touching.

She was certainly not among the beauties of her fellow pagan women who dress in 'red blanket' robes, the looks of many of whom are arresting indeed because of the flowing costume. It was because of her job in a Westernized household that, pagan though she was, she did not wear the traditional ochre-coloured garments but dressed in the manner of 'Christian, Westernized or *school* people'. Unsophisticated Xhosa rural women of her type like to wear the kind of ankle-length voluminous skirts that she had on, usually made of dark blue cotton spotted with white designs and formerly imported from Germany. They call it 'German (cloth) – *ijamani*', buy it by the yard at 'Kaffir Goods' stores everywhere. She tied a white apron round her waist, knotted the tapes in a bow at the back and the ends trailed behind. The sleeves of her blouse were pushed up to the elbow and enhanced the effect of industriousness and enthusiasm for her work. And of course she wore the married woman's big turban. An unremarkable person like millions of others. But for the man to add the epithet 'beautiful' to her clan salutation was one of the courtesies, styles of language that delighted me when I heard them again after being away from South Africa. And I almost guessed what he would say next in the pattern of such a conversation. He continued : '*Kaloku* this joy is shared, is it not so? Does not the presence of children at home warm the parental heart? That father of hers is *our person* – understand? But of course you understand; of *course*! We feel what he feels, what you must feel, friend, when flesh and blood comes home.'

The stranger looked intently at me and I looked at him. He was lean, scraggy, obviously not always able to afford to eat as much as he would like. MaDhlamini looked from him to me with a proprietary grin. Goodwill exuded. I was aware that the small boys smiled deferentially as they watched. It occurred to me that as they stood quietly in the background and daily saw such scenes, they absorbed the traditional behaviour and actions of elders, would unthinkingly reproduce it in their turn when grown up.

'I shall call on our professor, to pay my respects about this matter one of these days. Just now I am only in my working clothes, you see' . . . his hands dropped to his sides to point at the patched and ragged trousers, the long bare feet jutting from them. His gestures were expressive, reminding me of those that Goya captured in portraits despite the differences in subject and colours. It must have been because of the fingers – gnarled, long, slender; they looked like those of a deeply sensitive man.

'I am heading for my Europeans, going to work. There will be a time to put aside this threadbareness and make a seemly visit to the household and salute its prized arrivals,' he said, his voice taking on a tone of great dignity and seriousness. I had been home for over a month but people were still 'saluting and rejoicing' in the unhasty tempo of country life.

There was a silence brought on by that change of voice when he made the promise, for was it not allusion to a slightly ritualistic matter? In the silence he continued to gaze at me. I became self-conscious until presently I felt impelled to murmur something. It was politely ignored, however. Words from me were not called for. (Later, when I felt totally established again in the ways in which things were done at home I did not feel such embarrassments.) Everyone went on gazing. My presence aroused many thoughts about families, about the intricate balance of personalities within them in the kind of life we knew, whose customs were changing yet unchanging. Finally and with a loud sigh, he turned his gaze back to MaDhlamini. She again began to shake out her mats. And, released, I started to walk again to the house, to the doorway into the passage by the kitchen. Their comments rang on in my wake for they had not finished yet; the exchange had still to pass into another phase, a coda as it were, to round things off. The voices rose higher. I heard MaDhlamini declaim:

'Ah yes, brother, this household is now a *home* – with people who have *travelled* to return to it.'

'Thank God,' he declaimed back, 'that we people still *travel*! God gave us feet to use. Would we belong to this South Africa had we not been seasoned wayfarers in olden days? Travelled from far, not afraid of the road – oh, not we! Is it not Cape Town for this one, Jo'burg for that, a thousand miles from this Border province? Why, I too went to Queenstown year before last. I *move* too, in my ramshackle way! Not in cars or aeroplanes like the great among us but in third-class coaches, pounding my arse on those hard benches for Natives Only, packed tight like Sinners Burning in Hell – eh? But it is travel nevertheless. Let it always be so. Let our people go and come to one another, for do we not say "The foot hath no nose", dear friend?'

They were absolutely hollering by this time – the opening bars not having been strictly *piano* either. Their voices now seemed to fill the entire countryside, especially at the burst of laughter at that reference to low class Native railway transportation. And thinking of his earlier reference to the Europeans he worked for as gardener, I remembered the usual reaction of such employers to the noisy sociability of African servants, when they forbid the entertaining of friends or passers-by. It must be difficult indeed to tolerate these 'passings of the time of day' if you are not involved in the social structure that they mark. And

7

if you are deaf to the use of language, stranger to the intense pleasures of its subtleties, intricacies, overtones, allusions, the whole thing must seem indescribably tiresome. I could and did enjoy such encounters because I was part of the structure. The longer I lived abroad, the more I seemed to extract from it when home. 'Absence makes the heart grow fonder.' I felt something akin to a renewal, a strengthening, when I heard our maid shout back her 'finale' (for at last the man was going), 'God speed you, brother. "*The foot hath no nose*", that is the big truth. We are happy today because it has led our people back to us. *I* am doubly happy for I had not seen the maternal uncle nor this MaJili; I came to serve the family during her absence. Now the feet so-splendid have righted that!'

I passed into the house and thought of the friends in England who always ask how I could bear to revisit South Africa; so did many white friends in South Africa itself. But of these some, who had lived for generations in country hamlets like mine, could understand the influences that pulled. They had shared in the atmosphere that prevailed when I was growing up in a small town. Its inhabitants were of the various modern South African races: Africans, English, Jewish shopkeepers, Boers (who now wish to be called 'Afrikaans' but we cannot get used to it), Coloureds. There was even the isolated Indian shopkeeper. The distinctions had existed naturally, but did not threaten as now, to transcend the interest in individuals: their deeds or misdeeds, their setting in families established or newly arrived, their eccentricities, their efforts misguided or commendable; the wild hopes that some of them would on occasion suddenly entertain, the plans that sometimes came off, sometimes crashed. If you grew up in such personal contacts you liked to feel that even *apartheid* is only another framework, a transitory one – like other policies that had framed people's lives in other times. So to go home is for me always an experience.

My family elders were in the sitting-room. I joined them and found myself thinking about the way we used to live when I was young. I was 'adult' now, but so long as your parents are alive, when in their house you are never really regarded as such. You are not expected to speak until spoken to, for one thing. So while they talked among themselves I could follow the thoughts that the sight of them and sound of their voices provoked in my mind.

The three big people, elders in the house, my father, my uncle, my stepmother, had gone out after breakfast and, while I was sauntering outside the house, had been carrying out their own routine.

It was different now from when I was a child. But enough of it remained to make one's return seem like a journey back into the security and comforts of those days.

That was my feeling for instance earlier that day, when the story of this particular visit begins and of the changes that were to come in the months ahead.

The women servants had started on the housework before daybreak – and oh, how it had taken me back to hear them sweep passages, turn out the sitting-room, my father's study, the dining-room. So did even the way in which they muffled the sounds as much as possible and only spoke in whispers, if at all, because the family still slept; for I used to lie half awake listening – and now found myself doing so again.

Then they left off to get ready our morning cups of coffee in bed. After they had served these, they prepared our washing arrangements. My father liked to have his bath in the mornings, as did we all but had ours at nights in deference to him as head of the house. Ours was the kind of sprawling country *ménage* that lacked conveniences. Ten years before, when the family had taken the house my mother had had one of its rooms turned into a bathroom, installed bath, pipes, drainage system ready for the great day when we would have running water laid on. We were still waiting too for the electric company that proposed some day to put pylons across the veld. No doubt if we had had no help, we would by now have brought our own pump, windmill, generators. As it was, our cheerful maids had to bustle round and, among other things, bring water to our rooms morning and evening. They heated it on the oil and coal ranges in the kitchen. There was plenty of work for them but they never seemed to mind. My new stepmother, my uncle and I used the heavy old decorated porcelain jugs and basins and their companion foot-baths, bidets, with which the bedrooms were furnished. These Georgian and Victorian articles were part of my childhood. One set had been a wedding present to my parents from some elders, others had come down from my grandparents, even from the one or two of my sixteen great-grandparents, the ones we knew about because they had decided to abandon the pagan life and become 'school people', Christians.

When the servants had done that, and filled the bath with gallons of hot water for my father they next prepared the family's eight o'clock breakfast. On arrival I had been allotted one of the bedrooms used by the young and therefore near the noisy kitchen passage. So when breakfast was being got ready I sniffed comforting smells as when a child at our other house: brown millet (sorghum) being cooked as porridge, bacon and eggs, more coffee. And I thought of when my own mother had been alive. She had set the pace, trained all the servants in the method and order that they afterwards followed without supervision during the years many of them stayed with us. When the early work was finished and breakfast cleared away, the women went into the bedrooms which we had now left.

Nowadays after breakfast the big people went for a walk. Not so in the old days. My father had always gone up the campus to lecture and we children off to school. Now that he was a retired man he liked first to walk to the the family graves. On my first few mornings home I had gone too, 'to see my mother' where we had buried her five years previously. And since the year before when I had last been back the walk was also to 'see' my young brother where he now lay beside her, after he was shot dead in Johannesburg. These 'deprivations' as they are usually called, in addition to my father's altered way of life, had modified the household routines that I had known when we lived at the college at Fort Hare.

Here at Middledrift we no longer held morning prayers as in the old days. At that time, children, servants and other dependents used to gather in the dining-room to listen to my father as he read the Bible from his place at the head of the breakfast table. He did it in a monotone, unemotional. He would close the big black tome inherited from his grandfather, with birthdays and other family events written on the fly-leaves. We would all get down on our knees on the floor, then turn about and bury our faces in the chairs we had sat on. He or the next senior 'big person' present would pray. This my father always did quietly, briefly, succinctly; but other big people sometimes rambled, often wild, dramatic, hair-raising – about sin and hell-fire – so that the children stealthily opened eyes and looked round. Then my mother or some other 'mother' – a visiting aunt perhaps or woman of that generation – would lead our unaccompanied part-singing of the Lord's Prayer. It never occurred to anybody that the piano might be used at prayers. One gardener we used to employ had a memorable bass voice, rumbled contrapuntally against my father's baritone and the other voices, tenors, altos, shrill trebles.

Nowadays we held only evening prayers but even these were a modified version of the ones at Fort Hare. There, my father would often afterwards go to the piano to relax if he had had a particularly pressing day at work, and play his favourite music – a Chopin mazurka or polonaise. A feminine taste, and odd, I thought later when my own predilection developed for the masculine J. S. Bach. People living with us, including the servants, used to try to sing snatches of the melody in tonic sol-fa as he played, a practically impossible feat in such intensely capricious, pianistic music – but when the whisper went round that he was about to play, the servants would say to us older children, 'Good, let's hope father will hit "*Doh so-so-SOH! Soh-lah-t-doh-ray-ME, t DOH!*"' the household name for *Opus* 40, No. 1. And as for the youngest ones already in bed, they would creep out of a darkened night nursery in pyjamas and tip-toe guiltily into the sitting-room, nestle up to my mother imploring her with big brown eyes not to let the nurse send them back to bed.

My elders no longer got up early in the mornings as of old. And their after breakfast stroll to the graves, 'to see those who had gone on ahead' as they said, was really to sun themselves – everyone old now, no pressing engagements – and to stretch the legs, a constitutional, a limbering up for whatever the leisurely Arcadian day had in store.

On this particular day, the early afternoon was to bring to the house another of my 'uncles' – one who lived locally, Uncle Rosebery. He was to come in his car and pick up my Transkei uncle, take him over to Alice my little old home-town twelve miles away to look up relations, members of the Bokwe and Matthews families.

As the big people talked among themselves, I now gathered that I was to go with the uncles. I too was on a round of family visits – three altogether: first here to my own home; then I was to go to the Transkei; and after that to Johannesburg to my aunt, my late mother's eldest and only surviving sister.

My uncle was a farmer, and at the moment in between seasons; as for me, I was between seasons too as it were, taking time out between continents and school terms. My daughter was at boarding school in England and flew out each summer to join me and my husband in East Africa where we were living for the time being.

The big people spent the morning apparently doing nothing but sitting about. It was not idle or pointless, however, only a change. My father, as he said, was 'actively not writing' and my new mother delegating her usual household duties, because of the brother-in-law being present – which meant fresh angles on talk about family and South African affairs; people came to pay their respects about the matter of the arrivals; telephone calls about these were answered; mid-morning coffee was served, the mail was brought from the post office across the valley. . . .

I sat about in their company absorbing the atmosphere that elders generate, and felt as if involved in a kind of osmosis, not unlike when the little boys cleaning the car stopped to watch MaDhlamini and the passer-by and me.

So we spent the morning, against a background of willing hands oiling the wheels of life in the country.

2

LUNCHEON over and everyone rising from the table, my father exaggerated the physical infirmity of his age, pretended to groan, muttering, 'How recalcitrant one's limbs become, stiffen, take no account of the fact that you don't feel as old as *they* do – eh?' There was an exchange of big people's jokes about this since actually they liked getting old. Was not the veneration that it brought, everyone's ambition? Then he said to my uncle, serious again and repeating the decision taken that morning in the sitting-room; 'Yes-no, no-yes, she had better go with you, brother-in-law,' pointing at me and using the only word that now does for 'brother-in-law', the Afrikaans derivation, 'Her new mother and I will stay. We live here; *you* are "the ones who have been away and therefore need to be seen again, *you* the clouds of rain that will break the people's thirst and nostalgia for you". Let Zac Matthews and his wife have you to themselves.' He smiled at my stepmother as she agreed with him.

Her voice was musical, delightful to hear. And she had one of those very dark skins against which the teeth seem very white. Her eyes twinkled all the time. She loved joking and now leaned across to nudge me and said in a low tone out of respect for the men:

'Father tells the truth. Go and rain, dear Noni!"

I smiled back, but hoping it looked natural. It was my crisis on this visit to have discovered that I now resented her presence, although the year before when she and my father married shortly after my brother's murder I had thought her a marvel of support and sweetness in that most bitter family circumstance. She had continued to be its comforter. As people said, 'That is her nature, for which her role in this family's test of endurance was intended by the ancestors (*amawethu*). God sent you *a Person* in that one.'

I was not denying it; I could see how she loved, consoled,

13

cherished my father. He had become gay, contented, as when my mother had been alive. I had expected to be happy on being back again after their year of marriage. Instead I found I was seized by emotions that conflicted and bewildered me.

My uncle had alluded to a situation of this kind in a letter he had written me before I announced out of the blue that I was homesick and had booked a passage home. But letters from him were invariably terse, crisp. The allusion was a glancing one, cryptic. I had not taken it in. My uncle wrote to nieces and nephews in formal style, mostly about doings on the farm, and always ended with the English greeting, 'Your affectionate uncle, E. C. Makiwane.' At that distance I was filled only with happy anticipation of home, of taking up from where we had left off.

Uncle Cecil's chair scraped the floor when he too, rose stiffly to his feet. He was a heavier man than my father. He ignored the fun between me and my 'new mother' and said something to my parent recapitulating the fact of the awaited and imminent arrival of his and my kinsman.

He straightened to his full height. He had a solemn face, the very small nose of my mother's people, their sedate, reflective eyes – a wonderful, masculine version of my mother, darker than she had been for he was sunburnt and weathered by his rugged outdoor life, whereas she had had that pale coffee colouring that was called 'white' in Xhosa long before Europeans had been heard of.

He wore a plain grey suit that I remembered from years before. It looked rather tight now across his great chest and shoulder-blades. He sported a triangle of spotless white handkerchief at the top of his breast-pocket, wore an old knitted black tie on a white shirt. He dressed carefully when visiting even close relations because, he liked to say 'Part of holiday relaxation is the chance to dress neatly.' At the farm it was only on Sundays that one saw him look the dandy that my mother used to tell us he was as a young man.

He pulled a turnip watch out of his waistcoat-pocket, lowered his bullet-shaped head to consult it. I saw how he had got thin on top, and grey. His neck was thick and sturdy. He looked up, glanced at me then at my stepmother, and back again at me. I started. Did those glances mean he was thinking what I had just been thinking? Or about his letter? Since he arrived he had seemed to pay no attention to me or my stepmother. His manner was not effusive, least of all to 'those on the distaff side, *ababhinqileyo*: (literally *"those who tie round the waist"*)'. On the other hand one's maternal relations are 'attached to you by the navel', the figurative expression referring to 'the intuitive sense' that they are supposed to feel on your behalf, and about how they expect to help, protect, intercede for you when 'situations about blood' arise, and to correct your attitudes and behaviour if the fault is yours.

I and other maternal nieces and nephews were in tremendous awe of him yet felt drawn, compelled, fascinated because he *was* our mother's eldest brother, our 'male mother, *malume*'. We called him that, never the English word 'uncle'. The Xhosa title had terrific implications. *Kaloku* you are drawn by the power of that navel link. You accepted the imponderable without at first being aware that possibly you had been conditioned to do so.

Once my mother had said to us when we were young: 'You children need not *quake* before your uncle like frogs mesmerized by a serpent. I know that he is a man of few words. But he *loves* children and those of his sisters are particularly special. Get used to him, he has a giant sense of humour; your uncle is a lovely man. And if anyone ever wrecks your life he would be your support. That is *malume's* duty – yours too, little one,' sweeping my brother into her arms, 'towards the children of your two sisters!' He was only eight years old and looked bemused, puzzled; my mother laughed and hugged him.

When I caught *malume's* glance now I became quite frightened – lest he call me aside to 'speak with me' about the reactions that I was experiencing. But no; I realized with relief that this could not be. But his expression made me nervous for I was certain that an exhortation was to come; I looked away.

Strange, I thought, how like a child again I felt in the presence of the two men, my father and my mother's brother;

and conscious of the hierarchies they represented. They were standing side by side, my father tall, my uncle taller, and both straight like soldiers and only a few steps from me. Now that I was a woman they still seemed to me splendid, superior to any man I had ever known. Unlike other grown-ups, some of whom had seemed to shrink and become smaller with the passage of time, sometimes positively commonplace.

I watched them move out of the dining-room, my father leading the way. His figure was much less hefty than my uncle's because for years he had taken particular care about putting on weight. He ate sparingly, always talked about spartan discipline, self-indulgence; and never missed an opportunity to tease people about over-eating. 'Which is to talk to walls of stone,' he would say, 'in our society of gormandizers,' and make them nearly choke in mid-mouthful because he would lift a long finger in fun at them, laugh at his own joke and flash that most beautiful smile. He was slim, trim, in a favourite old brown suit with the Edwardian drain-pipe trousers that had delighted him by becoming fashionable again – 'You see,' he would cry to dandified young men, 'you who rush the shops and tailors at the advent of each new style? Behold the reward of thrift!' and disarm them with that smile so that they doubled up with laughter and teased him back by a pointed stare at his well-polished boots in order to draw him out about his eminently round-toed sensibility; old-fashioned lace-up ones like my uncle's. Their generation had no use for *shoes*: 'Bringers of corns, bunions. Those afflictions would not *know* you young stylists if you shod yourselves as we do.'

His Jabavu face, slender, mobile, sparkling, contrasted with Uncle Cecil's; Makiwane faces were heart-shaped, high-cheeked. My father's had 'the forehead of distinction' of the verse in the Xhosa song composed in his honour and sung at gatherings wherever he went. The eyes danced as if from nervous energy. And the smile, also publicly acclaimed: it captivated people – regular teeth framed by exceptionally well-shaped lips. His was a male film-star's mouth – which he did not know since he hardly ever went to the pictures, and then only to cowboys; and not for their smiles but their intrepid horsemanship.

16

I was profoundly pitied as a child for being a duckling, inheriting no good looks. 'Handsome man sires so ugly a child!' family friends used to exclaim, examining and giving their verdict. I had to listen without protesting. 'That learned forehead, in the child so debased,' they always blamed me for defaulting on the patrilinear, never the maternal side which did not count however good-looking, 'Why, it is *isiphongo*!' the harshest epithet they could find. I felt ashamed and, fighting back hot tears, buried my face in my mother's lap. But she might comfort me only by a surreptitious pressure of fingers while smiling with my tormentors since it was bad form to soften candid criticism which was intended to toughen a child and prevent conceit. I only began to escape attention when I was seven years old and my sister was born and two years later my brother. Their looks made up for my deficiencies, although even for them other aspects were picked on in order to 'bring them down a peg'.

My father walked to the study to take an afternoon nap on the battered leather sofa that had been his father's before him, and was placed under bookshelves as it had been in my grandfather's house. The rest of the study walls were hung with 'South African Railways and Harbours' maps, for my father adored trains.

My uncle strode off to put on outdoor things. My stepmother rang the little silver bell and we continued briefly to joke together until the maid came to take her orders. Then I left to get my coat and joined my uncle on the veranda where he stood, long-sightedly scanning the landscape for my other uncle's motor car.

Uncle Rosebery had suggested that during an off-duty period from his surgery he would take Uncle Cecil to visit the cemetery at Ntselamanzi, beyond Alice, where his mother was buried. She had been one of my maternal grandmothers, a 'classificatory' one. They would also stop at his sister Frieda's and her husband at Alice. I was a 'niece' of the Bokwes because their father and my (real) maternal grandmother shared an *Ama*Bamba clan relationship . . . I was well and truly back in the setting of relations which anthropological experts call 'fictitious siblings'. They were decidedly not fictitious but factual in our eyes; although so slightly related to us Uncle

Rosebery and Aunt Frieda are among those with whom we share drops of blood that can be traced and therefore may not intermarry. It is true that at times exogamy so strictly observed makes it seem as though you may marry absolutely nobody, and you wonder how long the people can maintain such a horror of 'incest'. But the attitude is drummed into you early and is afterwards practically impossible to shake off.

My uncle did not talk, so I passed the time thinking about the relations we were going to look up.

'Grandmother' had been a widow for as long as I had known her, a beautiful old lady, her family outstandingly handsome: four uncles, Barbour (now dead), Rosebery, Selborne and Waterstone the last born, and my playmate long ago, near enough to my age for me to call 'Woti'; we were taught to play piano duets together perched side by side on a bench. And two daughters: Frieda, now Mrs. Matthews, and Pearl, Mrs. Radebe. I used to call them '*oAuntana* – the Little Aunts', because they were much younger than my mother and had to call her '*Sisi*'.

'*Sis*' Tandiswa!' they used to cry, and tug my mother to the dressing-table in her bedroom to powder their noses after their long walk to our house. They used to arrive bubbling with stories of how they had spent the day. They were school-teachers at the time. And my Aunt Frieda also taught a few pupils the piano, as did my mother since anyone blessed with the slightest accomplishment in our small town invariably found themselves confronted with eager tyros.

The sisters had the most wonderful skins I had ever seen. I was struck dumb with admiration as a child gazing at their golden cheeks. They too had the prized 'coffee' colouring, were even lighter than my mother. Their eyes were great pools of light brown. And their hair, unlike my mother's, was thick and dark, a russet ruddy shade. My mother, like many Makiwanes had, as they said, '*rotten Hottentot hair*', tinged with ginger and knobbly, needing tremendous preparation to make it presentable – '*wretched Bushman stuff!*' My little aunts had pale, soft hands, shapely nails on small fingers. Their immaculate chic dazed me. I thought they smelt divine and Aunt Pearlie had such dimples.

They were *petite* but not fragile for although so tiny, their hips were wide – another feature which my mother who lacked it, teased them about in the privacy of her room, 'Hey, *mantombazana* – you girls will be brood mares one day.' Roars of laughter, blushes, with me looking on and listening. The prophecy was fulfilled for when they married they both had splendid quiverfuls. Standing on the veranda with Uncle Cecil and thinking of all those things, I remembered how I used to compare these aunts to the most beautiful pictures I knew as a child – ladies on chocolate boxes.

Years later I found a picture that really caught their loveliness. No chocolate box, instead the painting by Andrea del Sarto of his wife Lucrezia. I caught sight of it when shepherding my eighteen-year-old daughter round the galleries of the Prado Museum in Madrid, looked again; there in the young sixteenth-century Italian woman was my Aunt Frieda at her age – the same rare colouring, gentle cheeks, the dimples, dewy mouth, the softly moulded chin. I was staggered. I wanted to know more about Lucrezia and discovered that the painter's contemporaries had not all approved of her. That made her seem more than ever like my aunt as she had been; for not everyone had approved of her either when I was a child. I remember overhearing criticisms and puzzling over them. But politics afterwards changed all that. Her husband Z. K. Matthews, Professor of Law and Social Anthropology at Fort Hare, and at that moment also Acting Principal of the college was swooped upon in bed at night by police; my first knowledge of it was through banner headlines in newspapers abroad. He and his son, my brother's age – and former playmate – were imprisoned, then later charged in the famous Treason Trial together with one hundred and fifty other people, the ordeal that was to last for years. It was then that our small world saw the stuff my aunt was made of, and saluted her as a 'modern African'. As a matter of fact her generation and branch of the family were partly English and Scots; but Xhosa people have no complex about 'miscegenation'. They admired her courage and behaviour, 'an ornament to her clan'.

But before the Treason Trial, *apartheid* had already brought some of its problems to these particular relations. Some years before they had bought a house in our little town, within walking distance of Uncle Zac Matthews's work at Fort Hare. I looked forward that afternoon to seeing how her roses had done since I had been there last year and how the lawns she had laid out on taking the house had matured. But towns became scheduled under Dr. Verwoerd's Group Areas Act as 'European Ethnic Areas'. Other inhabitants had to move to 'black' ethnic areas. In some cases no decision had been declared as to where people were to go.

At last we saw my Uncle Rosebery's car bumping across the veld. His surgery and house were across the valley. We watched until he drew up at the front of our house. Uncle Cecil stepped down into the garden and along the little path to the gate. I followed. Uncle Rosebery was a small frail-looking man. As he smiled, leaning out of the window, I saw that his skin had darkened. For years his health had not been good. He 'looked black', as the expression goes when people look poorly. Southerners certainly do, especially Xhosa when ill, probably because of the Hottentot colouring. To look 'black' is comparable with looking sallow.

And my uncle's hairline had receded. My father said he was one of the hardest-worked in the land, that he was public-spirited to a fault and in danger of wearing himself out. I saw what he meant.

However, his eyes still shone, bright and large – the Bokwes all had those eyes. And when he got out of the car, gesticulating, his movements were still quick and birdlike as of old.

The uncles greeted each other tumultuously. Apart from blood links they had other ties. They had taught at Lovedale together before I was born. In family albums I had pored over pictures of such things as the staff cricket team in which they had both played. All my life the men in the family were cricket mad; when they 'rooted for South Africa' in Test Matches abroad and for provincial teams at home and followed their fortunes in newspapers and on radio despite the policy of *apartheid* in sport, they were the despair of the more single-minded women.

My mother too had taught at Lovedale with them before her marriage; all my elders were part of the net of people linked by

professions, business, blood, and for many of them Lovedale was
the *alma mater*, the cradle where they had shared a social and
political background inherited from earlier generations of
Bokwes, Jabavus, Makiwanes and others – tens, scores, hundreds, now thousands. It had been an all-embracing net when I
was growing up. And to see my uncles together and hear the
joyous way they recalled their old life (which they did immediately!) reminded me of the things families and friends used
to do; like the time we celebrated Uncle Rosebery's return from
years of training in Edinburgh.

What seemed to me at the time a multitude, a host, assembled
to go camping in the blue-looking Amatola Mountains on the
horizon from Alice and my present home at Middledrift. We
went in covered wagons drawn by teams of oxen. There was a
lot of walking on such trips, young ones trotting stoutly alongside the creaking wheels, darting about like puppies. We threw
stones at birds or rabbits, or picked bunches of everlasting
flowers, gazanias. The big people rode. We clambered into the
wagons too when we got tired but did not stay for long because
among the grown-ups you had to be quiet, behave.

Then we arrived at the spot, a green glade on the mountain-
side. The hired herdsmen and boys outspanned, grown-ups
talked and laughed; mothers and aunts cooked. We children
played games and entered a world of the imagination. But it was
not so imaginative after all, I find, looking back, for I see now
that it was influenced by our history reading at school about
pioneers, for we played at being Dutch Voortrekkers. Indeed
the sources of inspiration for such games were never far to seek
from the covered wagons. Some of us small girls were thrust into
cotton poke bonnets by our mothers to protect us from the sun.
These were like those worn by trek-Boer women travelling up-
country with their pioneer men in olden days. The little boys in
our party called out (in Afrikaans) to one another and to the
oxen. Such scenes were depicted in the school books where we
had read how 'the brave Boers formed their wagons into a
laager (strong point) at nights for safety. From there they shot
down the savage natives'. So we played and shouted, '*Basopani,
siyeza singama Bhulu!* Look out, we're the Boers and will get
you!' After dark we asked our mothers why our party had not

brought enough wagons to make a *laager*. But it was consoling, exciting to roast lumps of meat at the camp fire and later to be put to bed underneath the canvas hood.

But we outgrew the age of romantic *voortrekking*. Things were changing. Our families began to acquire motor cars. I remembered how these two uncles of mine had bought their first and afterwards no longer rode up to our house on horseback or in a Cape cart; the name 'cart, *ikari*,' had become the smart slang word for motor car, smarter than *imoto*, I cannot think why. Even the uncles were using it, I noticed. Presently everyone travelled by car all over the Eastern Cape and Transkei (we seemed never to go to the Western Cape and Free State and Transvaal: other worlds) to gatherings social, sporting, political. My own family was among the very last to go in for a motor car because of my father's blind devotion to horses and railway trains. But in the end he gave in – my mother wanted to be practical and we children wanted to be like other people. At first the cars were 'tourers' – open Buicks, Chevrolets, Dodges. We all called the tonneau cover a 'tent, *itentyi*.' Only the frivolous, the 'conspicuous consumers' bought English motor cars because as everyone declared, they were not suitable for South African conditions and distances. Later the tented tourers gave way to 'sedans', closed saloons. Uncle Rosebery's motor car was an American, naturally; a chocolate-brown Hudson, the kind advertised in the local paper as 'the only car that you can step down to get into'.

And we had to do just that. Uncle Cecil twitted the other about the design of 'this handsome cart', 'Not suitable at all for these stiff old bones of ours, man Krila! Why do you go in for this "*rumsha*, super-modernist's" thing?' Much noise over that, and teasing. My other uncle was lithe and sprightly, hopping round to pour the older man in, opening one of the doors at the back for me, then jumping in himself.

In no time at all he was calling Uncle Cecil by his English nickname 'Fish', picking up old threads. I knew the origin of that one. When Uncle Cecil was a schoolboy at Lovedale, a certain missionary teacher took the boys for compulsory swims in the River Tyumie. My uncle did not then subscribe to the teacher's enthusiasm about *Mens Sana in Corpore Sano* and rebelled, saying he was 'not a fish'; and the name had stuck.

We drove away and presently the car bumped off our veld track and glided into the dirt road, a dry, white, dusty one, typical of the Eastern Cape scene: cloudless skies, jagged dark mountains far away, and in the middle distance the veld dotted with bushes and gnarled, stunted thorn trees. Where its contours dipped into shallow depressions, there were clumps of candelabra euphorbia trees standing upright like sentinels – dark, stark, forbidding figures which I never saw without being reminded how grim and sinister the aura that their name bestows on any chief or man called after them, *uMhlontlo*, one of the handful of plant names which for some reason are classified in the grammar with humans.

We crossed the railway line from Port Elizabeth to East London; then another of the fords that were almost indistinguishable in a season of drought such as this one. The ford was bone dry, its bed covered with stones.

Crossing it, we now left the territory of the AmaGqhunuk-webe – the Xhosa clan of Middledrift and district, noted more than most for their Hottentot blood, which their name suggests. We now entered the territory of the Jingqhi clan, approached the outskirts of our first port of call, Alice. I gathered we were going to stop first at Aunt Frieda's, then go on past Lovedale to Ntselamanzi and to the grave. Uncle Cecil and I were to lay a stone.

3

'*Ilizwe lama Jingqhi,*' Uncle Cecil murmured sighing deeply, 'The country of the Jingqhi people.' He said it again and again, '*The people of the Chief, Maqoma*'; he was looking round savouring it, the way people do when they return to familiar places. It was a very different countryside from his own in the Transkei. 'But this over-population, Krila – just look at it.'

I looked at it too. There were huts everywhere, and great gullies of soil erosion, *dongas*, except in the areas set aside as European lands – my eye scanned rows of orange trees, dark, vivid, against the dun-coloured soil. Beyond their boundaries were African settlements, huts huddled together on rocky hillsides covered with boulders, aloes, and cattle, goats, red-blanketed pagans moving about.

'This Ciskei is just too *full* of people, Rosebery man! The Transkei too is like this now, you know. Not like when we were children. Too *full* of people. Crowding, crowding. What is to become of us?' We all knew the cause: 'the work of the 1913 Land Act, Native Trust Lands. Twelve millions must live in thirteen per cent of South Africa while the three million whites must live in the rest.' It was always on everyone's lips; did not need recapitulating. Uncle Cecil was laughing, and evidently Uncle Rosebery did not intend to launch into serious political talk either for he too laughed.

'But we doctors are always *telling* you Kaffirs: "there is that civilized device, birth control", for reducing these numbers. Why not *reduce* yourselves to *three* millions, instead of these troublesome twelve?'

They looked round at each other and roared, for the very idea of family limitation is about as acceptable to Xhosa minds as a jackal in a sheep-pen. Furthermore, it is odiously inseparable from the one that exhorts Africans to 'limit the numbers' of their cattle. It may seem an odd juxtaposition, but has to be faced – 'people and cattle are one'. Mention of either invariably pro-

24

vokes thought of the other; and did so now in the car, for is not a
right-minded, right-living man traditionally surrounded by
stock and offspring? Cattle spelt prestige, children continuity,
happiness. The delight of Xhosa men in their babes, toddlers
and young has to be seen to be appreciated. They are his calves,
his diamonds. We knew that Uncle Rosebery was referring to
these inherited ideas, to everyone's belief in them, powerful
conservatisms that are hard to break. Nor for that matter was he
attacking them. Neither he nor any other doctor in our circles
advocate small families. He was indulging in the big people's
mannerism of diverting feelings into laughter when confronted
by the need to fit obstinate traditional ideas into the modern
scene. The white Government's idea that there can be 'too
many Natives' makes people laugh, rightly or wrongly. My
uncles laughed at it now. They kept raising a hand or shouting
a greeting to some rural passer-by in red robes. Many of them
recognized and hailed 'the doctor's wagon'.

We passed through Fort Hare College Farm with its herd of
Friesian cattle, *amaFeslande*; fat cows with huge udders. They
lay about on the grass in their enclosure. I had forgotten how
Friesians seem always to 'lie about'; a very reclining breed we
thought them as children. Uncle Cecil's eye lit up and I saw
him lean forward to scrutinize the animals. He and Uncle
Rosebery fell to comparing the qualities of breeds: Shorthorn,
Afrikander, Jersey, Red Poll. In no time talk was about the
cattle that our people in this Border region once owned; for
contrary to official propaganda about South Africa having been
empty when the whites arrived, 'blacks travelling down while
whites travelled up', we were already settled here and beyond,
along the southern coast, to Longitude East 27–29 degrees; and
talk veered to the historical contests against encroaching Boers
on one hand, and on the other, the early nineteenth-century
British Government of the Colony of the Cape of Good Hope;
about the days when punitive expeditions of Commandos
would swoop and 'steal' cattle of the Jingqhi people, the clan
which had been the most southerly of the Xhosa – indeed of all
Africans – at the time of the great migrations. Lord Henry
Somerset's commandos confiscated seven thousand head here;
twelve thousand there; thirty thousand, fifty-three thousand

elsewhere. Huge stockades were prepared beforehand to round up our beloved animals. There had been one at Fort Beaufort not far from where we were at that moment. I had been taken to see the spot as a child – early 'conditioning', I suppose, into the ways in which we interpreted eighteenth – and nineteenth – century local historical turmoil. Children of English Settlers and of Boers no doubt learned other versions when *their* big people conducted them on similar sightseeing trips.

The uncles went on to talk about those 1820 Settlers, *Ama-Setlani,* who were brought into land thought to be unoccupied, 'empty'; they reviewed the event, one of those 'errors' which had led to Xhosa grazing grounds being 'annexed' as Settler territory, along with our water fountains and timbered mountain slopes. These annexations and cattle confiscations were preludes to the wars of 'pacification' we had all three read about in history lessons at school, which the British Colony Government had waged on our forbears who in turn, not surprisingly, felt mulcted and aggrieved.

'And people are supposed to limit cattle so as to prevent soil erosion. Yet do they not inherit the feelings of their progenitors, whose eyes were gladdened by the spectacle of thousands grazing, ambling, beautifying the land for miles?' and an uncle's arm swept the horizon in a great gesture.

'Oh, the ancestors possessed cattle all right. Our wealth, pride, glory, in the days when men were men.' How often had I heard such lyricism, and would it ever end? My feelings had developed no differently from those of other people who had also been exposed to it since infancy. My elders were talking as if resigned, since Xhosa speech when dealing with painful matters uses oblique constructions as I have said. I had to try to calm myself, think of other things when we now approached the College itself. We drove through it slowly. But the sight of it, too, failed to inspire calm. It was about to be taken over by the Government under the new 'Bantu Education Act', and be run as a college for students 'only of the Xhosa ethnic group', separating them from other black or coloured South Africans. That step backwards into tribalization has since been carried out. As we passed I thought of young relations of mine who were at that moment studying there and whom I hoped to look up while home.

Fort Hare seemed much as when I had lived on the campus; buildings of cream-washed walls, red-tiled roofs. We passed our old house. I peered out feeling the usual stir of emotion. It stands on the bank of the river, by the bridge, a large bungalow with a pillared veranda. I saw our old garden; the lawns and herbaceous borders my mother had established; the jacaranda tree we had tended, our youthful duty to cover them on winter nights with hoods made of sacking as protection from the frost. She had had a hard tennis court dug out, levelled and rolled. I thought of when we used to beg the gardener *Bhut* Wilson to let us water it in his place. My mother's lawns still stretched down almost to the Tyumie River. I remembered how she had concentrated on the problem of which grass to plant – studying the qualities claimed for Kikuyu or Paspalum and other species. And I saw that a dark green carpet of periwinkle still covered the wild jungly part beneath the willows outside the fence. We were strictly forbidden to go into it and used to hop about fearfully because it was infested with snakes, and if we got bitten our disobedience would be found out.

But we crossed the bridge, left those intimate scenes behind. The road into town has been tarred since those days, so we drove smoothly along the avenue of tall blue gum trees, past the dried-up *vlei* or semi-swamp whose Xhosa name *eDikeni*, is the one we use to this day for the town that the British later built near it and called Alice; past the office for recruiting natives to work on the mines, past the butcher's shop, the draper's and General Stores near the market square.

All was quiet and sleepy for it was early afternoon. A solitary car, lorry or shooting-brake bowl by; we pass a saddled horse fastened to a post; red-blanketed men striding in the middle of the road dart aside when we hoot, braces of knobkerries sloped on their shoulders; a Stetson-hatted, sun-tanned European looks into a shop window and lights a cigarette; unemployed African youths hang about outside the 'Whites Only' café on a corner, run by a Greek and new since my day. We pass the power station making its familiar thudding noise; the doors ajar, as of old, to let in the breeze so I catch sight of the machinery, the big, solid, metal wheels; and they are revolving, as ever, pumping away. Time to get myself ready for we were about to turn off to the Matthews' house. My uncles were in animated conversation and Uncle Rosebery did not turn but drove on, even past the European school. I had to interrupt. At the sound of my voice they were taken aback, immediately turned faces over their shoulders, looked at me, round-eyed. I quickly explained that we had overshot. Resounding exclamations. Then they looked about them, examined the buildings, hedges and trees we were passing, and agreed, 'My word, she is telling the truth!' They debated whether to turn back, Uncle Rosebery driving on the while. Uncle Cecil said, 'But they will be sitting there expecting us.' Uncle Rosebery slowed his car down and I began to gather my things. 'On the other hand they would *still* be expecting us if we went to Ntsela first, then to them for tea, man, on the way home. *Yes-no!* Might, it not now be as well to go *on*?' The car spurted forward. After it had travelled for several hundred yards, one uncle said: 'No-yes. Shall we *start* at Nsela, then?' They breathed again, mopped their foreheads. We drove on. So I settled down. They picked up the thread of their talk. I sat back to look at the passing scene again.

We crossed yet another bend of the winding Tyumie and arrived on the outer edge of the campus of Lovedale, the missionary institution: fir trees, oaks, elderly mission houses with neat, thatched roofs as well as dozens of modern new ones built since my day. The great school had continued to grow. As the sun's rays beat down on it the place looked established, solid. As indeed it should, for it was a hundred and fifteen years old; a venerable age in a young country. When my uncles and aunts, and even older Lovedalians, talk about it, they generate an atmosphere that reminds me of a similar one in England among people linked by an old school tie.

My uncles began to reminisce about principals and masters of other days – Stewart, Henderson, Hunter, the memorable boarding master Geddes. They spoke with affection about these good Scots names for it was a Scots mission. Uncle Rosebery's father John Knox Bokwe had, as a young man, been secretary for seventeen years to one of these splendid principals. I too could share in the 'old school tie atmosphere' that now prevailed, having been a day girl before going to England and walked from home at Fort Hare, along the path that had led over the suspension bridge that we called *'uvetyevetye'* as children, imitating the rhythmical squeaks it made when we swung on it, a game that was strictly forbidden. Now we drove up the hill. Over its crest, the great expanse of Victoria Hospital came into view. Nowadays it seems to spread like a town, the flowering of the early work of another Scotsman, Dr. Neil McVicar, long since dead; but 'continuing', as people said, because his son lived in the locality practising as a doctor at Alice. The district was conscious of its links down the generations. We approached Ntselamanzi village. The road became execrable. We raised the usual cloud of dust. Presently we had to crawl, picking our way through potholes, ruts, gashes of incipient *dongas*, and were almost in the 'location' – hideous name by which African villages in South Africa are officially called; though some, to be sure, are called 'townships'.

People walking towards us gave greetings; all knew the doctor. Nowadays a wire fence surrounds the village for it is now an 'enclosed location' as they will all be eventually, under *apartheid*, Dr. Verwoerd's policy of 'good neighbourliness'; the better to police and control. The houses were a collection of depressed-looking mud huts and square houses, *amaxande*, some thatched, others roofed with corrugated iron. People sat in the lee of their homes for it was a hot day. We seemed to drive for ages on the terrible road beside the fence before we reached the location gate for it takes time to negotiate bends of hills in this part of the Cape. The contours are deceptive and stretch farther than they seem to at first sight. The atmosphere being dry, clear, thin, you see far-off places as though they are close. As we went, my uncles talked about the future of the village.

'*Uthi u*Verwoerd! Verwoerd says!' I heard them declare as I scanned the landscape thinking of the pranks I used to get up to around here long ago. All conversations at home these days seemed to begin with or feature or end with that remark. Nobody could plan ahead to build or settle 'because Verwoerd was planning a decree'. Whether black or white you had to get permission from the Government authority that dealt with the Group Areas Act and wait until Verwoerd had decided where each 'ethnic group' was to live and work. Some Coloureds were uncertain about how individual members of their families would be classed – some might be counted as black, others white, in which case they would have to break up, separate. A number of Europeans had had the shock of their lives on being told officially that they were not white.

'*Verwoerd says* the people of this location will have to move. Says black people must vacate this side for the *other* side of the river, and live and work over *there*!'

We looked across; but could distinguish European farms by their size. 'Then what about those Europeans?'

'Verwoerd says *they* must move to *this* side. This is their correct *Ethnic area*.' There was a short silence. Then they began again.

'Man, but these Jingqhi of Maqoma are people who have been moved about! Several times in a century – Lord Henry Somerset; *Trek Boers* running away from the British in the Peninsula; 1820 Settlers.'

'Well, *kuthiwa ke ngoku* "they must trek again".' Once more laughter broke out which did not sound mirthful. My seniors shook their heads.

At last we arrived. There was the church, the little one-roomed shop, the children's crèche, all close together just inside the location gate. We drew up and Uncle Rosebery pointed ahead of us: 'My sister Frieda started that crèche, and that shop. Shall we pop into them on our way back from the graves? You should see what our ladies try to do. Later at the house she will tell you about these efforts. Our ladies *move* here, Gambu. They are like a veld fire, while they say we men "forget ourselves in cricket scores and Rugby football" – eh?'

A cloud of small boys rushed out of the shop, clambered up and over the bars of the metal gate, shrilly arguing about whose turn it was to catch the penny reward that car drivers throw to them for opening it. They pushed the gate open, shouting, pushing one another. Uncle Cecil looked beyond them and said, 'So that is the Bokwe Memorial Church?' My other uncle repeated the story of how the villagers had subscribed for and built it in memory of his father – their former Presbyterian minister and leader. He had been an accomplished musician, of a musical family. Congregations still sing music he composed.

The gate was now wide open. Uncle Rosebery started up the car, cautiously watching the excited small boys who jostled one another expectantly before him. He leaned out of the window and told them he would 'throw' later, on departure. Only then did they get out of the way and fall back, disappointed – but revived instantaneously, laughing and scuffling again as the car stopped alongside the shop and we got out.

4

A MAN came out of the shop and walked slowly towards us – a
tall figure, thin, gangling, dark-skinned. His lower lip hung
down and showed gaps where several front teeth were missing.
The clothes were too loose on his frame, fell well short at wrist
and ankles. As he came nearer I recognized him – a fellow
scholar in one of my classes at Lovedale; I had been among the
little girls who sat in a front row under the teacher's nose, he in a
sinister gang of bass-voiced big boys at the back of the room, the
terrors of our form mistress. She tried to bribe them by sending
them out to pick good-quality quince switches from the Institution's japonica hedges, on the all too many days when she meant
to thrash us over our multiplication tables, fractions, sums of
long division. Here now was one of those bullies, more than
twenty years on. His whole life since then seemed to be summed
up by his frame, and the exiguous clothes that he wore. To
recognize him was a shock. I wondered if he too did not feel embarrassed. But he paid me no attention. He looked at my uncles
and held his body in a way that suggested he was afraid, respectful, yet unable to prevent himself from approaching them.
His jaw worked, the lower lip, red and black from drinking
spirits, flopped even lower; he was trying to speak. At last in a
hoarse voice, and repeatedly raising his arm to rub his face with
his wrist, he offered to accompany us to the graveyard. The
uncles did not reply, only looked at him with hardly a flicker of
interest. Uncle Rosebery pointed the way to Uncle Cecil and
we started. The man fell in alongside.

It was a long walk. The man began to talk; apologized for the
state in which he said we would find the graves and told Uncle
Rosebery how he had remonstrated with the person responsible.
The uncles were looking down; they listened, but as if they had
stopped talking only to negotiate the stones and rough ground.
When he paused and waited for their response they ignored
him, not as coldly as this may sound, but in the manner of

senior men who might without offence leave him out of their conversation since in any case he had not been spoken to, let alone invited to take part. I was not surprised, in fact had begun to suspect he must be soft in the head. We walked on and gradually he put a distance between himself and them, as if at last taking his place.

When we reached the graves and found those of Grandmother Bokwe, and Uncle Barbour, we picked up clods of earth and crumbled them over the mounds. There was also that of Uncle Barbour's son, my young cousin Pumezo who had been killed in a motor accident. We greeted him too, our self-appointed escort watching.

Afterwards we moved about independently of one another, strolling and scrambling among thickets and rocks. Uncle Rosebery pulled up the more untidy weeds on his mother's grave and Uncle Cecil poked at others with the farmer's walking-stick which he always carried. They came together and stood talking in undertones. A breeze began to rise and I noticed how it fanned my school-mate's sad clothes making him look even thinner, forlorn. When I looked at him and then at the others, as if at flotsam and jetsam, the contrast seemed suddenly like one of social change, not only a matter of accidents of birth and heritage. My elders stood and talked quietly for a full hour, looking unhurried, prosperous, comfortable, paying their tributes according to custom. I liked seeing them do what they did. It was reassuring. But I was not sorry when at last they began to murmur about the rest of our programme for the afternoon for I was getting tired. They started to walk back. When we came to the car, I saw my uncle Rosebery looking in the direction of a little zinc-roofed square house that stood slightly apart from others, over on our right.

Following his gaze and looking too, I remembered the house. Years ago it had stood well apart from any other house, in a kind of dignity; but other huts and square houses had since crowded close to it.

It was the chief's house. Indeed the old man was there, at the door, and Uncle Rosebery had seen him and now told us about him in a low voice.

The old man began to walk, tottering almost, to the hedge of

33

aloes and cacti a few feet from his door. Uncle Rosebery said
(and in Xhosa it sounded a serious matter), 'We had better go
there, indeed start there after all, at the chief. I meant to take
you to visit the memorial church but he may have spotted my
car and would think, "Does Rosebery take travellers to see
inanimate objects first, and to greet human beings only afterwards?"' They chuckled and made surreptitious comments
about the hazards of trying to keep modern time-tables while
surrounded by conservative customs and Xhosa ideas about the
humanities. Uncle Rosebery stole a glance at his wrist-watch.
My heart sank. We would be lucky if we got through this ex-
traneous call in under another hour; it is not *done* tó swoop in
and out of old people's lives peremptorily. Since the plan was
to go to the Matthews', we would probably end by cutting out
church, shop, crèche. Meanwhile my school-mate had gone into
the shop and now reappeared bearing an enamel bowl of water.
He handed it to each of the uncles, then to me, to dip fingers
after the ritual at the graves. They did now acknowledge his
presence, for as we flicked fingers in the air (not wiping them
with handkerchiefs), they greeted him and formally inquired
after his health. He bore himself with the utmost punctilio and
deference. Not so soft in the head then, I registered. We
finished using the bowl, and immediately he barked at one of
the urchins hanging round waiting for that penny-throw, to
come and fetch it. Then he stood and looked at us, vacant
again.

The breeze had become stronger and was now a wind blowing
eddies of dust, whitening our shoes and his big feet. I saw the
way in which Uncle Rosebery stood as he watched the old
chief's slow progress. From his stance it was clear that he had
put his mind into gear for waits, delays. He and the other uncle
continued to murmur together, unhurried.

My school-mate eventually sloped back into the shop and
from where we were I could see him arrange himself on top of a
small mountain of bags of mealies, draw his long legs under
him like a spider, keeping an eye on us all the time. He called
out, swinging wild arms, 'It is going to *rain!*'

My uncles did not answer, except by glancing up at the sky.
It was clouding over, the sun about to be obscured. One

said to the other, 'He tells the truth. It looks like a possible storm.'

Uncle Rosebery took another look at the chief and now began to walk, setting the pace and we moved towards the house. The old man had reached the hedge at last. For a second he paused to scrutinize the approaching strangers. Then he turned his body and unbuttoned his trousers. I fell behind my uncles so as not to be seen, and they slowed down their pace so as not to come level with the old man before he was ready.

Finally he put his clothes in order again and turned and took steps towards us, his grey eyebrows knitted; then the face broke into a smile of recognition.

'*O?*' he called out in a shaking voice; not a long diphthong *oh* but the sharp, interrogative sound, like a tiny hammer-stroke. '*O?* Who are these who look as if I know them?' His wife was a member of the Bokwe family so he knew my doctor uncle like the back of his hand. This manner of greeting was only to ask who he was bringing. Chief Maqoma seemed terribly old, his hair snow-white. The trousers he wore were of harsh, common cloth. His ancient tweed jacket fitted very tightly. Uncle Rosebery smiled back, stepped up spryly and greeted in the style of commoner hailing chief, '*Ah-h! Ndab'em-fene; Ah-h!* Tshawe!' – the salutation for princes of the blood of the Right Hand House and their descendants. '*Ndab'emfene*' was a phrase from one of the lines of 'praise poems' of that clan and referred to the diplomacy and political skill of a forbear of this particular branch of the House, Maqoma, pagan and illiterate warrior, who had manœuvred prodigiously at critical moments of early nineteenth-century Xhosa history.

My other uncle hailed similarly.

I had come out from hiding behind them but kept quiet until the old man should speak to me; although if he did, my uncles would answer. I therefore had time to notice how he had changed since I had last met him. He had looked very poorly then but now had filled out and appeared to be in fine condition for a man of his age. His eyes twinkled in folds of flesh that gleamed, the skin shining as if polished. He held out his hand as Uncle Rosebery 'explained' Uncle Cecil; and tried to peer up into my uncle's face – which was not easy, being shorter, bent, and stiff. He echoed, 'Gambu? Makiwane?' The explanation was protracted because he confused him first with my grandfather who died in 1928 – then with my other and younger maternal uncle, Tennyson, a writer and better known to the Xhosa public than the elder because of his weekly newspaper, also because of a countryman's magazine that he edits, and an historical book he had written when he was private secretary to one of the great Pondo chiefs. But at last he understood, and at once eagerly pumped my uncle's hand up and down.

'*Cecil!* Oh, am I glad to see you?' and reeled off my mother's people's salutations, and in their proper order too, 'M'Suthu, Memela, Gambu, Ngwekazi, Bolontwini, Khondlo, Sikhukhuni! . . .' Here he drew breath, then wheezed with laughter that almost knocked him over. Then he teased my uncle about those wandering Sutho forbears of Sekukuniland and the Northern Transvaal, '*Nahiliza beSuthu-ndini!*' and wheezed away all over again.

Uncle Cecil visibly expanded at the recitation; people do when their background is acclaimed in this way.

At last it was my turn and I was brought forward.

'And this is Gambu's niece, the daughter of *Pro-fe-sa*; that one living in England married to the English.'

A different expression played on the old face at this news and for a moment he regarded me in silence; we all knew that my presence reminded him of many things. He had known both sides of my family for three generations. My brother had been his subject because born (at Fort Hare) in Jingqhi territory. He began to murmur about these facts as he clasped my hand, pressed it when he mentioned the names of my forbears, because for him it was thoughts of them that the sight of me inspired. Then he began to think of me as an individual – about my having gone to live in England – for his expression changed again, became gay; he said in fun, '*Kwek*'! The things one's offspring do – this slip of a girl marrying those treacherous English who uprooted, dislocated the lives of my progenitors.' He meant the Border contests between the Xhosa and The Colony Government; the 1820 Settlers. Pages of history that were vivid to him because he was a direct descendant of our great chiefs: Ngqika, Ndhlambe, Maqoma, Sarili, Sandile –

his own immediate ancestor had held out longest in the campaigns of the Hundred Years War, the battles that the British waged against our nation. During its intervals of truce, his father and uncles had endured 'the perfidy of the Colony Government': or of course, its 'pacificatory measures' – depending on which history books make sense to the reader. Men of his lineage were walking archives. They could quote chapter and verse (he quoted some now) giving the reasons why the English disappointed the Xhosa, ready though we were to have dealings with them rather than with the *Trek Boers*.

But it was banter. He did not hold these leaves of Cape History books against my husband. 'Our son-in-law' he called him, smilingly inquiring after his health; and at last led the way into the house.

I followed at the end of the single file.

5

THE square-house consisted of one main room and another which we did not see, partitioned off by a skimpy curtain of clean cotton cloth. Along a wall was a single-size iron bedstead covered with a thin mattress and woollen rug tasselled at the edges. A very young woman sat on it, little more than a girl, suckling a baby that looked about a year old. It lay in a peculiar position I thought (once having suckled one too) – on its stomach, chubby little legs dangling down the mother's lap; the head seemed attached to her breast as if that was its only hold on her, for her hand rested only lightly on the little bare buttock, almost indifferently. Her breast hung from the opening of a cheap shirt-blouse and the veins on it were distended, you could see them throbbing. The baby's head jerked up and down as it sucked, like clockwork. But the young mother seemed to have no vigour, no interest. She looked at us listlessly as we filed in.

In the middle of the room was an oblong deal table, on either side backless benches drawn up to it. On a stool at the head sat a boy of about sixteen. Textbooks were spread in front of him and he was writing in a lined exercise-book, dipping his pen into a dry-looking bottle of ink. He glanced up when we came in but promptly lowered his eyes again and worked on; we were no concern of his. The old man paid no attention to him or the young mother either, but led us across to a lady sitting on one of the benches at the table.

She looked ancient, very frail, her skin golden; and she re-mained motionless, bolt upright. But her neck! It was so thin that it was almost the first thing that you noticed about her: it seemed not flesh and blood at all but as if belonging to an apparition – it was all crinkled parchment drawn across power-ful ligaments, erectile tissue, a column pared down to absolute economy and bareness; skinny, craggy – frightening. Like a Rodin. I was suddenly struck for the first time in my life by

38

the thought (probably mistaken) that the anatomical purpose of those ligaments in the neck is strictly to support the head. Hers was crowned by a dark turban of dramatic size, swathed in superb folds reminding you of pictures of magnificent heads of Arabs – a noble spectacle, alert yet reposed. She turned her face towards us expectantly. Her gaze was curiously fixed, stark. The eyeballs reminded me momentarily of those of a Greek statue for they were oddly lifeless, as if colourless: in that instant I realized she was blind. . . .

The old chief tottered tenderly to her side as he announced us. Immediately he finished the room resounded with her exclamations and he then stepped back a little as if to let her have *her* share in the joy he had just experienced. He bent over her and smiled while she spoke. She overflowed with hospitality, crying out with voice raised to the pitch of a Wagnerian singer for all that she looked so fragile, '*Kwowu!* My Children! Doctor! A good deed you have done this day!' And she rose putting out an uncertain hand. Uncle Cecil reached to grasp it, quickly thrusting his walking-stick under an arm to do so, and moved close to her, holding her hand firmly. She tried to peer up at him. His shadow fell on her face. '*Kaloku* I no longer see, you understand; only shadows, my child, and dimly. Oh, sit down, sit down!' and turned cautiously, holding out her other hand so that we followed its direction and saw a bench lined along the wall. 'There are no children on it, are there?' she asked, head on one side, like a bird, until reassured. So we sat down crowded in a row; and our hosts then lowered themselves at benches on either side of the table, exclaiming, thanking God again and again for our coming. The young woman went on suckling her babe, the youth with his home-work. Neither of them were interrupted. The ancients and elders started talking about olden days. I listened and looked round.

'Yes indeed, I have eighty-seven years *as a man!*' . . . and went back to the Hundred Years War, his people's struggle against displacement, dispossession, to their final conquest and subjugation, to the beginning of the removals from pillar to post, a review in which he contrasted the freedom and nobility of the cattle pastoral life, its splendid horizons physical and spiritual – with the present 'bare existence' in fixed and enclosed villages.

He talked about the expiration of nationhood when those thousands upon thousands of cattle became the spoil of the victorious harrying English. Now the harriers were the Boers. Verwoerd had decreed yet another removal for the remnant of his tribe, his people. His wife interjected, her voice ringing:

'O, for the allegiances and aspirations of former days! But we are old. Our predecessors wait for us to join them, Gambu.' And she leaned forward towards my other uncle, 'They wait, Krila, you who already know how impatient we are, here at home, to be beside them.' Hospitable instincts prompted her to include me too and she added, 'You see us waiting, Jili, child of our children; you see us poised for departure, is not that the fact? You may not have known, girl, as your doctor uncle knows, that this was how you would find us. You have brought your young eyes from so far to see these things. As for ours, they are about to put themselves at rest, that we may follow the nation's progress from the other side, together with those who are no longer here.' She said it with gusto, gaiety, like an actress in an Elizabethan part. The surroundings were tawdry, but she imparted to them something inexpressibly fine – the effect of that grand turbaned head, the voice, the delicate body, its movements? It was poignant to see that like so many people at home she looked as though she had not lately eaten anything really nourishing. What food they got, I was thinking, probably went to their young people. Her voice rang like a descant above the ground basses of the men as they laughed with her; that oblique African laughter.

My attention hovered over the surroundings. The mud walls were plastered and well done. The earth floor was smooth, hard, smeared with cattle-dung in the usual pattern of chevrons which I had forgotten about in my absence, and guessed was the silent young mother's handiwork. The window was small and only approximately rectangular. Pictorial calendars hung on either side of it, a collection spanning several years. One was from the Natal Building Society, a picture of two European children of a type idealized by white South Africa – Nordic, flaxen-haired and I remembered how when I learned to read English, at about nine years old, I too became a sucker for Nordics, Vikings; and for years after was secretly in love with the idea of love for a

fair, blue-eyed god. In the calendar the young Aryans strolled
on a lawn of incredible greenness edged by herbaceous borders of
a dream garden in Europe: Russell lupins of every colour of the
rainbow, poppies, asters, gypsophila, geum. It seemed to represent a nostalgia for Europe in white South Africa not unlike that
in black South Africa which was represented by the kind of conversation I was listening to, about vanished nationhood; cattle.
Would these compulsive images ever be reconciled? Round the
calendars houseflies settled on walls. Others buzzed about our
faces and legs, dozens or scores probably, but seemed to me like
hundreds, millions. I kept waving them away but nobody else
seemed to be bothered. The teenage boy worked on undisturbed
while they crawled on his exercise-book, forehead, hands. The
young mother attracted them most because of the smell of milk.
She, suckling her infant motionlessly, must have long ago given
up the battle. I felt for her, wondering how my own spirits
would survive were I in her shoes.

I again paid attention to the big people. It really began to
look as if we would be here for hours – they had not yet touched
on the Bantu Authorities Act, the Suppression of Communism
Act. My uncles from time to time interjected 'Yes! No! *What?*
You don't say! That's the truth!' Uncle Cecil's voice nearly
overpowered the quavering octogenarians'.

But all of a sudden the clouds that had gathered when we
arrived obliterated the sun. A gust of wind stronger than before
blew in at the open doorway, an icy blast although until that
moment the day had been warm, getting closer. It swept in dry
aloe leaves that rustled at our feet. The sketchy partition curtain
billowed out and revealed a spartan little alcove furnished with
a bed and a trunk. Within minutes huge drops of rain pelted
the baked ground outside as I watched, and the distant hill
contours darkened; the whole countryside changed colour.

The old man's once bright brown eyes looked up at the sky
and he cried, '*O!* Why does it now look like rain?' and he
reached in his pocket, brought out a worn tobacco-pouch made
of baboon skin, unrolled a plug of cheap *Boer tabak*. There was
a tremendous thunder clap, a flash and a silence. The noise
ushered into the house a bevy of chickens and fowls cheeping
and clucking, their wings half raised as they scuttled between

our legs and across the room in a frenzy. Three small children followed, just as frightened, distended stomachs pushing out little shirts above spindly knees. At the patter of their feet the old lady exclaimed, 'Come inside then, little ones, come!' her voice instantly compassionate, warm; and she stood up. Her faded and voluminous Edwardian skirts surged as she moved. The children rushed to her. Two of them flung their little arms round her, buried their faces in her folds. But the biggest, who looked about six, halted in his tracks at the sight of strangers and seemed to hesitate. Then I saw his bright eyes steal from us to the old lady, then round to the curtain partition. You could read his thoughts. He expected to be told to go into that other little room, away from the big people and visitors. Children usually are. Sure enough, when the old woman had stroked the little heads that clung to her and had murmured words of comfort, her voice changed, took on the note of authority, 'Right, children – now run along. Into the *kamer* with you! There are big people in here.' The small fry disengaged themselves, darted off immediately, single file into the chamber. Not a protest. They even skipped as they went, swung the cotton cloth apart and plunged behind it, their movements all gaiety, assurance; 'their old person' had reaffirmed the affection with which they were surrounded; and the childish gestures seemed to declare that they felt secure, loved, even if they must make themselves scarce.

The storm broke, lashed the house, rattled on the roof. In a few minutes we could see outside only a foot or two for the rain hammered down in sheets. The noise it made on the corrugated zinc was deafening and forced us to sit silent in the now grey light because we could not hear ourselves speak. But in fifteen minutes the worst was over. The wind dropped, the rain stopped. Then as we looked out we saw the vapour rise from the ground. After the cold blasts the temperature became hot, close, stifling.

Uncle Rosebery stood up, took an agile step to the doorway, screwed his eyes upwards to examine the sky, and gave his verdict.

'*Prince!* this business has not left off yet. There is more rain coming. We had better be asking for the road.'

'*What?* Already? You have just come!'

'Tshawe, we must ask. We must beg leave to go, Handsome One! I know these storms. The ford will be flooded and we may be held up for four hours waiting for the torrent to subside. It has happened to me before.'

The old people were terribly disconcerted. The suddenness of our leave-taking was a shock. They complained that there had been no opportunity even to give us food, that they had barely tasted our presence.

But my Uncle Rosebery insisted, explained with infinite tact, patience: it was the fault of the ford. It was impressive to hear the technique he used in language and phrase as he advanced the claims of common sense. His deference was clearly not simulated but sprang from a deep respect for what his elders stood for. And he was their kinsman, of whom they were very proud. He manipulated their outraged feelings with skill so that at last they accepted and 'gave us the road'. As alarm, shock and displeasure subsided, their faces softened again.

And now the old man uttered the required speech of parting. Suddenly he sounded exhausted, but gamely sang out the styled phrases, '*Eh-weh hayi*, Krila; *nawe*, Gambu.' My other uncle also rose and I stood up too; so the old man included me as if summing up, '*Nawe*, Jili! Singawothi, Masengwa, Qabazi, Gabadzela, Mandeluhlwini' throwing in the rest of *my* salutations. He had the praise-names and styles of people at his finger-tips. Chiefs and councillors always have. By reciting those of my clan at this moment he was letting me know that I had played a part too in the pleasure the visit had brought, although etiquette had demanded that I sit in silence and be ignored. His gesture had its usual effect. I, too, at once felt elevated which must have been apparent for he nodded at me approvingly before turning back to the uncles and recapitulating. '*Yes-no*, good people; we acknowledge that you must leave. Go then, and may serenity travel with you.'

We stepped out and hurried to the car. As we approached the shop, I saw my old class-mate unfold himself from his perch on the mealie bags. He came out, loped towards us chewing his lips and lisping something. We climbed into the car. He walked alongside as it moved. The engine purred – a soft sound. The children who had hung about before, to open the gate, were not there. So he barked out their names. Heads immediately popped out of the doorway of a near-by hut; they had taken shelter from the rain. They ran from the hut like birds flushed out of a bush. My uncle now 'threw' for them as promised. There was a flurry. Small bodies jostled, knocked against each other, against the car. Some fell into puddles, trying to be first to reach the coins. Childlike, they forgot about the wheels and hurled themselves almost under them so that my school-mate shouted and swore; and Uncle Cecil called out in consternation, Uncle Rosebery jammed on the brake, put his head out of the window and scolded. 'What is the *matter* with you children? Don't you *see* the car? Do you want to *die* – eh?' That sobered them for a second and they moved back an inch, their eyes fixed on the ground for their prize. But as soon as we had moved past I saw them close in and again wrestle and fight. When we reached the good road through Lovedale my uncle accelerated. 'We must race the next instalment of the storm'. He took up the thread of talk back at the house.

'So he says he "has eighty-seven years *as a man*", in other words eighty-seven years since he was circumcised. But even if he was initiated earlier than most youths, say at fifteen, earliest, he would be over a hundred by that reckoning. Well, he cannot be that.'

Uncle Cecil said, 'No-o,' in English but drawing it out the Xhosa way, 'he is not. These old people like to make out that they are older than they are. On top of that, their memories get confused. He is *actually* eighty-six, in his eighty-seventh *year*; and that is counting from his birth, not initiation. I happen to have heard that he was born the year they discovered the diamonds at Kimberly, 1870.'

'My word, you tell the truth about how people equivocate about their ages. The guesswork and mental arithmetic I have to do when patients give only these cryptic hints they are so fond of! They will say, "*Kaloku* I was born in The Year of the Locusts, or Of the Prophet," or whatnot. And plenty of Christians even, like Ndab'emfene for instance, insist on calculating birthdays from their initiation. It is not only the pagans who behave as if the years of childhood – anything up to eighteen or even twenty-five – don't count at all, should not even be thought of.'

'*Ja*. But all the same that Prince *is* old.'

'*Ja*. And born of a House with that tradition for orderly government from where his forbears got the salutation – Noni, do you know about that?' He turned his face half over his shoulder. I collected my thoughts quickly. 'Do you know the meaning of that praise-name "Ndab'emfene, *"Palaver of Baboons"*? It marks what our remote ancestors observed about how those animals organize their society. They believe in strict protocol; order of seniority is followed at all times. They are ruthless about it. Young male baboons just must not *think* of wielding power while the senior dogs are alive. The most senior is the leader of the herd; out front; sets the pace; chooses the route. The young men may only keep the rear guard behind the women and children. . . .'

Uncle Cecil interrupted, chortling, 'Ho! Heaven help a young baboon that dares to eat *intlaka*, the resin of the thorn tree.' They both laughed loudly, since they were associated with the privileged not with the erring junior of my group; and Uncle Rosebery echoed, '*Ja*, resin is big people's special food, reserved.'

'And that disobedient youngster is not only thrashed; his elders force the illicit resin out of his stomach – he has to regurgitate the lot. Everyone in the group must behave according to the rules. That is why baboon herds are so strongly knit and can terrorize the land.' When we stopped laughing, one uncle wound up, 'Yet Europeans think they belittle us by calling us baboons. Those fellows do not study the phenomena of Africa. One day they will be sorry.'

Now that I had been brought into the conversation, I mentioned my pleasant surprise on seeing the chief look fit and well, his face filled out.

But Uncle Rosebery shook his head, looking before him with an anxious expression because raindrops had begun to fall, and said in a changed tone, 'He is not well, I must tell you, Nontando. Not well at all. He has filled out but I am afraid it is oedema. And the old lady has cataract – you saw those eyes? Too bad, for that condition could have been attended to. But they are putting all they have towards those grandchildren. And they are proud, that couple, and sensitive. It is difficult to help.'

His thoughts affected us and for a mile or two no one spoke. We sped through Alice. No mention was made about going to the Matthews and I did not like to butt in. At last Uncle Cecil spoke again. He harked back to the resin but in an absent manner as if talking only to push to one side the dismay that had crept up on us about the old couple and countless others like them. I sat back while they talked about rules that govern society and the behaviour of communities and individuals. I was thinking about how the visit to the old chief had wrecked our programme, and felt vexed. But when I remembered how he had chosen words calculated to elevate me too when we left, I suddenly thought, what do programmes matter? The Memorial Church, the crèche, the shop . . . there would be another time, as there would be to see Uncle Zac and Aunt Frieda too; truncated plans were one of the hazards of life in arcadia. 'Time always leaves us behind!' country people say, not worried. I guessed I must be falling into step for it now seemed better to be able to slide into the way people normally lived, not have things contrived for me because I was in a hurry about catching aeroplanes to keep appointments in my other life abroad.

By the time the car had turned off the road and on to the veld track that led to our house I had begun to feel less put out. The rain had settled into a steady drizzle and we passed villagers in tattered coats, shawls, children hooded in old mealie bags. I started to think about how I might catch up on the calls that we had missed.

6

I T was not going to be difficult, I thought, cheered now on getting back to the house. I had only to wait until my big people were satisfied that 'the long-absent calf had warmed it'. They would then 'lend' me to warm the kraals of others. Since that was what happened, I did visit Aunt Frieda and Uncle Zac shortly after that unpredictable outing with the uncles, because at Middledrift it was expected that after all these weeks I should be getting restless for the company of my 'age group, *iintanga*'. The shadow of the tradition that 'generations do not mix' hung over everything and my elders also wished to keep their own company, although the unusual circumstance of my living abroad made them want to see so much of me when I came. Enough is enough, however, and it was about time to get back to normal. But the next step had to be negotiated in a proper manner, which was that two members of my *iintanga* telephoned 'to ask the big people if they might come to ask for me'. I had to laugh when my father told me.

'How conventional we are,' I said. My long absences abroad had made possible a 'joking relationship' of this sort between us and he did not mind, on the contrary, welcomed any excuse to delve into the traditions he loved so that he smiled and began to elucidate:

'*Kaloku* human encounters are matters that should be handled artistically, delicately, with feeling. In proper style, an envoy would be sent – this household might even send a request to the other to *send* that envoy, to prepare the way. Pagans still do! These two age-mates of yours are properly brought up. They use telephones and such new-fangled things but only as adventitious aids to traditional observances.'

The couple he spoke of were actually many years older than I was, but it is not always only chronological order that counts. In the dim but – as my father suggested – still potent past, what chiefly mattered was who were the individuals with whom

47

your father was circumcised, initiated. A youth of eighteen
might, as the uncles had remarked when debating the old chief's
mistaken calculations of his age, be initiated with a group containing others of perhaps twenty-five. But from then on they
were 'coevals, age-mates' because they had entered into man's
estate at the same time. The male hierarchy was established and
the years of childhood were put away, rubbed out, forgotten,
did not count.

Their sweethearts (and later their wives – not necessarily the
same) grouped themselves accordingly. We never went in for
the horrors of female circumcision in order to initiate them
into the counterpart 'woman's estate'. True, on the first
appearance of the signal of fertility in a girl her family held
a ceremonial feast to celebrate the occasion. Their daughter
had passed from childhood. Now was the opportunity to
let the world know that she was marriageable, a potential
mother. No markings on her body were in any way imagined
necessary. It is an inheritance that seems to make one totally
irrational, aghast at the idea of female circumcision but ap-
proving adult male circumcision and the ritual that surrounds
it.

Nowadays of course among the Westernized (or 'school
Christians') a girl has no knowledge of when or where or if, the
men in her family are circumcised; and it is unthinkable to discuss the matter with any man whatsoever. The
ceremony came under strict proscription from the Christian
missionaries, though some of their converts – not all – adopted
the infant male circumcision introduced with the new religion.
But one cannot cross one's heart and declare that the latter
operation has wholly captured the imagination of even those
moderns who practise it, for what had counted traditionally was
not the hygienic reasons that are advanced in its favour; it was
the ritual, consisting as it did of physical endurance tests com-
bined with a long-drawn-out period of seclusion for the group of
youths involved. While in the heightened psychological state
induced by bodily pain, shock and discomfort they were exhorted by the elders in charge on the importance of becoming
'mature men', lectured on the moral obligations and social
responsibilities they would now bear. It was impressed upon the

group that they had put behind them for ever the status of 'carefree childhood' and that, as coevals they had jointly leapt on to the next rung of the ladder of the social hierarchy. In such a framework it was absolutely taboo for a man to marry uncircumcised.

Maybe it is atavistic to be in sympathy with the pagan idea that changes in personal status should be marked, as they are when dramatized by ceremony and ritual.[1] What is certain is that the attitude endures, is one that most powerfully colours the social fabric in which you find yourself. And I for one would be sceptical if told that it has been undermined by modern conditions or by Christianity. Like other women in the scene, I too shall never know about the circumcisions or lack of them in any of the men in my family. On the other hand I ask myself, 'Why should one expect to know everything and not be "capable of uncertainties"?'

The couple who telephoned, then, were children of men who were friends of my father's and always spoken of in the family as his age-mates. The husband, Mr. Mzamane, was a lecturer at Fort Hare, had been one of my father's language students when I was a small girl. Like most former schoolteachers, he was called *Teacher* by everybody – and that was what I called him, since he was too 'senior' for me to use his name. His wife Nompumelelo – *'Sisi'* to me for the same reason – was born a Balfour. Her parents and family belonged to the network of families that I mentioned earlier; and she too was once a student

---

[1] Perhaps I should explain that I do qualify this atavistic approval—only of the Xhosa form of the operation. Doctors describe it as the simple kind such as is performed in Europe on baby boys with a quick clean stroke. I have to admit that once, at a public showing of a colour film of an appallingly elaborate, physically extensive, and long-drawn-out operation practised by a tribe in East Africa, on Mount Elgon, I was among those in the audience who fainted dead away. And later, I did not disbelieve when Government officers working among that particular tribe declared that initiation did not seem to integrate the personalities of those involved, that on the contrary it seemed to disrupt not only them but society, and set up unbearable tensions in the community for months before the holding of a ceremony and enduring emotional stresses afterwards.

at Fort Hare. Like many of these, they both treated my parents as their own.

They came to tea at four o'clock on the day of the pre-arranged errand. My stepmother baked a cake the day before, rock-cakes and other things on the morning; and we sat and talked until nearly sunset about every imaginable current topic, mainly to put my uncle in the picture of what was going on in our part of the world.

It was not until they were about to leave that Teacher made the awaited request. There had been laughter and gaiety, so that the 'speech' when he made it, was in light vein. We were all putting on something of a performance since it is not to be denied that we take pleasure in dramatizing.

'Father, we would like to ask if we might have Noni's company at Fort Hare for a few days.'

'*O?*'

'May she not rest from being with "old people, *amaxhego namaxhe'ukazi*"?'

'*O?*' my father lay back in his armchair and smiled.

'And Fort Hare youngsters too want to see her. *Kaloku* Jili, we *all* want to be refreshed by the rain of overseas.' My father shut his eyes tight, nodding and smiling more broadly – a favourite gesture when pretending to be stuck for an answer or caught on the hop.

'Then what is the position here-at-home? Can she be spared?' There was play at a pretence of a pause to consider the proposal, my uncle watching, aloof but not quite unsmiling, my step-mother and *Sis*' Nompumelelo giggling like irrepressible school-girls, Teacher 'anxious'. At last my father opened his eyes.

'Well, *perhaps* in the society of greybeards she *is* starved of the real news. Perhaps you had better take her, that *iintanga* may unravel your things of Caesar' . . . the room rang because he was overtaken by the celebrated stutter, and Teacher pretended to be forced to help him out with the troublesome words.

The Mzamanes knew different sides of my father's character. As he well knew they liked to mimic him – as most of his old students did; he would say, laughing, 'To imitate is to honour!' Listening to their present pleasure, I saw again in my mind the occasions when the Mzamanes had come to our house and worked like beavers helping with the avalanche of visitors and mourners when my mother died and later my brother. And my father had afterwards thanked them in one of the semi-ritualistic styles that are resorted to when an almost unbearable human crisis has to be faced; and he ended that speech to which the whole gathering had listened in stricken silence. 'As for you, M'Simang (Mzamane's salutation), and you MamKwayi (his wife's), I am not going to attempt to thank you for the support which you have given; am I not your parent, your fathers' co-eval? *"What therefore can I say to you? Ndithini ke ngoku?"'* ... and among the women present, those who might have broken down were forced to control themselves for he had throughout exhorted us all to be Stoics, had himself set the example. The affection shown to Teacher and his wife at the afternoon's tea-party had firm foundations.

I noticed now another expression cross my father's face. The smile did not leave it but became wistful and his voice changed subtly. Not stammering now. For some reason that difficulty overtook him mainly when he was in playful mood; he said smoothly, quietly:

'Take her. And may you, being older, find an opportunity to help your age-mate.' He turned slightly towards my new mother, towards my uncle. Delicate gestures but instantly registered. Xhosa sounds wordy but it also uses carefully timed silences and there was one now. This was the first mention of maladjustment between me and my stepmother; and was in order, because first broached in the presence of intermediaries. Nevertheless I was startled, as when my uncle had given us both that look without speaking. One's feelings are not made easier to control by the fact of belonging to a society that takes infinite pains to help adjust them when they go wrong. My new mother nodded in accord with my father. I noticed, and it mortified me, that they looked at each other with affection and understanding.

He went on, 'Her mother-here, her uncle, and I: we know what we may expect from you who were of-this-home when late Mama was still-here. *u*Noni and her sister had to be emzini, at their homes-of-marriage. So you children of my age-mates represent continuity for them; you the bridge across which these girls can link themselves with our new family, theirs, yours.'

Everyone knew that this was so. But the blood rushed to my ears. One of my new mother's daughters was expected to arrive next day. I had not felt enthusiastic when told of her coming visit. So far I had met (the year before) only one other of her children, a charming married girl. The meeting had been at her house far off, in another province. When told about this other daughter coming to *my* home, I found myself crying out, 'But – will she sleep in *my sister's* room?'

Now that my father was making this ritual reference about new families ('ours, yours, hers'), I understood what he had meant when he had laughingly talked about conventions by which a household in difficulty might send a request to its friends asking them to *send* their envoy, he who was to open a way to discuss matters which it had already been felt and agreed should be straightened. . . . The Mzamane household was one of those that were ready to do anything for ours. I listened in a panic, knowing what I ought to feel, but unable to let myself feel it, until I suddenly realized I was no longer sitting composed and motionless as the others in proper African manner.

What my father was saying is difficult to convey in English for it all sounds self-conscious, 'too awfully embarrassing' as some English friends of mine have put it, whose adult lives are tragedies of family hatreds, resentments which they refuse to even try to demolish because of the embarrassment of *talking*. Xhosa is fortunate in talk. Because of its structure it avoids 'embarrassment'. The inflexions, the shape of the sentence, the flexibility of the verb, the alliterative concord, the euphony of constructions that sound like arabesques and weave in and out like counterpoint – its characteristics can confer grace on expressions of the heart's emotions. I was ashamed for I was aware of being far indeed from a state of grace. Perhaps because much of my life had to be spent away from the influence of the language and all that it implied? But no, there are plenty of reasons for being in a state of bloody-mindedness.

I heard my new mother say, her voice melodious as ever, her Xhosa impeccable, 'You "Speak the truth", father' – a phrase inviting him to continue:

'*Kaloku* we old have been savouring this young person's presence. We have been greedy, and she has been patient, *u*Majili; we have not as yet made the opportunity to *speak* of these delicate matters in the way that is needed. Time is necessary. But that is the element which perpetually "leaves us behind", here *emaXhoseni*; while her life is one of time-tables. That is the problem! No so?' The note was amicable throughout, conciliatory, skating over the tenseness. The Mzamanes and my new mother called out my father's salutations to show that they appreciated his having put it like that. My strong silent uncle said nothing, only joined them in looking at me. They were smiling, but I felt *he* was saving himself to lecture me later, when I went to him in the Transkei. The tensions over which the whole rigmarole was tiding us overwhelmed me and I found I had risen from my chair. Upon which Mzamane said swiftly, as if in banter, 'Aha! *u*MaJili has heard, you see? Is on her feet, wasting no time. Yes, go, girl and pack. Your father consents, bids us take you. Let us push off while the going is good, you know what these old people are like, liable to change their minds.' We all knew it was not so, that he said it for a purpose.

My new mother heaved herself out of her armchair.

'Let her be given a hand with the packing. Is that not what mothers are for?' – gay as usual. Thus the 'pleasantries' propelled me to my room to collect myself, calm my agitation – for I had of course already packed. In my room my new mother talked, kept up the atmosphere that was intended to prevent any outbreak of emotional storms. We even joked, for as I have said she was a laughter-loving woman. My mother also, I thought, but this one's laughter is different. What could a woman do in her shoes? I was in a daze. When I again passed through the sitting-room, she insisted on carrying my little case, and came out with me and the Mzamanes to their car. She helped us get into it. When Mzamane swung the nose of the motor car round, she stood and waved, smiling. One of our dogs rushed from the back-yard and leapt beside her, barking and wagging his tail. I saw in my mind's eye the other times when my mother used to see us off, young people going to a dance or a concert. She too used to bend down as MamSwazi did now to quell the dog's excitement.

MamSwazi exhorted us in the customary phrases, '*Nigcinane torwana! Nonwabe!* Look after one another. And Be Happy.' Then she began to giggle, peals of musical laughter because the engine spluttered in anticlimax, and gave out, the exhaust pipe emitting clouds of blue smoke.

'*Yo!* Will this broken horse of yours make it, Teacher?' Their motor car was an ancient second-hand one, a proper '*noxesha*, old-timer' that had to be nursed along. It recovered and we moved off in the rapidly falling dusk.

The track from our house to the road went west so the sky ahead was ablaze with the colours of sunset. Against them the dark mountain-peaks looked like giants. One dominates the rest and is called 'Mountain of Man, *Intaba ka Ndoda*', because according to local tradition, it represented an idealized councillor of state: wise, experienced, ancient witness of historical events. The district being packed with history and local people always ready to talk about the great battles that had been fought on the veld below these slopes, I looked at the scenery; and put disturbing thoughts to one side.

It was dark when we arrived at the Mzamanes' house. They lived in one of the modern staff houses at Fort Hare, near the river, a few steps above my former home, and on an edge of the campus. Their garden and yard adjoined a piece of veld between the college and Lovedale – not far from graves of English soldiers fallen in one or other of the Xhosa wars. I used to pass them years before when walking to school. The windows of their house were bright. We went in to find a crackling wood and coal fire. The night was cold, the children of the house were toasting their fingers and toes. The Mzamanes had three of their own, and in term time two teenage girls lived with them who were day-girls at Lovedale and belonged to friends and relations in the Transkei. As we came in through the kitchen where they all were, they scuttled to the walls of the room, behind chairs, anywhere to efface themselves before big people and make way for them to pass. I smiled for their action reminded me of when I was young. We too had always had other people's children living with us, their parents wanting them to be educated at Lovedale and also because, they would say to mine, 'We hope that by being with you Jili, MaGambu, they will absorb your atmosphere and become as *you* are.' Years later my mother told me this, saying, 'What appeal could be more disarming than that from people who were sometimes not even relations of ours?'

We greeted the young people, at which they tried to retreat even more, to obliterate themselves out of 'respect', the youngest of them so abashed that they looked away or even closed their eyes tight. And Mzamane disappeared into his study – again as my father used to do, I thought, into the sacred room totally forbidden to children, and away from domestic noises. When not doing college work Teacher was writing a novel in Xhosa (since published, and very fine), or working on a thesis on the structure of one of the nearly extinct archaic Northern Sutho dialects of South Africa. His wife rolled up her sleeves, set about supervising the workings of the household. The teenage girls had already started cooking the grown-ups' evening meal and to eat their own, which they stood up at, close to the stove so as to watch the pans. We had heard them all talking at the tops of their voices when we approached but now they observed a good-mannered hush in the presence of the mistress of the house. She looked round with a practised eye, congratulated them because everything was going according to plan: checked that the youngest was about to take a bath (this house had running water, unlike ours in the bush at Middledrift). She checked that the older girls had first done their school work before starting on their home duties. Next went through these: had they remembered to feed her Rhode Island Reds? Had the young apprentice garden-boy brought the milk cow home from the veld and tethered it for the night in its shed under cover by the garage? And had the day's washing been collected off the clothes line and put in the zinc container ready for the daily woman to iron next day?

Sis' Nompumelelo was a tall woman, built in proportion, a Juno, and comfortable-looking in her woolly cardigan and cotton dress; she was the sort who laughed uproariously and all the time. Even now as the children and young people answered her questions in proper subdued manner, they kept stealing glances at one another, dying to laugh with her but trying to hold back out of respect.

Then she took me to her bedroom. Chairs and bed had the usual heaps of sewing and knitting that she did for her family. 'These children *eat* clothes like goats,' she said and roared. She showed me her small knitting-machine, a recent acquisition. I saw her treadle machine along the wall draped with pairs of trousers. 'They belong to students,' she said. Students were always asking her to '*tsotsa*, taper' them since the craze for Edwardian drainpipes had displaced South African Oxford bags. 'How can you refuse these youngsters when they *know* that you have a sewing-machine?' We settled down to sew and mend and talk and laugh. As my father had said, I wanted to know about things which it would be inappropriate to allude to when with big people or with those of a younger 'generation' than my own and who regard *me* as a big person. However, when I put certain questions she laughed and protested, again on that semi-serious play-acting note:

'Those "things of Caesar" are not for you, Noni, man! You overseas people live an elevated life, not this of ours filled with deviations, schisms, political rivalries. We are *suffocating* in this South Africa of ours, becoming like cannibals, I tell you. *Apartheid* atmosphere is making us devour one another. Jockeying for position in all things. Disruption. Even in church affairs, imagine. "*I* frustration *isipethe*, girl, it really grips us; why should I drag your head down into all that?'

But I wanted to *know* how frustration gripped and said, 'Why should you hold things back from me? What makes you imagine that life overseas is untroubled? People there are not so different. They may not be exposed to *apartheid*, but do you imagine other things don't consume *their* minds and emotions? There is frustration, cannibalism, manœuvring and jockeying for positions there too.'

'*What?*' she raised her hands high, sewing fluttering in the air, 'Don't *say* that. You disillusion me. *Kaloku* you are "*Europeans of the water*", of the first water at that, Ntando *wam*!' We laughed and made so much noise that her husband called out from the next room. We tried to whisper, but would forget and find ourselves yelling again, her voice one of the most boisterous I have ever known. At last one of the school-girls knocked on the door and announced supper. We three sat down to eat, waited on by the girls. There was a moment when their faces were suddenly creased in amazement and disbelief when I 'exercised my privilege as a long absent person-of-the-house' and begged *Sis'* Nompumelelo to let them bring me a dish of common *umvubo*, boiled mealies with sour milk. I had seen them eat it for their suppers. The girls could not imagine I was serious. At the door they hesitated, looked back, eyes bright. But Teacher shouted and teased them, 'What is the *matter* with you children? Do you not know that overseas, *umvubo* is a treat – a pudding?' They scuttled off, and in the passage beyond burst out laughing. And presently brought my treat, their faces wreathed in smiles.

I fell to talking with Teacher about the state of the nation. But before I could draw him out, his wife interjected:

'Nontando, save up Teacher for the other talk that I know he wants to have with you – about archaic dialects. *I* am the one to tell you about "the state of the nation", *from its beginnings*, my dear girl, which is with these poor children that you see in our black homes. Oh, Ntando, oh, Noni! You'll never know what this *apartheid* atmosphere does to young people. Their little ambitions, so lively; their dreams of the exciting professions and careers they read or hear about on the wireless or see at the bioscope. These two girls for instance – one wants to be an air hostess. The little chap in the garden wants to be a pilot. What is there to say to them?'

The Nationalist Government made no bones these days about what it intended them to be when they grow up: servants to the whites. No engineering courses for keen black boys or careers as air hostesses for their sisters, who knew that if they had been born in Ghana or India the colour of their skin would not have prevented them.

'When your children begin to realize what lies ahead, they feel at a dead end. They get sad and depressed; then perhaps cheeky, as the iron begins to enter their little souls. Some get obstreperous. Others become withdrawn, apologetic, lose their curiosity and initiative. We seem to be growing into a new type of African, Noni. Even if one is only a housewife and mother as I am these days, one is up against it without even going out to meet *apartheid* in the street. Your children pester you: "Mama, why *can't* I be a wireless operator? Why can't I drive a Saracen

57

tank? Look at the smashing one in this magazine." And wishing you had no tongue with which to devastate them, all you can say is, "My child, don't dream those dreams. Don't break my heart – what do you expect me to do? It is strictly forbidden for black boys to do those jobs and that's all there is to it." That is the kind of answer you have to give your young hopefuls. Oh, it makes me envy white South African mothers. Do they realize how blessed they are, who do not have to crush their own children?' I imagined how I would feel if my circumstances had not by chance been different.

'And these students now at the college. I compare their hopes with mine at this same place years ago.' She and I shared her room that night, Teacher goodnaturedly banishing himself to the couch in his study so that we might go on talking. We did not stop until the small hours.

Next morning when the household had eaten and gone to school or college, the daily woman came, announcing her arrival in the usual stentorian tones of Xhosa language.

Mrs. Mzamane lifted her head and shouted back in kind, bidding the woman come through to the sitting-room 'to greet Jili's daughter'. She came, talking hard as she stamped thunderously on the polished floor-boards of the passage, her voice raised to the rafters about her journey on the lorry that had brought her into town from her village; only she called it a 'rolly'. Later she did it again. (Why, I asked myself, do people in unconnected parts of the world who can pronounce the sounds of the *l* and *r* phoneme, invariably interchange them in a language not their own? A journalist friend of mine in London told me how in the Far East he was without fail directed to 'The Pless Crub'. 'Most mysterious', he called it.)

The woman shook me by the hand, praised my father and my family menfolk. She was a younger version of the 'dressed' pagan women who worked for us at Middledrift. She wore the usual skirts under her apron, and a big turban that set off her splendidly poised neck and shoulders.

Sis' Nompumelelo said to her, 'My friend, just tell us something in Xhosa that Professor's daughter here asked me yesterday and I am ashamed to confess I could not answer,' and to me, 'Now here is a person for you to ask, Noni, the name of that plant of yours.' I ran to the bedroom to extract it from an envelope in my handbag. I had dried it but it was recognizable – a plant that I used to know as a child, picking it in the veld on walks but whose existence I had forgotten until this visit when it happened to be in flower. My late mother would have told me, but my father when I asked only peered at it over his bifocals, shrugged shoulders and jokingly affected not to know, or rather, to pretend that because he was a man he did not know.

'Ask one of the women folk, the waisted ones of the house,' he said. 'It was they in the past who combed the veld picking edible wild greens for themselves and the children. We men do not eat greens and therefore do not know these things.' I smiled; he was working on a book about the past, so this was one of the moments when in his mind I knew he was back in the traditional life of his beloved, ochre-daubed, milk-drinking, game-eating, vegetable-despising pastoralists. He certainly did eat vegetables and exhort people to grow them – had he not coaxed me when I was small and disliked them, with forkfuls of spinach or cabbage off his own plate? Romantic man! Now he dismissed me with a 'You should ask your new mother, Mam-Swazi.'

Mrs. Mzamane's servant examined the specimen with enormous concentration. We waited. At last she said, somewhat uncertainly although of course ear-splittingly loudly, 'Isn't its name "bromtjies"?' I looked at her; the word sounded totally un-Xhosa. But she reaffirmed it, nodding her head so that she had to lift up her arms to adjust the turban.

'"Bromtjies"?' I asked. 'Do you mean "blomtjie"?'

'Ja, *yi* bromtjies *le*, that's what it is.' Mrs. Mzamane thanked her but looked at me and winked. Later when Teacher came back and heard, he cried, 'My goodness, what is the *matter* with you people?' (a favourite admonition, often on people's lips). 'Do you not realize that this new-style pagan woman is teaching you Afrikaans? What Xhosa is this? "Blom" is Dutch, man; "flower, bloom"! Even her Afrikaans is no good, she only half-knows that plural diminutive.' And he snatched it away, galvanized into making independent inquiries; Teacher could no more abide faulty linguistics than my father.

Meantime the woman had gone back to her work, talking

59

with scarcely a pause for breath. As she heaved furniture then scrubbed floors beyond doors that were sociably ajar, her conversation rang out. She was really thinking aloud. Once I looked up to see her momentarily leaning forward on the hand that wielded the scrubbing-brush, eyes fixed in the middle distance of the floor she was working on while soapy water trickled over her brown wrist, and she hollered as if to someone across a valley, 'O, Lord God of the people! How on-earth will my poor children learn proper English or even proper Afrikaans now that our schools must instruct only in "mother-tongue", and only teach enough white people's language to make them "good servants"? How will they better themselves and *rise* from this kneeling posture of *my* life? Oh, this Bantu Education of Verwoerd!' In an undertone I asked *Sis'* Nompumelelo, 'If she is typical of the dormant unsophisticates who accepted "gradualism" in politics or social change, what are people of our sort supposed to feel under the pressure of this Verwoerd of hers?' But she could not comment for her woman continued in ringing tones, 'The *things* these Boers say! "Delicacy" is no word known to them, I swear to God. They only know brutality, burst on us like thunderbolts in that language of theirs. As for Verwoerd? A proper Boer!' She paused to wipe the sweat off her face with a wet arm, '"*Li Bhulu kakuhle elo*, no mistaking him for a 'European' (Englishman) that one".' *Sis'* Nompumelelo reminded her that it was time she rested and ate her mid-morning snack; a plate of porridge left warm in the pan from the family breakfast, bread and dripping and tea. She collected her thoughts and heaved a great sigh.

'I thank you, *Sis'* MamKwayi. You are right. Let me put Verwoerd aside and instead fill my empty belly with your good polish.' I had to look away for *Sis'* Nompumelelo too was suppressing a smile. It seemed an apt moment to change the subject, and *Sis'* Nompumelelo knew I was doing partly that when I now asked permission to go into Alice to do some shopping. It had already been arranged that I should, for my afternoon would be occupied – one of my cousins at the college was taking me to a students' tennis match. She 'gave me the road', but insisted that her young apprentice garden-boy (of the heart-breaking dreams about being a pilot) should accompany me; it was not polite, traditionally, for a grown woman to go on errands without a young escort to carry her parcels – or, if a bride, also someone who might pronounce the names of her husband or his family (which she herself might not) in unexpected conversations with people on the way.

I set off, my escort dropping his hoe to follow. He looked about fifteen, and neat in patched khaki shorts and old panama hat. It took only a few minutes to reach the shops, along the main road where I had driven with the uncles. But once in town I loitered, stared, listened, savoured the atmosphere now that I was on my own. I bought presents for the Mzamane children and their other young people.

Then I made for my main objective, a 'native' or 'Kaffir Goods Store', the sort where our servants buy yards of 'German' – the cheap blue cotton print that they sew up into those graceful voluminous skirts. There had been two or three such stores in Alice for as long as I could remember but I had never set foot in them. As children of 'school, civilized people', our nannies or nurse-girls kept a firm hold on us when out for walks and did not allow us to wander among the red-blanketed pagans who filled them. 'The *imbola* that they daub on themselves will dirty your clothes. And the language of those unconverted people is improper.' But now few – even among prim nannies – are ashamed of or despise the pagan half of the nation. My father's attitude towards them had not undergone any change, however, for he had always said, 'They are the fountain of Xhosa life and language, custom' and of him they in turn said he was a 'Lover-of-the-*people*'. Other sophisticates had caught up with him, thanks to *apartheid* which was imbuing everyone with national consciousness; *u*Verwoerd was closing the ranks and divisions. It was thanks to him that I drew no glances of curiosity when I arrived at the most popular Kaffir store in town.

It was like hundreds of others in country towns or isolated in villages in the Ciskei and Transkei, even on the outskirts of the big cities. At the doorway men stood about, blankets draped over their shoulders like togas and carrying knobkerries in their hands. There were women among them, in turbans, enormous structures of heavy cotton, dark blue or bottle green decorated with rows of white stitching in linear patterns which they machined on the portable Singer sewing-machine that every woman possesses as part of her bridal bottom drawer. One woman's turban was a striped Turkish towel, a fairly recent affectation in head-wear. It seemed to acquire importance, like a fashion note, and set off the rest of her costume: a red-ochred shawl the size of a bed sheet, folded in half across her shoulders; a long rectangular white bib tied above her breasts and dropping down over them to below the knees – the modesty bib prescribed, together with the turban, for women on marriage. Then there was the ankle-length ochred skirt, copiously flared, cut so that the straight edges, picked out with bead-work, were in front and all the fullness swathed to the back where the folds swung from heel to heel as a woman walked. And in the eyes of those brought up to appreciate the niceties of the costume, the swing of those provocative folds depended on how she carried herself. Pagan society was lynx-eyed about the sexual attraction of carriage. The folds at the bottom of the skirt were decorated with row upon row of spaced black braiding – a touch that enhanced the flow of a really fine step and walk.

There were unmarried girls in the crowd too. Their skirt was only knee-length and straight, not voluminous. Girls like to sport a man's leather belt at the waist. They wear no turban, and no shawl except in cold weather. Their breasts are bare, for when firm they are the proud sign of 'not having been spoilt and borne an illegitimate child', since those of mothers who have nursed droop for ever.

The entire body of every man, woman and child was smeared with the mixture of animal fat and ochre which our nurse-maids had objected to. The reason for it: to protect the skin from sunburn and from getting chapped in South Africa's very dry atmosphere which is often bitterly cold. They also daub their garments with the ochre, since once your body is covered with it you may as well go the whole hog because your clothes will be stained.

And they wore bead necklaces, some broad and deep over the collar-bone, reminiscent of the neckwear one sees in paintings on pyramids, of ancient Egyptians. The women's arms were covered with brass bangles graded to fit tightly from wrist to elbow and often even on the upper arm. As a child I had not admired what I saw, being staunch 'School' in attitude, hostile to things pagan – closer then to the rigid outlook of my nurse than to my father's since I was much with her. But I had since travelled in other lands and changed my mind. The red-robed people had come to seem to me magnificent. The men in togas reminded me of the Romans that I visualize when I read the novels of Robert Graves; and the women were like the figures on frescoes of ancient vessels – all the movement was there, the flow and grace, on backgrounds of terracotta and black. The *only* trouble with the crowd I now admired: it smelt to high heaven! Rancid fat, acrid smoke of wood, cattle-dung fires – for of course huts have no chimneys. When visiting the homes of relations of ours who are pagans and superb representatives of all those forefathers in our myths and legends, my 'school Christian' eyes smart and stream; I choke and gasp. Even in the shop, mixing freely and identifying myself with our people, I had been warned not to breathe too deeply.

And the ochre, now so beautiful to my eyes was a menace to my white dress. The people were aware of this and as I stepped between them they made way and cracked good-humoured jokes about not staining 'the immaculate convert' in their midst, making me laugh with them and feel welcome.

Inside it was semi-dark, the light from windows high up the wall almost blotted out by thick piles of blankets which hung from racks suspended from the ceiling. The shelves round the walls were stacked from top to bottom with bolts of 'German' and many varieties of cheap cotton prints, and 'Kaffir sheeting' – the heavy off-white twill from Manchester. And there was 'Kaffir' hardware – black three-legged iron pots (from Birmingham no doubt), tied together and strung from hooks. They looked like strings of Breton onions. Next to them were billy cans and zinc buckets that shone. And rows of combs and bangles of every colour of the rainbow, mostly pink, blue, red and pale green.

I had come to buy some Kaffir sheeting, and had arranged with a pagan relation of one of our women at Middledrift to decorate it with the black braid that they use. (My own pagan relations live on the Natal border, at Harding, where the Jilis really originate.) I wanted to take it overseas to make curtains; exotic, smart, to remind me of home. When my eyes became adjusted to the subdued light I saw two Europeans at the far end, in short-sleeved khaki shirts, serving behind the counter. Blanketed customers crowded in front of them, packed into the available space. Some leant elbows on the counter and supported their chins with their hands as they examined the goods. They did this with concentration, with the unselfconsciousness that is often mistaken for 'childlikeness'; and with an air of having all the time in the world to decide. The hum of conversation was deafening. Every buyer was helped to make his or her choice by the others standing about, and who all spoke in the usual terrific tones as if addressing people far off up mountains. From time to time, someone would turn aside, remove his or her pipe that was as long as your arm from the mouth and indulge in a splendid hard jet-like spit on to the floor-boards. You had to keep a sharp look-out and leap out of the way.

The Europeans spoke Xhosa, and as locals usually were, seemed relaxed, unhurried, like their customers. I pushed my way through and stood at the counter next to a woman in the act of announcing that she had at last reached 'the moment of being about to buy'. She shouted, 'Come, European, I am ready for you.'

Her shoulders were bare, for she had wound her shawl under her armpits and over the married woman's modesty bib in order to free her hands. She now lifted them to her huge turban. The brass bangles from wrist to forearm gleamed. She felt in the folds of the turban, extracted a knotted piece of rag which she placed on the counter before her, then resettled her turban, patting the folds back into place – all the while keeping up a powerful running commentary on the reasons why she had decided on the goods she had picked in preference to other specimens of the same, interrupting it to repeat, 'Come, European.'

Then she began to untie the knotted rag. She took out of it some pound and ten-shilling notes. They were grubby, and wrapped around coins : half-crowns, florins, shillings, sixpences, even 'tickeys' – the tiny silver threepenny bits.

'*Come*, man! What is the matter with this European – is he pretending not to want money?' Her every move was watched, men and women sucking their long pipes, eyes glued on her fingers as she fumbled. One man called out after the last tickey had been unwrapped, 'Where are the pennies and halfpennies?'

'Oh, I keep those in my purse,' she said. That in turn was inside a twill bag decorated with black piping and suspended from her waist. She counted out the money. One of the Europeans now sauntered up and joined in the watching. She counted the money a second time, and a third time through, then paused. She raised her face to the ceiling and burst out in loud lament, 'Oh God, these Europeans are killing me! Why do you kill me, European, taking all my money?'

I leapt back a step for she 'threw' her voice like an actress, within inches of my ear. You could have heard her from the back row of a theatre, yet the shopkeeper was only across the counter. He was not disturbed but replied quietly, blandly, in Xhosa, his brown eyes scanning the money spread out in front of him, 'Have you not come of your own volition then, to be killed?'

'But you are *truly* killing me!'

He did not answer immediately and a chorus of male and female voices rumbled in jovial laughter. People shook themselves to be more comfortable and take part. They stood at ease, mothers hoisting babies more securely on backs or hips, men changed knobkerries from one hand to the other, and taking pipes out of mouths, commented, 'Are you deaf, European? Did you not hear what she said? She has worked a whole month for the money which you stand looking at as if you would like to swallow it.'

'Look at his Adam's apple, how it moves up and down. Swallowing already. She is right. Being killed we are, wretched black people. We toil, kill ourselves for you. Then you kill us again, swallowing the money back – eh?'

The shopkeeper said, as if making an effort not to smile, '*Of course* I must swallow, if you force your money down my throat. Now look here, lady, what about it, are you buying or not? Because I will put these things back on the shelf if you don't want them.'

'No, oh, no! Why such a hurry? I am still *counting*, man.'

'*She is still counting*, man European! Leave her. It is not your dinner-time yet.' A burst of laughter, for pagans do not eat at midday, only morning and evening and think Europeans (and 'school' people) very soft. The woman was arranging the coins in little heaps, pausing now and again to stroke her chin. She seemed thoughtful of a sudden and at last cried, 'My! But I have not *got* the money you want, don't you see, European? *Andinayo mos!* Oh, problem, problem! To be solved *how?*' Her tone was no longer bantering. Again that unselfconsciousness. There was a hush. Everybody counted the coins with their eyes, saw that she was a few shillings short. She had made more purchases than planned when originally wrapping the money into the rag, then turban, then setting off for town. Now she moaned, '*Yu-u-u!* I have walked all this way – nine miles! Even stinged myself the bus-fare, and now not enough money. Yet I *need* those things!' She looked at them, gave a low whistle and shook her head dolefully from side to side. The hush around her deepened in sympathy until it seemed reverential. Everyone participated in her predicament. I too found myself agonized. The atmosphere was tense.

At last the European made a suggestion, quietly at first and with a straight face, '*Tandaza*', then repeated more clearly that everyone should hear, '*Pray*, good lady.' However tense, the people are ever ready to laugh and the advice brought the house down. The woman jumped, looked at her shopkeeper. The onlookers laughed still more. Their laughter made her turn and she swept an arm round at them and cried out, but now with a broad smile, 'You hear him. *Hey!* – these Europeans are *silly* – eh? Are they not getting out of hand? What does *he* know of prayers?' She moved farther as she spoke and now her back was turned to him. His face was stern, but the eyes twinkled while his customer harangued the crowd. At last he broke into a laugh, exclaimed 'Well-well!' in Xhosa, "*Yeh-haa!*"' You, a pagan, ask me a Christian such a question. Who is the silly one? Tell me that! You know *well* that I know prayer.'

'*Where*-from?'

'Church of course. Me, I kneel every Sunday. My knees are red with kneeling every Sunday.' The chorus echoed, splitting its sides, '*His knees are red!*' But the European went on, his face

66

expressionless. 'Here is my advice, since you ask me to solve this problem that you have made for yourself: Put your hand in that turban again and feel for *t-h-a-t O-T-H-E-R* money that you are still saving in there, doubtless for your church collection, since it seems I am getting praying church-women in my shop these days. Pay me from that, and you can take your goods home. Then pray for your church, dear red girl who is much-prized – because you will have squandered its money.' His Xhosa was exquisite. She clapped her hands together as if too scandalized to speak. When she found her tongue, she made comments tart and coarse, bucolic. Then she doubled up with laughter – kaleidoscope of mood changes – at the jokes he was making against her; and everyone joined in her laughter – a tremendous din. But I noticed that in the hubbub, the trader started to wrap the goods in a parcel. While he tied the string round it, he muttered under his breath making idiomatic jokes. He was the sort of South African that I have sometimes run into in Europe, who have approached me tentatively, and finding I was a fellow countrywoman, unburdened a load of homesickness. 'Overseas' lacked the tang of their small town back home.

He trimmed the string off and pushed the parcel towards the woman, who now seemed overcome. But she composed herself and made a proper little speech, 'O, *danke*, European. You have helped me. Truly you are a person of-ours after all. You have humanity!' I thought to myself: Probably one of those whose boast is, 'I'd kill the native who wanted to marry my sister.' But other elements were in him too, as in many such people. He arranged that she should pay the money she owed next month – a crippling sum: 3*s*. 6*d*. At last it was my turn to be served.

I took a short cut back to Fort Hare, 'time was leaving me behind,' made for a spot where there was a ford of stepping-stones across the river almost opposite the Mzamanes' house. The young boy followed, carrying my bulky bolt of twill.

Before we reached the ford, at a grove of oak trees, we passed a woman in a German print skirt and black turban. She was bending over, scrutinizing the ground exactly like one of Millet's figures in *The Gleaners*. She was collecting acorns, tossing them into a billy can by her feet. She raised her face to watch us pass, her body still bent over. We walked several steps beyond then heard her call. I turned, she straightened up and stood still, with one hand extended questioningly, with acorns in it. She seemed unsure . . . now suddenly I recognized her: one who years ago had come to our house on Mondays and Tuesdays to do the family washing and ironing. She lived at a village, *kwa* Gaga, some miles up a hill in the other direction out of Alice from Middledrift.

The chance encounter overwhelmed her. She was not a very old woman but her face was worn, especially noticeable in her case for she had one of those freckled reddish pomegranate-tinted 'thin' skins that chap in winter and in summer peel quite severely. And I knew that under her widow's turban she had the absolutely ginger hair that went with it. And when we had made our salutations and she had to wipe her eyes, I noticed while the tears stood in them that the pupils were grey-blue flecked with brown; and remembered how we used to remark on them as children and be told they went with the rest of her colouring. Now they looked old and weary; and I too was moved. We stood and talked. Gradually she controlled the feelings that had overtaken her on the unlooked-for reminder of her former mistress and happier times, declaiming as she mopped her face, 'O, the happenings on this earth, this eternity!' At last she had recovered enough to begin to chaff me about my looks. She had been with us when I was young enough to have had to listen to those comments about how ugly I was; and commented on my appearance now that I was a grown woman.

'But Ntando, child of our late one, your body has remained so slight – like an unmarried girl only. When will you acquire a *presence*? O, you married people of these days! Is it true then that people overseas eat only water? You look as if that is all you do eat. Shame. Are you not happy? Yet they say you have a good husband; have you?'

She on the other hand looked 'mature matron', the style of dress accentuating her size which she now compared with mine. She was small-boned, covered with soft flesh that looked any-thing but firm, healthy. Her bosom was motherly indeed – like a bolster. And her upper arms bulged; the hips swelled. She took pride in it all, as women do since that is what the men

admire, and was sorry that my frame did not 'display contentment in the state of marriage and motherhood'. I could not
say that my size was due to chance, to a different life; it was not
that I 'ate water' but foods that were nourishing and varied;
and not compelled, as she was, to survive on starch almost
to the exclusion of other things. I could indulge my caprice
when home and sentimental for thick milk and mealies, corn on
the cob and the rest. I joked about how I was making good my
deficiency of these during my long visit but thought, as I spoke
about our fates; and, not for the first time, how lacking in envy
people were when I came home. They reflected no less on these
fates but ascribed them, as she now did, to the Will of God;
and she added the usual rider, 'Time is on our side in South
Africa,' and that black people would all one day enjoy the
opportunities that were so far available to the few. She laughed
and teased about all that. Then, her voice changing to the tones
appropriate to a statement more solemn and semi-ritual, and
also more personal because of her former connection with us
which she said used to be 'her weekly uplift of the soul', she
thanked God for families such as mine because of what they
portended, and said, 'They are the leaves wafted beforehand by
the oncoming gale of progress.' It was deeply touching when
people spoke in such ways and I was thankful that we were
each brought up to feel ourselves a symbol, 'a representative
of a group" not of a family only, and not as a private person.
'*Umntu ngumntu ngabantu.* A person is a person (is what he is)
because of and through other people.' Otherwise success too
often leads to conceit and failure to humiliation that would be
an intolerably lonely burden. As it was, the sharing gave a sense of
proportion. While she was in the middle of her speech my
young escort gave an enormous sigh. I looked round at him.
He was shifting his weight from foot to foot, restless. The
woman noticed too. She stopped speaking immediately, in mid-
sentence, and turned to attend to him but saying to me, 'Wait,
Ntando, I have not finished,' then to the boy, in gentle concern,
'Forgive me, my father, my son, for delaying you in this way.
You see, this is a person I have not seen for *too* long, not since
she was so high. And believe me, my heart overflowed just
now because of her. That is why I have tired you. But I have

nearly finished, "Child of people who-have-trained-you-like-a-treasure"; who have made a gentleman of you; brought you up to *know respect*, patience, tolerance. You have shown it towards an old woman dwelling on matters that do not interest. Your people are to be congratulated.'

He, startled because his mind had been far away (probably looping the loop at the controls of some aeroplane) tried to smile. But we went on looking at him, now as subject of a prized 'upbringing, *ukuqeqesha*', embellishment to the unknown family in his background; he could stand it no longer and blushed, lowered his eyes, began to dig with his toe among the oak leaves on the ground. His youthful confusion imprinted the interview even more in my mind because of the way it took me back. For the washerwoman's manners, courtliness towards him were part of what haunted my mind about home: the idea underlying the life of the people about 'the child being father to the man' – expressed, of course, differently in the language. She might have been saying this out loud for the thought was apparent on her face and I had heard elders many times give voice to it, 'Do not children represent continuity? Are they not "the jewels" in the life of a right-thinking man because closer in time to the ancestors from whom they have newly arrived to join us who are on our way back to them?' And they asserted at all times the importance of *all* generations in the social organism, even in the act of punishing children when naughty (training, incidentally, which must always be inflicted in public – never in private), or giving them tiresome tasks to perform, because it was their duty to obey in their present place in the hierarchical system, as this young boy had been given by his employer and guardian, *Sis'* Nompumelelo when she sent him to accompany me. But being 'put upon' by one's seniors and grown-ups fell into perspective in childhood, as I knew myself. The boy had been bored to death during this errand, yet he knew that his big people where he worked, laughter-loving but strict, sympathized with his hopeless little ambitions; and also thought well enough of him to thrust upon him responsible duties like this morning's.

I stole a glance at my watch. It was long past time to ask for the road. But we spent several more minutes before I did so. It was not likely that we would meet again.

7

WHEN we got back to the house my mood dispelled because *Sis'* Nompumelelo greeted us with her brand of uproarious, infectious laghter.

'Aha! Late, 'Ntando. You see how it is here at home? *"Ixesha alisoKUZE laziwe,* time can *never* be controlled", we don't *know* that thing, man.' Luckily the Mzamanes were not in the habit of dishing out meals on individual plates to wait – so that they turn into small mountains of stone-cold food. Having been so often thus confronted in South Africa, I have come to the sad conclusion that we are not among the sensitive nations of the world. We are no gastronomes; no Chinese, no French.

As we pulled chairs up to the dining table, they said that a programme had been arranged for me by my student cousins. Teacher had been at the lecture hall that morning and been approached by them for permission to entertain me.

'These youngsters are *formal,* man. They made a deputation, as if I were an old man.' I smiled; had he not formally asked *his* elders?

His wife laughed, 'But to them you *are* old, *Titshala.* It's only this courtesy title, "Teacher", that misleads. They would call you "father", but *kaloku* they are modern.'

We ate meat with *umngqush' onembotyi,* mealies and brown beans, pumpkin and greens from their garden, while they described my programme. Immediately after lunch I was to be taken to the court house at Alice because a case was being tried involving a Fort Hare student who had scuffled with police and black detectives at a political meeting held recently in a local rural village. In the cool of the late afternoon I was to go to a college tennis match; and in the evening to a dance at one of the students' hostels.

'They talk about getting a taste of "overseas" from you but clearly intend to give you a slice of their own life too.' Teacher said, 'We are a self-centred lot; typical *dorp* mentality.'

All the same I thought the programme did not only reflect what he said about small towns. It reflected the personalities of the cousins concerned. The one who wished to take me to the magistrate's court was Mzimkhulu Makiwane. By Western standards he was only a second cousin. But our grandfathers had been brothers, so we were 'brothers and sisters' all down the line. When I was two years old and my mother had gone to England a second time to continue music studies which she had begun when engaged to my father, I lived until the age of four with Mzimkhulu's mother. She had a girl my age, now married and living in Bechuanaland. Mzimkhulu had not yet been born; he 'had appeared', I learnt years later, shortly after my mother came back and fetched me home. And now he arrived at the Mzamanes and they presented him to me. This was our first real meeting. Hitherto I had seen him only at great family gatherings and never talked.

He was a tall slim man wearing a shaggy black moustache that contrasted with a light brown skin; the most noticeable feature about him his eyes. They were intense, flashing, unusual among his family. Mr. Mzamane said of them, 'Always on the look out for politics" for no sooner had we welcomed him than Mzimkhulu was launched on a description of the political threads of the case to which he was taking me. The Mzamanes cut him short with laughter. 'This one is a proper Makiwane – one of those forefathers of yours come back again.' They teased us about our ancestors who, in becoming Christians, had been radical revolutionaries; a ferocious step to take when you had been born and bred as pagans. Succeeding Makiwane generations were moderates politically, content with their inheritance which was British rule (the Colony Government) – even 'protection' in our case since Makiwanes and Jabavus were really Fingos, Zulu tribes in dispersal and only Xhosa by absorption, with a tendency at first to vacillate in their loyalties – a phase we later preferred to forget in the 'gradual evolution' that westernization promised for Fingo and Xhosa alike. Far greater numbers of Xhosa were conservative, not having been broken up by northern despots as we had been before Europeans came on the scene and therefore already rootless. Mzimkhulu was a throw-back – with other Gambus of our generation – more revolutionary than his father. In the family we all knew the conflict between these two. The son thought the father a stick in the mud because like all our fathers he clung to the British principle of constitutionalism, gradualism; whereas my cousin's hopes were anything but constitutional or gradual.

He had started adult life as a country teacher. Then he moved to the big city to do other work, anything he could find that was better paid in order to save up more quickly for what he wanted: a university degree. Like many contemporaries, he 'went back to school', to Fort Hare, although married by then and with a young family. He was reading for his B.A. and Diploma in Education, wanting to teach; a 'born teacher'; but higher qualifications would throw open to him more interesting, better paid teaching jobs. While a world's worker in the city, he had been imprisoned for the usual offence – Failing to Produce a Pass when Challenged by the Police. That touched him off, put the 'fire' in his eyes. He became a 'live wire', a rebel who refused to take *apartheid* lying down, or even accommodate himself to it. His father had chanted at him in that special Xhosa tone that expresses exasperation, the refrain so often on the lips of elders trying to equip their young for a livelihood that we absolutely know it by heart, 'Leave politics a-lone awhile, young people. They will st-ill be with us when you finish your studies. First get your qualifications, afterwards indulge in the luxury, if you must. Else how will you earn your bread and butter?' And hot young men like my cousin look away and clench their teeth in silence – for you do not answer elders back. When he and I were alone presently and talked about that, he said laughing, 'It puts you in a fix, not being allowed to remind them to their faces that "Man cannot live by bread alone" or that they quoted it practically daily at prayers, when we young ones knelt on the floor and were all ears. You feel like asking: "Did you think we would not listen, or want to act?" Old people do not analyse anything, that is the trouble with them.'

I had already been told how Mzimkhulu had had to promise the family that while at Fort Hare he would 'stay quiet'. Yet I knew that university students were like their kind the world over: they reacted like litmus paper to their environment.

They hoped and dreamed; yet the future that was now prescribed for them was such as to open the eyes of even unlettered
house-servants. The night before, I had been hearing about
repeated outbreaks of 'strikes' on the campus, alcoholism,
boycotting of meals in hall and of lectures, violence, expulsions,
every kind of unrest; and often coinciding with each new wave
of 'Bantu Legislation'. I wondered how, with his temperament,
he was managing to keep the promise to be, so to speak, 'a
quietist'. He gave a rueful smile, spun his hat round in his long
Makiwane fingers.

'*Sis*' Nontando, don't ask. I'm managing – by the skin of my
teeth. Things are too hot at Fort Hare these days. I am always
suspected of being near the centre of whatever trouble there is.
Am supposed to be a ring-leader even when I have done
nothing. "*Sendifile kakade*, am dead (convicted) anyway." Yet
knowing I have not done my bit. MaJili, I tell you, "*ifrustration
indipethe!*"'

Not everybody approved of him, but I was enjoying his company. He might be idiosyncratic but he had courage, humour.
I could believe what I had been told, how in prison his personality had cheered the hearts of other 'law-breakers'. No one
regarded him as a law-breaker; race legislation sooner or later
lands everybody in jail – they do not have to be criminals. And
however often he 'went inside', my cousin certainly had not the
look of a potential anti-social type; I had only to listen to his
wry jokes and look at his carefully pressed grey flannels; brown
shoes gleaming; shirt spotless. You could see that his neatness
was not come by without effort. The clothes were worn, the
flannels of ancient cut, not even *tsotsa'd* – his money went on
books, pamphlets, and sheet music. He was the sort of person
who looks presentable yet nonchalant, 'born a dandy, *ukuhomba*',
with a distinguished bearing because of his carriage, figure,
height: especially carriage – *umkhita*. When we got up to leave
for Alice, Teacher remarked on it in a manner that was
evidently habitual in people who saw him regularly, 'So you are
taking her to this police case of yours, Gambu. Look after her,
man, *umnta' ka Profesa!* But you will – just look at your brother's
walk, Noni. A soldier. That back of his – they say he lashes it to
a plank, that's why it is as it is.'

74

We started off, retracing my steps of that morning. I began to feel proud as we went for I became aware that my relation was something of a celebrity. People hailed him, not only fellow students but mature Africans, even pagans. In the end I asked, 'How do the ochred ones know you, Gambu?'

He smiled and said, blushing, '*Kaloku* some of us these days try to emulate your father, *Sis'* Noni. Everybody tells how when he lectured at Fort Hare, he used on Sunday afternoons to go into the villages round about to talk with pagans; sat with them right by the cattle-kraal – to *convert* them, to religion if possible even though he wasn't a minister, but mainly to the idea of educating their children. *u*Jili was making sure of a supply of future Fort Harians, I suppose. Anyway some of us now see the importance of that field-work. We go among the pagans and try, in our way, to carry on where he left off. That's how they know me.'

'Do *you* convert people to religion? Since when did you become that way?'

'Ah, you don't know the full story of my misdeeds – why should you? Well, I *am* religious, sort of. It's the music, really. I like these prayer meetings because of the chance they give me to organize the music, conduct the singing – choirs, quartets. Do you realize the kick people get out of it? The way they *go* for it, close harmony, rhythm, syncopation, counterpoint! It is next door to "*umbhayizelo*, the dance" – that is the tradition they build on. You might call it a case of music taming the savage breast, the way it fits in with these secular matters of Verwoerd's.'

'Verwoerd? Even at *umbhayizelo*? And fitting in?'

'After the singing – and there are wonderful voices hidden in those huts, it is utter pleasure – you naturally sit around and talk. And these days everybody, pagans included, wants to "Read the Lesson"; in other words the new "Bantu Laws"! People are supposed to know and understand them, are they not? "Ignorance is no Defence!" But pagans cannot read. So they take advantage of *our* acquaintance with the *a b c*. They get us to read aloud and explain these new edicts; the same way they ask "school" people to write letters for them, you know. *Apartheid* legislation winkles everybody out. The "idyllic"

Native Reserves are just like the urban areas these days, harassed, restless, on fire. But of course we are all proper blacks, we have to mix the harassment and instruction with music.'

Four years later back in England, I had news about Mzimkhulu, finished at Fort Hare and living in the Transkei. It was when trouble broke out there over the enforcement of part of the torrent of new laws he had talked about – this time the 'Bantu Authorities Act' to create 'Bantu States' in the overcrowded Reserves in order that blacks 'should develop along their own lines'. He was on the point of arrest. He had 'done nothing'; so, like others of my relations who were arrested and detained under the Emergency, he was charged with no specific offence; he was assumed to be a ring-leader. Red-blanketed music-loving friends went to him by stealth one night to give him warning: that one of the Africans employed by the Government as spies and detectives had 'bitten them in the ear' (told them secretly) that his apprehension was imminent. 'There is no time to lose, Gambu,' they whispered, and produced an ochre-stained toga, beads, knobkerries for him to carry – an entire costume to disguise their choirmaster who must take flight immediately. He must have looked magnificent. They had also brought him a horse ready saddled. And to see the operation through, they rode with him, 'daggers in cloaks', to the border of the British Protectorate. Eventually he reached an Arab town in North Africa, where I, on a visit and knowing nothing of all this, missed bumping into him in a French-named boulevard by a single day. I was not surprised when I heard of those adventures, for as we walked to the court house that afternoon I was catching a glimpse of the life he and our contemporaries found themselves living.

The Court House was not far from my Kaffir Goods Store of the morning, on another side of the central space in the middle of the town, Market Square, to which in the old days wagons and Scotch-carts had brought farm produce for sale once a week. Later, lorries were used, the wide dirt roads modernized. On one side of the square an expanse of grass was now edged with flowering plants. Civic buildings gave on to it. They seemed never to change, I thought, looking at them.

There, as of old, was the Magistrate's Office, and Post

Office with people's P.O. Box safes in the wall; ours used to be P.O. Box 8. But Fort Hare had its own Post Office now. Opposite was the Town Hall – where we used to go to the 'bioscope' – and shops; also the Standard Bank of South Africa, and Barclay's D.C.O. My father, and for some reason most people, 'were Standard Bank', so I was rather odd in now 'being D.C.O.' because I cashed my travellers cheques there. They were taken aback to discover that in London I refrained, because opposed to my country's Government's policies, from using a South African bank.

On another side of the green, the jail house was still there under leafy oaks a few steps from the tiny Public Library (Europeans Only). Alice looked better kept than ever. I could see at a glance that the community had prospered. Whoever was in charge of the municipal gardens and pathways had funds to make a good job of them. He and the town councillors were white. Like other long-established towns inhabited by blacks and white, our little *dorp* was now a 'White Ethnic Group Area', supposed to be on its way to the dream condition: 'inhabited by Europeans Only, day and night'. However, because I had been born and brought up in it I found it an effort to remember this. I could see Mrs. Tremeer's butcher's shop across the road from where my cousin and I now stood outside the court house waiting for the doors to open. She and my mother used to discuss not only cuts of meat but how their toddlers were doing, her son Rhodes and I, while we, meantime, eyed each other's tricycles on the pavement beyond the shop's fly-screen. I always went to greet her when I came home from overseas – perhaps now breaking one of the new laws in doing so. Rhodes had blossomed into a celebrated South African photographer and had made a gift to my family of pictures that he took of the funerals when my mother and brother died. My cousin commented, 'If there is no law against that kind of neighbourliness wait till Verwoerd hears about it. He'll frame and pass one so quick, you'll blink.'

I could see the attorney's office, old Mr. Burl's, my father's lawyer, adviser and friend for forty years. The town was made up of such people. I saw the garage proprietor walking across the street, Mr. Petzer, a Boer. He still looked strong and rugged though now his jet black hair was streaked with grey. The sight of him reminded me of how my father used to speak of him when he was younger and we were children, and say, 'The kindest-hearted man on earth; and what a Rugby-footballer, with that *neck*' (demonstrating its leonine proportions), 'those biceps, those calves, legs.' The sight of Mr. Petzer inevitably called to mind his old father-in-law, '*u*Botha', everyone called him with something like affection. His character had many aspects; he was a Boer, but we all had dealings with him; he dovetailed into our lives and movement often at hectic moments – for he ran a taxi. The law had not been passed yet – it has since – that taxis must ply for passengers only within their own racial group. We all swore that '*itexi ka* Botha' was the most reliable of them all. He never let you down. And you engaged his even in place of those run by friends or relations, especially if you wanted to be sure to catch a train. And the old man was one of the finest idiomatic Xhosa speakers in the district; like old Mr. Glass, of English Settler descent, who even wrote it so beautifully that despite the changes in its orthography during his life-time in the town, it flowed 'like pagan cattle-kraal language'.

Standing there waiting set me talking in reminiscent mood, 'Like a big person', my cousin laughed as I possibly bored him about the town's inhabitants when I was small. I now saw them all as 'South Africans', starting with old Mr. Salaai, whose salutation is I *think* Cira, who still worked as messenger at Taylor's Stores across the road, which belonged to the cultivated family whose name it bore, and where my mother had always shopped.

And I talked about the *predikant* of Alice's (Whites Only) Dutch Reformed Church on the slope of the hill on the west, an ardent musician. Once when on holiday from school in England where I had learnt to play the violin, I took my fiddle and bicycled across this square to his house. In those days he caused no sensation in the town when he invited me to come of a morning and practise the Double Concerto by Bach with him. Mzimkhulu pretended to be shocked to hear it.

'You even stopped for a rest from practising, at eleven o'clock and drank coffee together? Cousie, today you would both get the lash – fraternizing across the race and sex bars in that way. Fifteen strokes. No, ten only, because the "Opposition", the United Party secured *that* amendment! Did you hear about it overseas? When the Government Minister of Justice, Swart, just smiled and said, "Very well, gentlemen, *make* it ten, if that is what you prefer. After all, what is five strokes, between friends?" or jolly words to that effect.'

The atmosphere had been different in my young days, and because of that I tried to describe to my cousin the pleasures that the sight of my home-town brought me. Their intricacies drew a smile from him. I had the impression that he understood, but he made no comment.

People were arriving in numbers now at the court house and a crowd was gathering outside the old stone building. It was Victorian and looked colonial. The zinc roof was painted dark red, its window shutters an ugly brown. The gum trees and green bushes in the park a few yards away seemed to set off its sombre colours. We were joined by a host of boisterous students in their black and yellow Fort Hare blazers. I noticed the way the townspeople looked at them as they talked and laughed and commented about general affairs and offered one another ideas about how the world might be put right – as young people like to do. The locals, black and white, paid no attention. They were used to them. One or two Europeans were clearly not locals though, for they watched and listened in surprise. There were several African manual workers, municipal gardens employees and some mine-boys wearing the rough cotton trousers knotted below the knee. They were '*ama*-Join-*i*', recruits to the gold-mines (joiners) killing time from their business of signing on at the Native recruiting office near by. There were also Africans in collars and ties – clerks or teachers. And there were the ubiquitous red pagans who stood about, picked their teeth with thorns and emitted lightning jets of spit on the dusty ground. All of these listened to the students' chatter, not with indifference or surprise but approval. The expressions on their faces reminded me of the housemaid at the Mzamanes, of the energy that she concentrated on the problem of 'educating our children that they might rise in the world'. The students seemed equally energetic, yearning for life's experiences – of which they had come here to sample yet another kind, that of the Law in Action.

At last the doors opened and they trooped in, not waiting as they should, I noticed, for their elders to go in first. They heaved and pushed, we all pushed – red-ochred, collar-and-tied, blazered, along with the sweaty, trouser-knotted brigade who tried to hide billy cans and knobkerries politely under the folds of blankets draped over one shoulder and falling with a curious grace over their version of proletarian trousers.

Indoors the moderate-sized country court house was warm and stuffy from the preprandial session, despite windows having been left wide open. We shuffled along towards rows of wooden benches. The races observed the usual segregation in seating themselves but did so perfunctorily since people knew one another in the small town and were not impelled to make an issue of racial protocol as they would with strangers; they only wanted to be next to friends. The better seats – for whites – were near where Mzimkhulu and I found places and he whispered, 'In the big cities, Jo'burg or even Port Elizabeth, court officials are strict about this seating business these days.'

After the magistrate came in (a correct, unruffled, legal-looking man called Mr. Schwabe whose status we acknowledged by the usual rising to our feet and not sitting down again until he had sat down), I heard the prosecutor Mr. Stofelberg murmur as he wiped his brow with a large, clean, white handkerchief, 'This place is getting a little bit *shushu*.' It gave me one of my pangs of obstinate pleasure to hear that spontaneous, and apparently unconscious, use of the Xhosa word for 'hot'; it reminded me of a passage I had read somewhere about 'modifications taking place in the cultural life of the Europeans of South Africa owing to their contacts with the Natives'. I settled down to watch, for the court scene illustrated some of these contacts and the modifying of the inheritances of the different racial groups.

The case opened. Everyone seemed to follow the languages used, Xhosa, Afrikaans, English, despite the formal use of interpreters for people reacted – exclaimed or laughed – even before one of these men opened their mouths to translate.

The majesty of the Law, its procedures and officers – all that was 'white'. But culture contact was inexorable for in the Law's ranks there were some blacks: informers, detectives, policemen. The students giggled sneeringly at these and hissed in undertones, 'Stooge! Sell-out!' whenever one of them took the oath before giving evidence against their fellow.

To me the contacts seemed emphatic because I had not realized until then, never having been to court, how the Xhosa words and phrases that had to be used would sound in context when translated from the English legal terms. I was startled by the beam of light that they threw on our inherited attitude towards the whole function of the law. But nobody else seemed surprised when for example, for the term 'defending lawyer', interpreters said '*igqwetha* – twister'; or for 'prosecutor', '*umtshutshisi* – torturer, harrier'. Such words and their meanings are the natural ones in current present-day Xhosa, not archaic or stylized. And I gasped, for need one look farther to see that what seems a fair, balanced, unemotional process in the eyes of our white fellow countrymen looks to us like 'a system of trickery'.

Ours was of another principle and attitudes to it are ingrained in everybody because all took part in legal actions; the law had no professionals; therefore 'big people' handed down the attitudes it expressed, along with all the other which influenced our lives.

In a Xhosa customary court a litigant announced to the Chief who sat in Council with elders, '"*Ndimangele!* I have brought a complaint!"'

And a member of the council would 'encourage' him (linguistically) by uttering one of those expectant words, '"*Yitsho!* Say it!"' or '"*Qhuba!* Continue!"' The complainant would unfold his case step by step, encouraged in that manner from phrase to phrase – even if it took days. When finished, he used the familiar expression. '"There I pause, rest my case!"'

It would then be the accused's turn to state his. That too might take days. Time was no object. At the end of that, the elders – and male members of the public – would cross-examine the contenders and their witnesses. These were present throughout, not at any time sent out of earshot as during the processes of white people's litigation – no 'trickery'. All speakers were allowed their full say however tediously they might digress. Finally the Chief would give his verdict, a summing-up of the decision arrived at by the elders' council and delivered in language that everyone could follow, including the women and junior (uncircumcised) men who might take part by listening from a distance but under no circumstances speak.

But the court case at Alice expressed another idiom. From the beginning of the proceedings, if you were an African involved or looking on, you felt slightly out of tune. Too many people seemed to talk, even shout, at once; which was partly because of the translating which clearly cannot be dispensed with; but mainly because nobody giving evidence was allowed to express himself according to our ideas of completeness. Tradition and custom prepared us for the hazards of interminable boredom and repetitiousness that that might entail.

The atmosphere of 'white' brusqueness and harassment was aggravated and heightened – in our minds – by what was *not* meant to happen but often did: that officers holding the floor, or leaping up to interrupt, would round on an interpreter immediately on detecting an imperfect rendering of their words or their client's for they understood the original as well as the translation. Thus what sounded like a squabble broke out and resounded in that hot, stuffy chamber and made all of us squirm and glance at one another – for nothing could sound more improper; according to custom, at all times one voice only should be heard and that was never to be interrupted however mendacious, evasive.

'Let a man have his say and in his own words get out of his system all that is within,' was the motif. The people, assembled to watch him like hawks, believed they would later arrive at the truth.

In the box, the African witnesses slipped into traditional ways of giving evidence – rambled, made flowery speeches; they prolonged dialogue through the luckless interpreter by counterposing parable or analogy to questions that had been put: a natural temptation for the interpreters were all Africans, therefore witnesses slipped into the error of treating them as if they were men in their own right – not, as the European law required, impersonal mediums. At one such point the European lawyer cried out in understandable exasperation, '*Must* there be a long conversation between the witness and the interpreter every time I ask a simple question?' and banged the table with the palm of his hand, a theatrical gesture that he had to stoop to perform, face red with anger, impatience. As a member of the audience you felt for him even if you had to stifle a guffaw, and were thankful that his was not the job you were saddled with – to get at the facts. He shouted, 'Answer the question "Yes" or "No"!'

Dumbfounded, hurt, frustrated, could the African in the box look anything but evasive? I was not legally minded, nor on the law's side as the case unfolded. Yet I was aware that we were listening to distortions. Misunderstandings seemed inevitable. A black policeman being cross-examined became indignant because his colleague implied that he had not co-operated, could conceivably have been 'the prisoner's friend', that the scuffle (on which hung everything) that was being described might have been staged on purpose to allow the prisoner's initial escape.

We watched the man's dark face flush darker, his eyes burn; he could scarcely contain himself; a policeman's lot was not a happy one when white colleagues mistrusted him because of race; and in addition was himself a leper among his own because he worked 'for the other side, a stooge, a sell-out'. He exploded, 'What is the *matter* with this fellow? If I was not co-operating with him then what was that prisoner's shoe looking for in my hand, *what was it doing with ME – besifuna ntoni ke esasihlangu KUM?*'

The interpreter: 'Allegation incorrect, your worship.' The burst of laughter that greeted the condensation provoked the policeman intolerably and he yelled, 'This white fellow is trying to *fix* me because we were *both* fooled by that prisoner. And he has said to himself (acting it out): "*Which* of us is going to be in the soup when this thing becomes known?"' In his agitation he threw in the English noun but in Xhosa locative form, the whites of his eyes bulging.

I looked at my watch, thinking that days later when I left for the Transkei the drama would probably still be on. Mzimkhulu noticed my glance. As soon as he could he led me out. He obviously longed to stay but was torn, reluctant to let me walk back to Fort Hare alone, saying, '*Titshala* will be vexed and call me a savage; and rightly, if I let you go unescorted.'

'But we are not in Johannesburg, Gambu. There are no gangsters here – it's my home town.'

My cousin still demurred. In the end I fell back on what he could not dispute, my privilege as his senior; and made him stay.

8

My other cousin was waiting when I got back to the Mzamanes'
house. Now he really was a cousin, in English – my uncle Cecil's
third son and last born. He had 'appeared' when I was seventeen. Because he was that much younger, he did not comment
on my lateness. When I ran into the room he just smiled and
shambled shyly to his feet. He treated me rather more gingerly
than the gap in our ages really called for because in his eyes I
was almost of the older generation, the reason being that his
only sister, now about twenty-five, was regarded in the family
as 'my' child. When she was five, I had left school in England
and was home for eighteen months. Uncle Cecil and Aunt
Valetta and their children came to stay. The little girl took to
following me everywhere, became my 'tail' as everybody called
it. Years later my mother told me that when I was seen to submit to the attachment and the obligations that it entailed, the
fact was noted with satisfaction. Everyone had noticed some of
the Western mannerisms that I had acquired and were dis-
mayed, feared they might cause difficulties in the future; my
acceptance of the infant encumbrance was observed with
approval by the elders.

'You sometimes turned down invitations to dances if your
little tail fretted,' my mother said – to my amazement, for not
only had I forgotten the incidents but I had been unaware, as
one is at that age, how people watched and analysed behaviour.

'It was seen that you were still basically like other girls. They
do not go about scot-free of obligations as white girls do. The
ideal is, to be sure, to acquire *some* of the characteristics of
Western life : to be methodical, businesslike, use one's brains and
so on; but not to become hard, selfish, as they are. None of us
want to be *too* different from our ancestors. It was a relief to
see that you had not become wholly English'. So when my
uncle and aunt returned home they took only their three boys,
left the daughter behind, to encourage my sense of African

responsibility. After I went back to England she lived on with my family and joined the children who, as I have said, were intermittently part of the household being brought up with my sister and brother. But she was still 'my child and charge'; and on the visit I was to make this time to the Transkei in a few days when Uncle Cecil returned, I intended to screw up courage to ask if I might arrange for her – now teaching domestic science at a boarding-school in Natal Province – to come to England.

Although that tie did not exist between her younger brother and myself, he knew how fond of him I became at the time of my brother's death, when Uncle Cecil 'lent' him to my father to help soothe the wound. His college vacation had been spent with us. This year also he continued to be 'a child of the house'. My stepmother had joked about his role.

'*Kaloku singu* Darby *no* Joan,' she said, 'I and father would have been forced to steal some young person to warm this house if youngest Gambu could not pop over constantly from Fort Hare at week-ends and if your uncle did not spare him for us during his vacations.'

When she had said this in his presence at Middledrift I wondered if she knew that before she had come into our lives, our household had already felt a special affection for him. For unlike his sister and brothers he was the image of my sister, who my father asserted was 'a Makiwane in every detail, down to the ears and fingers'. Yet he had always liked *her* best, although my brother and I had grown into recognizable Jabavu types. We accepted her favoured status – or did we inherit the attitude since everybody else did? For if I ever felt pangs of jealousy I have not remembered them; the structure of the family system probably conditioned us. In any case it allowed you to escape from time to time for you were free to go and live with your other 'mothers and fathers' when the yearning overtook you, or when in their wisdom they 'asked for you'. I had often gone to my beloved Aunt Valetta in the Transkei, not knowing at the time why.

Nevertheless, feelings and passions, not unlike complexes, maladjustments as they are called in English, did arise despite the infinite pains society took to regulate personal and social balances. As I greeted my young cousin, breathlessly for I had been hurrying from the court house – almost running at the end – I was thinking about something my father had said about him after one of his visits to us. Talking about Uncle Cecil's having ended his widowerhood too since I was last home, he said:

'This cousin of yours does better to live with us for the present, at any rate until he gets accustomed. Your uncle lent him to me last year at the time of your brother, as you know. But when he married, the minute he spoke of tensions he noticed in the boy at home I asked for the loan of him back. Young people do not always accept changes smoothly when a new mother is installed. Also this boy was too young when he watched his late mother's years as an invalid, helpless and in pain.' That had made me tremble for it was near the bone. Now that the sight of his bashful smile brought it back to my mind I tried to shut it out.

He had been named after both his grandfathers, Elijah Makiwane and Mtobi Mapikela of Bloemfontein. Charming, but it meant that none of us could call him by his names, neither the big people nor we of the younger generation since we had to 'respect' or 'avoid, *hlonipa*'. I was shocked presently at the tennis match to hear his fellow-students call him point-blank 'Mtobi', although I knew very well it was in order for them to do so; they were under none of the taboos that applied to his relations. Later his own sister and brothers shattered me by using his name among themselves. He had always been called *Kehle* instead, a neat form of 'avoidance by substitution', because the word means 'Old Man' as well as 'Old Men'.

We embraced and I apologized for my lateness, flinging myself into an easy chair to get my breath back. He started to sit down again too but rose, confused, for I jumped up almost at once, seeing from his anxious face that I should not tarry – the tennis courts were at the far end of the campus, over the hill, and he had been keen for me to see the match. He was twenty but looked a puppy, not full grown, his clothes fitting tight over a chubby body. He had my uncle's neck and head and eyes, was clearly going to be a carbon copy of him if he grew taller. My brother had added another two inches to his height at the age of twenty-three, a sudden sprouting that was supposed to be a trait of Makiwane blood.

Out of deference, he would at first only speak when I spoke to him, a custom which puts young people in a less than favourable light if one forgets or does not know of it. We strode up the hill fast. I was quite puffed with having to do most of the talking. Apart from the matter of age which inhibited him he was 'a proper Makiwane', not loquacious like Mzimkhulu. We talked about his father's visit to my home, then about *his* home. I had to watch what I said, being aware of his difficulties and of the unending strictures, pointed by proverbs, about the arts of conciliation.

Yet I was in difficulties myself, which I had been unable to hint at to anyone least of all to him whose stepmother had been 'found' for his father by *my* stepmother. I had yet to meet her. In talking we naturally linked them, having to use collective as well as reciprocal forms of speech. Whatever the nature of our innermost feelings, these devices forced us to express sentiments which we knew we ought to feel towards the new maternal figures in our lives. The conciliatory sound of the plural forms was helpful, and hearing myself utter them, I could not help remembering how people declare that 'the more often you *speak* as you know you ought to feel, the more likely you are eventually to come to truly *feel* as you speak'. I wondered how long it would be before my cousin and I succeeded.

But I had not realized, as I now began to do from his answers to questions or comments on my assertions, that he was under another stress. The revelation came when we had almost reached the tennis courts and I was looking on a scene of gaiety in the sunshine, laughing students, some seated on benches, others standing or milling round, all turned out in white or cream-coloured sports clothes. My attention was straying to the jolliness ahead of us when I heard my cousin saying he doubted whether he would stay on at Fort Hare to finish his course.

'*U*-Daddy (but pronounced *uDe-di*) is being difficult about the fees, *Sis'* Nontando. I cannot see how my brother Cobham will be able to pay for me. His wife has had another baby.'

I stopped dead. My maternal uncle, a Makiwane, recalcitrant about educating his young? To say I was staggered is to put it mildly. It was like a thunder-clap. Faces in the crowd were already turning to look as we approached. I collected my wits.

We had only a few steps and there was no time for me to reply. I thought, rather vexed, that only an immature young man could broach an intricate subject as he had done. We reached the crowd and 'Old Man' began to introduce me to friends. They scrambled up, cutting short their animated conversations.

One of them gave me his seat which I was glad to drop into. A strenuous silence descended. They were polite young people and I again had to take the initiative in order to put them at ease, and thought, no wonder generations prefer to keep their own company; I was finding it exhausting to behave as a senior towards the young. Had my reactions atrophied because of the 'lack of ritual of that life overseas'?

I asked about the game and who the players were, but my brain kept humming back to the matter of the bombshell about my cousin's education. His friends began to respond to my talk. Finally they thawed and regained their original mood.

They were watching a singles match, the last of the afternoon, which Kehle was pleased we had arrived in time to see for it was a contest between the best of all student tennis players not only of Fort Hare but of Fort Cox, Lovedale, Healdtown, St. Matthews and other great institutions in the Eastern Cape, breeding grounds of *aficionados* of sports and athletics. Adjusting my sun-spectacles and getting my bearings, I was attracted by one of the players, a stylishly turned out young man in very short shorts that set off the light brown skin of his legs, like a fashionable young Frenchman in summer at Antibes.

'That is Makalima,' my cousin said. He was another of those we call 'red-complexioned' at home, brown-haired, grey-eyed. As if that were not enough he had also the physique of a Greek figurine – for he was small. When his supporters rooted for him he acknowledged with the engaging smile of a bashful, dark, golden, confident Hermes.

However, his less striking opponent played a subtler game; a man called Hani, I was told. He had a curious gait, reminiscent of the South American professional, Segura. His fellow students who had seen Hani play a hundred times were not reconciled to the figure he cut either, for they talked among themselves about his extraordinary, painful-looking movements.

'How can a chap *play* this tennis, walking and running like that?'

I told them he was in good company, one of the champions of the world functioned under the same disability.

'Segura? *How!* He too looks stiff like Hani, this *non-elegant – eli qhitalaekunxibeni?*' They were incredulous, but delighted to hear that their colleague's tennis was as thrilling to me. I did not say that merely to flatter. Hani's placing was astute, his ball found remote spots, was delivered over the net with hair's breadth precision and a style the more scintillating because of the contrast with his awkward movements. He held his watchers spellbound. They forgot about my irruption in their midst and I was glad; it gave me the chance to see them as they really were.

They mostly talked in English. I knew of course that they came from all over South Africa but had forgotten how vividly at Fort Hare you saw the tribes welding into a new nation. You had only to listen to the exclamations and shouts. Their various English accents gave you a sense of the vast spread of South Africa. There were the clipped, sharp Sutho of Basutoland and the Transvaal; the staccato and glottal-stopped Chwana – from Bechuanaland and the Orange Free State; mellower silky Zulu – from Natal; soft sophisticated Western – from the faraway Cape Peninsula, 'Capetonians'; and of course the abrupt and masculine Xhosa tones of locals of the Eastern Cape and Transkeians. You could even detect the different gestures.

I listened to comments on the play cast in satirical quips, in private jokes which had to be explained to me; I saw a young woman's finger raised in exclamation, a young man beside her leap up and reel in ecstasy like an *umbhayizelo* dancer, because of a successful backhand smash stroke at the net; heard remarks that illuminated attitudes which I had forgotten could be modified by the regions people came from, up and down the country. A series of rallies got under way. Everyone became entranced, only breaking out in their pleasure by moaning, grunting; squeaks that sprang from different languages and their tonality. A rally collapsed with a point to Makalima, upon which a young man rose, his eyes twinkling like a bird's; and he prepared to 'give a speech' as a big person might.

'Friends, Romans, countrymen, lend me your ears,' he started in English, then slipped into a torrent of congratulations in Afrikaans mixed with English. Applause. His audience obviously loved the campus clown for burlesquing tradition. The next service began. Another rally. He was about to sit down and was poised on bent knees, leaning forward, shouting unfinished sentences in a Jo'burg accent. Some of his up-to-the-minute slang went over my head, but slayed those who knew what it meant. The ball streaked, almost invisible; necks craned; tension mounted, until another young man jumped up unable to contain himself and thrust the first one down by the shoulders, crying,

'Man, what justice can *YOU* do to *this* piece of tennis? Away with you! Allow *me*, friends, to take the floor!' His oration, delivered in yet another regional accent, shed still more light on the complexity of current student humour for he played on a different set of assumptions. They were recognized as he linked the game with political issues, Verwoerd – inevitably; the forthcoming truncation of their normal study courses under the Bantu Education Act. He touched lightly on the existing ambivalence towards 'emancipated women', and I was told, amid laughter, that the pretty girl beside him was his fiancée and a leading college feminist. When the match ended and we all went home, dusk falling, I realized that the sport acted like a catharsis. It helped release some of the pressures, '*ii*frustrations' about the future that everybody was faced with. The rebellion masquerading as laughter was frightening and tempted me to remember only the laughter.

9

THAT night I was in my bath getting ready for the dance with the other cousins when my father telephoned. But from down the corridor and behind the closed doors Teacher's voice could be heard as they exchanged stentorian greetings. I pictured the scene at the Middledrift end, my father standing up at our old-fashioned rural party system instrument. It was fixed high up on a wall, on a clumsy brown ledge.

He would wind the handle round and round to call the operator; and being unmechanically minded manipulated it awkwardly as if not trusting it and would give the contraption apprehensive glances as if it might be dangerous, some kind of booby trap. And when finally connected he would lean over with an air of tremendous urgency and shout down the mouthpiece exactly as I had once seen him shout to a gardener who had fallen down a disused well we used to have at the house at Fort Hare.

Teacher at his end was equally ebullient, he too speaking in Xhosa. I tried to imagine myself a South African telephone operator – how to keep a straight face at multilingual eccentricities over the rural lines.

When I came out and dressed and joined the Mzamanes I knew that the conversation had been about my uncle: he was setting off for the Transkei in the morning. I had heard Teacher echo my father's words and say, '*O*? Gambu has already pulled out tomorrow, then? *u*Gambu *selendulukile ngomso, kanti?*' a construction that I had almost forgotten. However, Teacher now retold the entire news and re-emphasized its principal message.

'The old man said that your uncle says he expects you at-your-home at Tsolo within a week and is therefore not bidding you good-bye.' He looked at me. We were in the sitting-room before the fire, waiting for my escorts to arrive. The children of the house were in the kitchen round the wood stove and we could hear them make their usual and permitted merriment when not in danger of disturbing grown-ups. We too were laughing and joking. But soon I was aware that the Mzamanes had moved the talk on to another plane, had steered it almost imperceptibly from where it had started – the telephone call, then mention of my uncle, then reference to 'my' home at Tsolo, until it was now weaving round that other subject: my stepmother. It probably sounds strange, in English, to say it could happen almost imperceptibly. But the language used was full of such capabilities. For instance, references to my uncle were not in the general, rather inexact term: 'uncle' (it does not exist in Xhosa), but in the particular: *'malume,* male mother'. Paternal uncles are called something different, implying another set of obligations, other loyalties, expectations; while *'malume'* carried its own load of connotations. Again, when Teacher referred to 'your home at Tsolo', he used a plural possessive, so that he meant the 'home and refuge' of children of an extended family – those of a man's sisters. In the context, the grammatical constructions and what they implied developed an enormous emotional impetus. They juxtaposed the ideas underlying the fact that one 'belongs to various homes'. And since the situation at Middledrift had been broached when the Mzamanes came, we were all more than aware of the 'refuge' that my other home stood for. The words stirred up in the mind all those latent moral obligations peculiar to the patriarchal background. In its setting, one's mother's people, 'those of the umbilical cord', had certain functions to perform. When one of their number was confronted by difficult adjustments within his or her lineal family, the 'maternals' were expected to act as conciliators. My mother's people had absolutely no right; why should they have, in a paternalist society? But everyone accepted that social 'rights' only work when the affections of the human heart have been satisfied or else regulated.

It was in the light of all this that a conversation like the one between me and Teacher and *Sis'* Nompumelelo could take place; and be elliptical in language yet electrifying in clarity. Once on the plane we now reached – and I had become very nervous – other elements to do with the structure of the

93

language enabled us to glide on from thought to thought, mood
to mood.

It is perhaps time I explained about that structure, since the
whole of life at home is enclosed in it. But one is liable to envelop
everything in a fog denser than before. I can only say that it is
based on inflexion – as in Latin; alliterative concord between
certain syllables in certain words in the sentence. This allows
meaning to advance by allusion, suggestion, where direct
statement would be crude, 'savage', as we call it. The language
seems to have been almost invented to handle situations that
involve personal relationships and the imponderables that
intensify emotions. So my father's telephoning, which had set us
laughing about our elders' attitudes towards 'the new-fangled
machine for speaking', also set in motion all our dormant
thoughts about attitudes and adjustments in other matters;
until I suddenly realized with a beating of the heart, that my
hosts had turned the talk into 'the opportunity' that my father
had exhorted them to take to 'speak with me, *ukundithethisa*'.
They murmured phrases about leaving doors ajar, about room
to manœuvre, about the need for 'unhaste'. Apart from the inflexion and alliteration and the system of verb 'extensions' that
make for remarkable flexibility and sensitivity the language is
also pre-eminently figurative. But it is misleading to try to
translate into English the words that the Mzamanes used to
express the ideas involved because the figures and metaphors
sound plain silly; they either carry different overtones or convey
nothing and confuse because they dip into a different 'rag-bag
of culture, history, myths', social assumptions.

'Part of the trouble is the time element these days when
people try to deal with one another's feelings,' Mzamane said.
'The big people rely on *time* to do its work when relationships
are awry. They bring us up to behave in the manner in which
they were trained, when there was leisure. People did not
have to get accustomed to changed situations in five minutes.
There were months, seasons, years. If the individuals concerned died before things were put right, then those 'representing' them would carry on until the difficulty was either
resolved or forgotten. Then balance, equilibrium, civilized attitudes would be restored among the groups of people who are

embarrassed or flung into disorder by the maladjusted among them.'

He paused, I thought waiting for me to say something but as I did not speak he went on in a very quiet voice: 'But *we* have to be in a hurry over everything now, like savages. You especially, Nontando. After all, *we* are always here and are less pressed.' I did not answer. I wanted to, because with them I was free to express myself; was that not the whole idea of 'preparing a way through one's age-group'? But I was unable. Against my will, the thought of my stepmother made me 'switch off'. I was ashamed because what seemed to happen as I listened was that memories crowded in and made me writhe.

They took me to the day I left Middledrift with the Mzamanes; when my stepmother stood at the gate seeing us off and stooped to pat our excited black dog. Now why should that particular scene trouble me, about the Labrador mongrel whom a wag in our household had named *Umfana* (literally 'young man' but with connotations of roguish, carefree)? He had been my mother's favourite. The nickname no longer applied since her death because he was now twenty-eight years older, in dog years. But I was filled with thoughts of how he used to follow her around when she tended her plants, when she would declare that he too liked gardening. And my father would tease her, 'He is only watching that you do not disturb his buried bones.' And my mother would chaff him back because she regarded his attitude towards animals as deficient indeed. Like most of his equals he did not approve of domesticated pets, thought the place for dogs and cats was out of doors. He liked only the idea of traditional hunting-dogs which the pastoral ancestors had treasured. He perpetually 'bawled out' any of our cats that were so ill-informed as to set foot in his study – and they never seemed to learn. One winter when he was taking an afternoon nap on his sofa, we were congregated round a fire in another part of the house and suddenly heard cries of alarm from him as if a robber had broken in, '*Bantwana bam, ncedani Impaka!* – Children, help! A cat!' (even using its archaic name as if wild-cat); and we rushed, only to find that one had jumped on to the skin kaross over his legs. Dogs were more sensible. As puppies they learnt to skirt round the house, never

95

venture in. Not that he was ever cruel to them; he just gave them looks when my mother fondled them, then laughed at himself until they both laughed at his out-dated attitudes. When I saw *Umfana* with my stepmother that day, I had remembered my great surprise a day or two before that, on noticing among the small sheaf of annotated postcards my father took out of his waistcoat pocket, a snapshot of the dog and my mother. I had taken it a few weeks before her sudden death. She had been transplanting seedlings with the dog beside her looking on, front paw uplifted.

At last I heard *Sis'* Nompumelelo murmur, for once not at the top of her voice, '*uTitshala* means, Ntando, that you are mistaken to expect *not* to feel resentments on your first visit home under the new order. You are bound to feel them; so do not struggle; admit that you do, and face them – the only way to conquer them, eliminate the poison inside. The struggle to conceal and suppress is useless. It will only fester whereas it must be cast out. We must pray for you to be given patience even in this atmosphere of haste and hurry.' At that I could hold back no more and burst out. *Sis'* Nompumelelo leaned forward: 'O, Noni – take care.'

My voice rose, I suppose; I was overwhelmed by all kinds of things big and small that *I* knew even at that moment were trivial: like 'the banishment' of old family photographs, that for instance of my eldest sister (whom I had never known), taken as a baby before she died in the great 'flu of the First World War and whose picture had never never been moved. When Teacher interrupted with a sibilant 'Hush!' the room was suddenly deafeningly still. He uttered the little cluck that people make when in a dilemma, '*Kwek!*' But it only set me off again and I became carried away by the stream of my own interpretation. Whatever my stepmother had done in our house seemed to reflect on my mother and the old order of our life. I did not stop to remember the intricacies of my relationship with my late mother, its ups and downs, or of how Aunt Valetta had suggested when I went to her that a mother's task to *train* her children could never be unalloyed joy on either side; 'whereas with fathers, distance renders them immune. And in this man's world of ours, they have the advantage; to his offspring a man *can* be a source of pleasurable emotions if, like your father, he is indulgent and kind and beautiful to behold as well. He will be feared, rightly, but also adored'. I thought of none of that. My mother now occupied a special place in my feelings. But I could only express all this in futile terms for it was a jumble in my mind, and I could only harp on goods and chattels, the introduction to our house of new ones, dismissal of familiar old ones. I was unable to consider the deeper levels with which the Mzamanes were concerned. I knew that I was being stupid, wrong-headed, but could not stop.

Teacher took on a stern voice, the way you do to ward off hysteria in someone you are fond of. 'Now look here. Your tastes are naturally late-Mama's tastes – those of new-Mama are bound to be different, you know that. Must we treat you like an idiot? Why must you conclude that father is in league with her, with anybody, to erase the memory of the old home life? How can you let yourself think like that? *Kwek!* Don't you realize – don't you *allow* for the fact that men are helpless in these chattel matters? Pictures, vases, chairs, crockery – all those things are women's province. She is trying to make father comfortable in *her* way. uJili could not interfere, even if it occurred to him to do so.'

I could think of no answer to that and only trembled. Teacher leaned forward, an expression of anxiety on his face and asked point blank, 'Have you said any of this to *anyone* at home?' I shook my head. I saw him breathe deeply, as if relieved. 'Ah. Then at least war has not been declared.' There was a pause.

But his wife said uneasily, 'It may not be war but people feel, *know* in the bowels.' He interrupted her, leaning back now, and thoughtful: 'Of that Ntando is aware. MamSwazi and the old man naturally know. Nontando, do not *your* bowels tell you of the hurt your hostility causes her?'

It was no use, I now fell headlong down the slope and shrieked out a sentence.

There was a terrible silence. It was as if somebody else had cried out, not me, for I was bowled over by the words I had uttered. It was the unforgivable, a thing that 'should never be spoken even when one *may* speak' – as people say, since permitted freedoms have their rules and beyond a certain point the

expression of certain emotions and irrationalities is taboo because it puts too great a strain on the peace that is essential for
social balance. 'Words cannot be recalled, therefore those who
heard what you should not have uttered are embarrassed when
confronted with you' is a saying dinned into your ears from
childhood, that you may try to regulate your behaviour according to an ideal.

Mzamane shifted uneasily in his seat. At last he murmured,
hoarsely this time, '*Kwek!*' I did not know what to do. I saw him
surreptitiously glance at his wrist-watch. It suddenly reminded
me of the cousins who were coming to take me dancing. He
looked at his wife and whispered, '*Kwek! Yint' eyizak'th'wani le?*
What is to be done?'

She did not answer. I found I was shivering now, in spite of
the sparkling fire. And, as if at the end of his resource, he
finished, '*Impi ye* dance will be here before we can straighten
this mess.' I tried to collect myself – and realized, to my
astonishment, that I was feeling partly relieved, some of 'the
poison' had that moment been 'cast out'. At the same time, my
discomfort was acute, acute. What about the ethical offence I
had committed in gaining relief? Could I hope they would forgive, erase from their minds the words they should not have
heard? Was it too much to pray that they might ascribe my
error in uttering them not to viciousness but to 'the mixed
behaviour of these days' that he had talked about? I struggled
in a state of contradictions, knowing I deserved nothing.

Sis' Nompumelelo took over. Her mind worked on a practical
level as well as on his more analytical planes. She started on a
series of concrete suggestions. As I listened I could not help
thinking that she and her husband had 'inherited' some of my
parents' capabilities: they saw people's ordinary problems,
however personal, as reflections of 'our changing society'.

Suddenly I heard *Sis'* Nompumelelo call me '*Sisi wam*' – the
dignity of the title that our ages prescribed that *I* give *her*. I was
moved almost more by that than by anything that had been said
so far. Was it not an instinctive offering – conciliation, concern,
delicacy, affection? Much later, wondering at the effect of so
gentle a gesture I remembered our old washerwoman when she
had turned to soothe the feelings of the little boy who carried my

parcel; she had made a similar approach when she had called him '*Bawo wam* – my father'. But at that moment, I realized only that I had not after all put myself beyond the pale as I deserved; that I was to understand that my impulsive, hideous utterance was erased from their minds, they would continue as if they had not heard my unspeakable threat never to like, let alone want, a new mother. I could breathe again, pay more successful attention to the rest of what she said. And when she had finished, how I longed to say I did indeed agree with their sentiment – was it not common sense, decency? But I could not trust myself to speak, only nodded, able to look not at them but ahead of me, into the fire.

We were all silent – and the fire was going down, needed more logs. I got up to take some from the basket. When I finished and found both the Mzamanes looking at me as if in hopes and 'willing' me to change, a violent desire swept over me to 'conquer this thing'. I made to speak – but *Sis*' Nompumelelo struck her hands softly together, a familiar signal; and her husband smiled and murmured something which, in a kind of haze, I gradually recognized to be a line, impersonal exhortatory, from the clan praise-poem: . . . 'Jili, Qabazi. *Mal-ukohlulwa*' – one alluding to a phase of 'resistance to defeat'. Actually it referred not to contests with emotions but, as the verb implied, to my male ancestors' battle exploits and struggle to survive during the Scattering of The Tribes, events which, if they happened, were earlier than the historically known ones of the eighteenth century. But Mzamane was putting poetic archaicisms to legitimate use, for praise-verses are not invariably laudatory or flattering; they were often used to provoke and goad warriors to fury so as to 'challenge their prowess and sting them into a will to conquer'.

In this case the line he had picked out had the intended effect. As my mind cleared, I found I was goaded into a resolve along the lines they had discussed. When I return to Middledrift, I promised myself, I will 'open the heart'. So I was able to try and look the Mzamanes in the eyes again. We were all three glad, for now we heard a trample of feet on the gravel outside and gay young voices. My cousins came.

But I cannot truthfully say that on the next day, I arrived

99

home at Middledrift as one restored. In the car driving back, those resolutions swayed and wavered. It was deeply disappointing. It may have been then or later that I was tempted to wonder how some of those forbears of mine succeeded in living up to what was expected of them. They must have failed dismally at times. We choose to idealize their conduct. But it was too awful to attack the foundations under one's feet; a line of reasoning one did not care to pursue and I avoided doing so. I longed to see my father again, yet thought in the same instant of pushing on to the Transkei almost immediately; although even there at 'the refuge', I was afraid of my uncle. These constantly changing states of mind were exhausting.

10

I spent only two days more at home. And because of the way
in which our family life finally ended in Eastern Cape Province,
the beloved 'Border' (since chapters of local history must eventually end), my memory of those two days is almost entirely
confined to my father. As I had found in the car coming back,
my heart proved for the moment to be ineffectually opened and
cannot have received sufficient impact from the other people in
the house. But his was not suffering from these defects; and
as I have mentioned he was called by the pagans 'Lover of
people'. When he and I were discussing my journey to Tsolo, he
would call out if Nomangesi happened to be in another part of
the house, 'Girls, girls', in the Xhosa way as if she and I were together, 'Come and entertain your father', and she would join us.

I doubt if we entertained him. It was he who talked until his
particular magic captivated us and we would momentarily
leave off cautiously eyeing each other and instead laugh and be
happy. Because I was about to go to my maternal relations he
talked about hers too, for as luck would have it they were in a
part of the province where his own had lived when he was a
child, in the country district of Peddie. That was where he had
been taken 'to be indulged'. And when talking to us of it he
could tease about the *'spoliation* that *abatshana* (nieces and
nephews, himself and contemporaries') received, and say to
me, laughing, 'You rush now from here like lightning, after
only a few weeks, barely two months. You think your uncle will
tolerate that? Not he. That umbilical cord truly binds him to
you young people. None are more possessive than umbilicals.
Just because they have no rights, they wield a power. Listen.
My father once came all the way on horseback from King to
Peddie to prise me and my brothers from our grandmother and
uncles because they could not bear to part with us after he had
sent us to visit. And besides, *emaXhoseni e-*Transkei, there is no
respect for your modern time-tables.'

We were on the veranda and he was joking about these truths to tide us over tricky moments. He levered himself up from the cane deck-chair he had brought from Madeira years ago and went to get maps and railway guides. Plotting journeys was a favourite hobby. Coming back to sit down again at the outdoor table that was laid for tea with bread and butter, jams and *konfyts* and scones and cakes that my new mother had baked he said: 'Ah, but I am mistaken, am forgetting. *Malume* will not be able to hold you indefinitely. I was forgetting about your going to "Big Mother" in Johannesburg. Now *there's* the one person in the family who can lay down the law for Cecil, for me, for all of us.' He unfolded a map and turned to my new sister but saying to her mother who now joined us, 'Had we not better explain these relations of Noni's to Nomangesi?' Mam-Swazi nodded, smiling. So he lifted a finger to his new daughter:

'It is like this, 'Ngesi. *u*Noni is going to her mother's people at Tsolo' . . . Nomangesi's name means 'Englishwoman', as you might say in French, *l'anglaise*, because she had an exceptionally fair skin as light as her mother's was velvety dark; its intimate abbreviation struck me as equally engaging, simply: *'English* – 'Ngesi.'

My new mother reminded him, *'Kaloku* Jili, *u*Ngesi knows about that uncle – how can you forget? – from the time of MaDhlomo!' She was referring to having 'found' my uncle's new wife', to having suggested and arranged the match, introduced them. My young cousin Kehle and I had been recalling the event only the other day, also the piece of news connected with it which MamSwazi had related to us both, and which she did not appear to realize had seemed to us extraordinary: that his father 'had driven in his car from Tsolo to East London on purpose to meet the proposed new person for the first time, over a cup of tea at the smart, recently opened Milner Hotel for Non-Europeans'.

I had been stunned to hear it, for we had been brought up in the shadow of some terribly old-fashioned 'country' people's ideas about hotels, and as children had only ever stayed, occasionally, at one, acceptable because it had been run for decades by friends of my grandfather, old Mr. Pelem and his wife. They died in harness at a great age. Going there had been more like 'visiting', no overtones of raffishness or impropriety. I had not dared look at my cousin when we heard the astonishing news for I felt for him, knowing that with him as with me the innocuous rendezvous aggravated one of our difficulties about getting used to the new mothers. They were 'town' people; and in the country it had been one of those unstated assumptions that the best people are rural, that in towns there is no moral control, a life of anonymity, and privacy – which is suspect; no discipline. And those of the distaff side, 'the beautiful dishes of a family's honour' who should be watched and protected could even possess households in their own names. Unthinkable in the country.

Was it not irrational to be influenced as we undeniably were by the unnamable implications lurking behind those thoughts, for had not the fathers in question themselves adapted, 'advanced'? And had not I myself the year before, when Mam-Swazi appeared on the scene, thrust those conditioned reactions from my mind? I found myself in pain, from thinking of all that again, now that she alluded to the happy part she had played in my uncle's life; and also when I saw from the glance that she and my father exchanged, that the whole matter was to them ineffably delightful, romantic. I looked away, but heard him snap his fingers, smite himself and laugh at his forgetfulness; then say, stuttering a little because excited:

'Then let me explain about Noni's "big mother" in Jo'burg. Now that mother of hers is the last surviving individual who has authority in this union of families, Makiwane with Jabavu; *u*Mrs. Daisy Majombozi. *Sis'* Daisy is old, getting on for eighty, the eldest sister of Noni's uncles. When I was a mere boy she was already a young woman. The first African girl in this country to sit for the matriculation, which was a tough examination in those days. And passed with distinction in mathematics. She wished to train and be a mathematician, but in our country there is no such career for a black woman. In fact, in the 1880s it was thought a miracle that a woman of her race should sit for any examination!' His eyes became bright, gestures enthusiastic; he had a great admiration for my aunt and her sister Marian*tjie* who had died long ago, she too having been another 'first' on becoming a State Registered hospital nurse at the time of her sister's triumph. I found myself wondering if his enthusiasm would not bore my new sister. Scholastic achievements were not everybody's main interest. In the circles we moved in, as in others, there were people who were not particularly 'earnest' but liked 'good times' and 'fun' instead. My father was carried away and went happily on. However, as I watched, his gaiety seemed to communicate itself to her – to her mother too; and I saw, with self-reproach, that I was again yielding to the dreadful temptation to be unjust.

'Anyhow *Sis*' Daisy did not let that frustrate her. She trained to be a teacher. But after my father started his weekly paper in 1884, *Imvo Zabantsundu* – again another "pioneer venture for an African" in our country – her father allowed her to join the staff as reporter and feature writer. *Kaloku* the old men were friends; very adventurous; united by love of country and nation; and of progress, advance. And I tell you such men – they were not alone – did things that would seem modern even to *this* generation. Yet these communistic youngsters of nowadays who take no account of historical settings, call them "running dogs, lackeys of imperialism" and what not.' He stopped, laughed hugely; then continued, 'How many women do you think were journalists at that time in South Africa, 'Ngesi? You should have seen Daisy Makiwane when I and my brothers were little boys' – and he counted the brothers off on his fingers: 'Richard Rose Innes, whom they called *u*Dick*e*, Alexander Macauley, called *u*Mac; and Wilson Weir, called *u*Mtshetshi.' And interrupted his story to tell how he and my uncles had been named: mostly after my grandfather's friends and fellow Cape Liberal politicians: 'Rose Innes' and 'Weir' were prominent names in King William's Town, but the youngest brother earned his family nickname when he grew into a devoted teenage church-goer, although 'terribly *naughty*', because he had a passion for church singing. And 'Macauley' had been after an American Negro singer who had visited South Africa at the end of the century with a Negro Spiritual Choir; his bass voice had gone down in local history. Here came digression within digression: an account of what his brothers did in later life. Only after that did we go back to the story of my aunt.

'We used to watch her of a Monday morning: step out of our

other house at Breidbach and climb up into our hooded Cape
cart to sit beside my father, who took the reins. And they would
drive into "King" to his office. We boys and our mother
followed in the other carts or on horses; my father kept superb
horses. We were escorted home to town by the servants. My
father had two houses; men could live in style those days!'
Here came a description of the house at which the family spent
week-ends, at Briedbach a village a few miles away; an area,
that had been settled by Germans, *Amajamani*. Nomangesi did
not know about these things, so my father explained them; then
told her about his real paternal home in 'King', at 7 Alexandra
Road. 'You can still see it. But it is in a European Area now in
these days of Verwoerd's ethnic grouping; which means I
may not sleep a night in my old home town without obtaining a
Special pass beforehand – and lucky if granted!' We all murmured about Verwoerd.

'*Sis*' Daisy lived there with us when she worked for my father.
She held the job until she married – grew skilled in all sections
of the paper; became a leader-writer. But marriage removed
her. The husband, Mr. Majombozi, worked far-off, up in the
Transvaal; a school-teacher. She was widowed more than
thirty years ago but has stayed on up there. Went back to
teaching to bring up her children, the cousins of *this* one.' Here
he turned to me and again snapped his fingers, remembering
something – 'By the way, that photograph!' and asked me to
fetch it. In his excitement he called me by a succession of all his
children's names, even that of his grand-daughter – confusion
bred of affection, which made MamSwazi smile, and say he had
truly reached old age and at this rate would soon be 'adding *her*
children's names to the roll call'.

I saw him give her a startled look; then throw his head back
in a great laugh and again smite his thigh. MamSwazi had
uttered a memorable thing, and appropriate. 'Ngesi and I
joined in his laughter. When it had tided us over the almost
unbearably tricky moment, I went to the study as bidden, to
fetch the particular photograph which he wanted Nomangesi to
see, of my grandfather and his newspaper staff at the *Imvo*.
In there, although knowing where everything was, I stood for
a moment, to calm myself. Photographs lived in a chest of

drawers along with family records. At last I went to it and dug
out the one I knew he had in mind, a solemn group posed outside the old office of my grandfather's newspaper. He was only
in his early thirties, but he looked imposing, old, established,
wearing a big Victorian moustache, in buttoned-up jacket,
wing-collar. The other men, sub-editors, reporters, were in full
fig – frock coats, cravats, spats.

My aunt was the only woman in the group. She wore a
dimity dress belted with a wide band round a handspan waist.
The skirt reached to her boots; they looked to me elegant for
those days, pointed at the toe and buttoning up at the side. Her
high-necked collar was picked out with a narrow lace band;
and there was a cameo brooch at her throat. Her small Makiwane face was framed by huge mutton-chop sleeves, and a neat
head of short, cropped hair (which a career girl like herself
would now grow as long as possible and stretch or press straight,
and make *bouffant* if necessary with adventitious aids of nylon
switches).

I loved poring over old photographs. They revealed unexpected likenesses recurring in the family. For instance in the
picture my father wanted, my aunt was like my cousin Funeka,
her niece, daughter of her brother, Uncle Tennyson. And my
grandfather did not look in the least like my father but was the
image of my late uncle, the so-called 'Churchman', jolliest,
noisiest man I have ever known; when he came to our house my
mother used to declare that those two brothers made it *shake*!
It was odd to see the carbon-copy resemblance between Uncle
'Churchman' of all people and their father; for I had heard
how serious, solemn a man my grandfather was. But now I
supposed that when young, as here, he must sometimes have
'doubled up with laughter, *akikitheke!*' as the sons did.

I glanced at another picture in the drawer, of my father and
uncles as children with their parents in which their mother
held a baby boy dressed in a flowing christening robe. I
realized that the new generation – my daughter and my
sister's son whose 'maternal refuge' was this home of ours at
Middledrift – they too were represented in some of those small
boys' faces. I lingered at the chest. At last I heard my father
shout, 'Hey, *what has happened?*' But as I sprang back to the

group on the veranda bringing the photograph, a visitor appeared at the gate and my father's attention was diverted; and I followed his gaze. It was one of the villagers, whom I recognized with a constriction of the heart because of the last time I had encountered him.

11

HE was one of the grey-haired men who had carried my
brother's coffin into our house the year before. I had watched
him help carry my mother's too, four years before that. We
sometimes did not see him for a long time and when away he
was not the sort who wrote letters. He was simply one of those
who were always 'present and at hand' at a crisis in any local
family. They seemed to materialize out of thin air and gather
round. As I watched him come, I thought how he and my
father and others living in huts and square-houses near by had
been through tribulations or triumphs together which I would
never know about; a knowledge of one another's personalities
and the tempering of them by hardships and joys which would
for ever be a closed book to me.

My father's face broke into a smile of welcome. The usual
shouts of gaiety were exchanged. My father tipped his ancient
panama hat over his eyes to shade them for his friend was in
the rays of the late afternoon sun. He shuffled leisurely up the
little gravelled path between flowers and shrubs, my father
uttering salutations – he was a Cira. He reached the veranda,
climbed up the steps, lowered himself into the chair that
Nomangesi vacated, and sat down to pass the time of day,
looking at my father expectantly.

MamSwazi started to offer him tea but noticed that the pot
had gone cold; we had become engrossed in the stories about
my aunt.

She went indoors to make a fresh pot and her daughter went
with her.

When it was brought back by the maid and I started to pour
out, my father interrupted the conversation to signal and point
at the buttered scones and jam and other things and say, 'Just
bring-yourself-close, person of ours, to these things-to-be-eaten.'
The idiom was another that rang fresh in my ears and made me
smile. The old man was in the act of shuffling to make himself

more comfortable in his chair but stiffened, recoiling at 'the things-to-be-eaten' and waved them right away with a gnarled hand, crying, '*Yo!* Jili. Don't you know that these delicacies are not for me? Cup of tea will suffice. *Kaloku* we are people accustomed to plain "boiled mealie grains, *inkobe*". You know that. These *lekese* (sweets) only rouse the fury of our miserable tooth stubs.' My father and I had to laugh at his cajolery on the imported Afrikaans word 'lekkers' conveying as it did the traditionalists' nostalgia for sweet cane and their disdain of modern sugary food, even though they eat it with relish. In the same tone of irony my father withdrew the offer, then added in another voice, 'But *inkobe* have other connections, my friend. We may disparage and call them the food of our indigence. But if you had been taught *isi*Latini, I would recite passages in that golden tongue which speak of how Roman warriors, on the march conquering the whole of the then known world, when they halted to eat, chewed these very grains of boiled maize.'

'*A fact?*' – the other became serious.

'A fact,' my father nodded. 'When I taught our young men and women Latin at Fort Hare, the discovery amazed them also. They would construe, translate, mystified for sentences at a time. Then suddenly cry, "*Tyini!* This food described here, *zinkobe*, Jili. So these Romans were *people* – like us?" And I would say, Ja, *makwedini!* At last you are getting educated – eh? You are seeing that you in this lecture room, coming from these kraals of ours, are *people* as those Romans were, *abantu!*' The old man seemed as incredulous as the students had been.

'Are you speaking of the Romans of the Holy Bible?'

'The same. *AmaRoma* – the glorious, the infamous.'

At last the visitor believed, and did not speak; only gestures could communicate what he felt. Biblical characters meant something to him. His generation of primary school-children had learnt to read Xhosa largely from Bible, hymn and prayer books although his children and grandchildren at Fort Hare and elsewhere might be weaned on secular classical matter as well. Once again I saw how the outlook of ordinary people was moulded not only by the myths and legends of our pagan background but by Old and New Testament, however unconsciously, imperfectly; for of course we are defective Christians – unlike the ardent flocks of the Dutch Reformed Church whose official pronouncements insist that Western Christian ideas can be absorbed only by white people, not by others living alongside them in South Africa.

Old man Cira rubbed his hands with pleasure. My father looked delighted that the little illustration had struck home. I could see that his friend was still turning Romans over in his mind. His face was the same colour as my father's, but fuller. Remembering what my Uncle Rosebery had said about the old chief's face I now mistrusted appearances of good health, especially amid the uncomplaining talk about poverty-stricken diets. That and the sight of his white hair made me sad. Yet he was not sorry for himself; he looked happy to be chatting with his age-mate. It was not that they were satisfied with things as they were – far from it; but what matterered most just then was the enjoyment of friendship. And because the style of their communion was leisurely, the visitor did not hurry on to another subject. He grasped the tea cup I offered him, gave thanks for it, then took up the point again.

'No, truly you have surprised me. So *AmaRoma* who persecuted Christians were eaters of *inkobe*? Fancy!'

'Well, that is how it is – *emhlabeni*. When we "learnt the Bible" we did not realize that it was a story of things happening "in this eternity".'

'Yes-no indeed. It seemed of another world. Take that "wilderness", for example, Jili. Did I not first set eyes on a wilderness only when I travelled to Cape Town and the train crossed that unbelievable Karroo desert; and only *then* understand about *uYohane*, the Baptist, his honey and locusts? And understand about Our Lord Himself?'

'Aha, you have it. To travel is to see for oneself. You saw a physical desert. The Baptist's story was also about the spiritual desert; of heart and mind; of his indecision. And the experience of The Son of Man Himself; the doubts, discouragements that we sinners are subject to. Is that not what you are saying?'

'Just so, Jili. Hard to visualize even this Karroo of-here in South Africa. How much more difficult for our pagan people to accept the concept of this other desert of the uncertain mind?

Because when you are pagan your mind *is* made up; admits no uncertainties. In paganism all is accounted for: sorcery brings the bad, disaster, death; ancestors bring the good when they approach The Almighty after we ask them to intercede for us. If you and your fellows accept that logic, what shortcomings can you see in your religion?'

'Yet did not the missionaries achieve that miracle, in converting as they did even only half our nation?'

'You can say that again with vigour, Jili.'

'*Punga, mfo,*' my father pressed him to drink, for the old man was holding his cup absentmindedly, wrapped in these thoughts.

'I said *drink*, man!' my father repeated; at which his friend bent his head down, about to obey; but again paused to remind the other, 'Yes, yes – I must drink. But as I said, tea is sufficient, sufficient! No need for these other things. They are not wholesome; are poison; would *kill* me. So please forgive if I ignore *that* side of your hospitality. You see, it is my teeth, man, "*live coals underneath innocuous ashes :* lying doggo until provoked". Oh, those sweet things are no good at all, handsome one.' He gave the rejected platefuls such a look that my father burst out laughing.

'All right age-mate, turn your eyes away from the sweets' – both men merry.

Nevertheless, like a typical South African he ladled several teaspoonfuls of sugar into his cup, stirred it thoroughly, then poured some into his saucer to cool, and drank from the edge of it with great sucking noises. We watched to make sure that it was to his taste. His aged eyes strained to meet ours as he drank. They registered contentment.

Like most of our neighbours in the village which was as unprosperous as any in the eroded Ciskei, he wore clothes that were threadbare and carefully tended. His shirt bore skilful patches; and an L-tear on his frayed jacket was darned with the precision that his schoolgirl grandchildren were taught – as I had been in sewing class at Lovedale. His shoes were crisscrossed with cracks which the dust showed up. The trousers were wide-bottomed Oxford-bag style, of indifferent material thin with wear. My father's drain-pipes were of an even earlier vintage for he too preserved clothes with care, was devoted to an ancient oak trouser-press that he possessed. His friend's had the horizontal crease above and below the knee where he folded and laid them under his mattress at night. My father's responded better to treatment being of more durable material. The contrast lowered my spirits. But not for long, for they radiated the atmosphere of the deep accord possible between old people. The sight of them reminded me of a Rembrandt portrait. They were not occupied by what they lacked but by life's other aspects; and dipped into these as into a treasure. My father prepared to elaborate on one of them for he lifted a friendly finger and began, 'Cira!' (the celebrated salutation of the senior Xhosa clan, and now also threw in some of its resounding auxiliary phrases in order to soften what he was about to express), '"Time is *pass*-ing, for such as you".' He raised his voice to that special pitch favoured by elders in amiable talk, high but unhurried, each syllable drawn out into what sounds like the longest in the world; and now that the conversation was going into this phase he used the collective 'ye' – archaic in English and giving the wrong impression and therefore I avoid it, 'You are *leav*-ing us, one by one. And when you depart, we who are left behind will be in a veritable fix. For we do not *know* these experiences of yours. Too many of them are locked up inside your grey heads. And, alas, you will take them with you. *Spe-ak* of them while you may.'

His friend sucked the last drop from the saucer, put the empty cup on it, reached over to put them on the table, then sat back. The expression on his face was as if his soul was expanding. The two men treated each other with enormous respect, courtesy. When not using clan names they called each other '*Bawo*', the ceremonial form of 'father', conducting their conversation with the delicacy and elegance derived from 'tradition, the higher things'. Yet they mingled colloquialisms with them like 'fix', 'age-mate, *ntanga*', and 'man', the jolly vocative, '*mfo!*' or '*mfondini!*' The whole style seemed to give form to their relationship; you felt that they 'connected', as E. M. Forster has put it. Cira replied, 'Aha! But let me *remind* you, Jili, handsome one: we are *all* quitting this world. "*Ngomso ngulo*", day after that it will be me, or another; you too, "*mfo wam*"' and referred to my father's head which was also grey. They chuckled, looked at each other thoughtfully. Again I had one of those intimations of experiences shared and beyond my reach.

When they took up their conversation again, I realized that the topic was one they had discussed many times. Cira exclaimed, 'O, Jili, you are after me again.' And I gathered that my father had often urged him to 'jot down his experiences, even in a little exercise book' for his descendants, that they might know their background. His friend no longer worked. He was supported by sons working in the big cities, and had leisure for he only pottered a little in the fields; and during the months of drought could not even do that, but was forced to sit idle. Who knows but that he might not use up such moments, hours, days, by roughly putting down his memories? A body of Xhosa literature had grown from such beginnings. Both my grandfathers had stimulated some of their own age-mates to write. Knowledge of the fact had been handed down to my generation of the family because a contemporary of theirs had told it to my father and his brothers when they were small boys at King William's Town. He was a man whom we young ones had seen only in very old age, James Ntshona, the head of an able Eastern Cape family, *o*Nkomo by salutation, one of those scores of families who made up our fabric of life in the Border, and gave us the setting in which none of us felt isolated or like pioneers among pagans, or among Philistines.

Mr. Ntshona had been for nearly sixty years a serious journalist, feature writer, outliving my grandfathers by more than thirty years. Throughout he had made it almost a mission to urge others to 'write down what they knew'. He had contributed a weekly literary article to our paper for decades, continued it when my grandfather died and my Uncle Mac took over. He was still writing now at 93. My father admired him beyond words and had got up from a sick bed, before I arrived to visit Mr. Ntshona who had been ill at the same time.

'At his age that illness might have been his last. I took no chances. For where Xhosa life and literature are concerned, uNkomo is a "*ntsha-ntliziyo*, fresh-in-heart". Wrote for years a column about Xhosa ideas in English for a weekly European paper, until recently these Verwoerds put a stop to it in pursuit

of their dedicated mission to ban "multi-racial activities".
Heart-breaking; one of the most hurtful wounds the
Nationalists have inflicted.' When I saw my father's eyes grow
sad and heard him use that arresting idiom for the enthusiasm
of his senior, I realized that when James Ntshona died the loss
would be poignant. He did die shortly after this, and for my
father's generation it was the end of an era. But when I afterwards thought of this particular afternoon at home, I felt I had
at least seen an influence at work. For old Cira was responding.
My father turned and they both looked at me so that once
more, I realized that because I happened to be there, I was
'representing my fellow young' in now listening to the things
that my father hoped Cira might pass on to his descendants. He
said, 'You see, this village of ours, like all these dusty-looking
undistinguished villages of-here, is full of people like this
father,' pointing at his friend. '*He* knows the history of every
nook and cranny of this worn-out countryside,' swinging his
arm in an arc and naming neighbouring localities. 'He will take
to his grave knowledge that he has *not* handed on. Cira, will not
these young people blame you and ask why?' Cira looked
down, scratched his head and sighed as if reluctant to delve into
that deplorable dereliction of duty. But all the same he proceeded to do so, and addressed me as if I had indeed put the
question.

'*Kaloku* MaJili, young men do not any longer gather to sit
within earshot when elders reminisce by the side of the kraal,
which was where much of the "handing down" went on.
"*Baxakekile*",' he declared in slang, '"they are up a creek".
People are getting *other* sorts of education to be sure, girl. They
have to learn how to live with the times that are upon us.'

'Mm-M!' My father uttered the soft moan that 'encourages'
a speaker once he has started to put his case; and alternately
threw in the other expressions, '*Kawutsho, Qhuba* – Say so,
Continue' or used the etymological echo. And his friend went
on:

'Learn to *live* despite the white man.'
'*Continue!*'
'The white man and his attitudes.'
'*Attitudes!*'

'The white man and his works.'

'*His works.*' A pause. How to develop his theme? He put it in this way. 'The life needs a new technique, Jili. This white man has made a *problem* of his presence here in South Africa.'

'*A problem. Continue.*' Throughout Cira spoke as if to me, yet was really exchanging ideas with his age-mate.

'The white man has not the faintest idea how to "live-with-others". His attitude is that of dog in manger, do you hear?' My father went on echoing, '*Dog in manger. You say so.*'

'I say so, indeed. Yet we black people, here-before-they-came, made an art of how tribes should "live-side-by-side, *ukuhlalisana*". When new people arrived in a locality during the great migrations, did not Africans allot the strangers a space in which to live?'

'*A space.*'

'Our chief exchanged a gift of cattle with their chief, then pointed to an area and said "Graze there, settle, live your life. Your people and mine will confer – when matters arise that have to be discussed; will rejoice together – when matters for rejoicing arise". *We* did not war for the *sake* of warring, no! If the new-comers were refugees, as in the time of those northern despots – *o*Tshaka who turned their nation into despoilers, savages, scattering people for no reason – we welcomed the refugees; for that was our code. We "*adopted them: Sabangeniisa*".'

'*We adopted them.*'

'And they lived in peace; became part of us; added their strength to ours; domestic and political security – do I not speak aright, Jili? Your own people were similar "enterers" – no so?' My father nodded.

'Yet now these whites bring *their* outlook to our scene. Do they know how to share? Do they want to? Is it their code? Ho! Even as refugees (for what are Poor Whites but that), they rake quarrels with us; growl continually; push us out of jobs as Smuts did with his "Civilized Labour" policy, instead of properly developing the country so that *all* could have jobs, graze in fair play instead of this robbing of black Peter to pay white Paul. And now the people's tolerance is giving out. We are beginning to retaliate: "*baya* defy*a*! *baya* boycott*a*!" – new techniques forced on us which we will doubtless learn to perfect; but for what? For destruction. All because of the disruption these Europeans have brought!'

'*Disruption.*'

'Europeans are *anti-social*, the bitterest thing conceivable – eh?'

'*Continue.*'

'I speak of the turmoil their decrees are causing all over our country. What is the black man to do?' He was so moved that he broke into a rhythmic exhortation which I afterwards wrote down and asked my father to check. His trained ear enabled him to recall it word for word.[1]

And he ended on a note the more telling because it fell to almost a whisper, 'Nowhere is there security, verily we do not *know* what it is that we may do.'

A fierce light burnt in his old eyes for all that he disciplined his words. It brought a lump to my throat for he spoke of his vision of the world as one who had lived the experiences, digested them and had finally distilled the feelings they had provoked. They were woven into a lifetime of changes he had seen in the Cape, a Province once full of promise. He summed up, 'No, man, Jili! How can *I* speak to my children and grandchildren about what is in store?'

They looked at each other in silence. At last my father cleared his throat and said, gently because his friend was agitated, 'All

[1]
   'Wahlal edolophini —
   'Baya citw abant' edolophini!
   'Wahlal emaXhoseni —
   'Baya citw abant emaXhoseni!
   'Wahlal e *Trust*ini —
   '*Be*FAK*w*' e *Trust*ini —
   'Nalapho umi ngamlenze mnye
   'Akukho kuqiniseka . . .
   'AndiYAZ eyona ntw esinokuyenza!'

The theme of his poetic outburst was the Government's population shifting decrees: "Africans going to towns to work, there being disrupted and ejected (the new 'work permits'); similarly on going to the Reserves (lack of work and living room); finally trying to settle in the Trust Lands, there only balancing on one leg, a tight rope (because of the frustrating legal conditions of residence there)". The last line is especially moving to a Xhosa speaker because of specialized stress, tonal emphasis and dying cadence.

the same, Cira, we can try to provide them with the equilibrium that comes from self-respect. Despite all appearances, the young people of now *do* absorb the equilibrium that *we* absorbed from *our* elders. And in it lies a strength that they will *need* under the new order.'

'*O?* You say so?'

And at that, my father turned to me saying, 'Here is what I want you young people to know: you are looking at a man,' craning his neck to indicate him to me, 'whose curiosity impelled him in youth to walk great distances. That is how for instance he knows the history of all these cairns dotted about the district, past which you people drive unseeingly as you rush to Alice or King, or East London, Grahamstown.' He mentioned many such items locked away in the authoritative head of his friend; and my eyes opened. Then he turned to him again with a smile, admonishing, 'Yet you are telling this generation of my daughter's that you have no opportunity to impart to your sons what such things stand for "because your boys and girls are up creeks in Johannesburg and Cape Town" – eh?' The other confirmed it with a rueful nod, but smiling too as though my father's imminent laughter communicated itself.

'That is what I say.'

'You say, "Gone are the days of handing down by mouth"?'

'*Ja!*'

'Yet there is this thing called "writing" brought to us by the patient missionaries who accompanied these "anti-social destroyers". For did not you, just now, commend the work of the teachers who argued with our pagan forbears?'

'I did.'

'And you, my friend, went to school.'

'*To school.*'

'Were educated, taught to read and write.'

'*And write.*'

'Good money was spent on this?'

'Oh yes, *was spent.*'

'Your father sold the odd ox, perhaps even the apple of his eye: his racing ox? Perhaps your mother, like others, took in Europeans' washing to pay for those books and slates?'

'Took in washing – "*kwek!*" You've finished me! Get away, man, Jili! Do not remind me of accomplishments hard won, about which I have been remiss, my beautiful friend!' And at last they absolutely burst out laughing together, as if they had reached the climax of a vaudeville act. In fact, the exchange had been on the lines of a typical 'act' that you often see. People suddenly strike it up anywhere, out on the veld, in a shop such as the one I had gone to in Alice, on a street corner in town like a jolly whirlwind. You join a crowd of passers-by, listen and watch, and go on your way reeling too at the fun and self-criticism.

The kernel of their communion could now be extracted and they became serious again, my father saying, 'Well then, Cira, have you forgotten the parable of the Talents? Is it not true that when "the mouth is sewn up"' (as people say of political oppression, censorship), 'the hand can still write? Let me tell you something. One white man who studies codes of human behaviour, Malinowski, an anthropologist, once remarked: "The vision of the past in human memory and tribal legend is something which has to be studied. It has a psychological influence active in present-day African society. People are swayed by the *errors* they *feel*, and not by the *truth* which they *ignore*".' My father put it in language that struck home and his friend exclaimed.

'A white man said that? My! Those words fall like a soft rain. Truly these Europeans can elevate sometimes despite their destructive nature. Which of them said this, do you say? Do I know him? Never mind, it does not matter. Even a white man can speak the truth when not barking, growling, which cannot last. God sent them as a plague to try us, for sure, to temper our national character so that finally it may *deal* with the condition that we are in today. By the time of the new men of Africa, you and I will have passed on, Jili, and will be watching from the other side.'

'*Ja*, with the ancestors.'

They agreed on that with the confidence one could not fail to notice when people remembered about 'time being on our side'. They could feel that, as ancestors, they would share the eventual triumph. The idea of continuity was always implicit.

It was late now and our shadows on the veranda were slanting, like the lengthening ones of the spiky succulents at the bottom of the path. Everything in the changing light looked cool, secure – the grass, the trees, the darkening mountains. The two men fell to looking on the scene too. They had refreshed themselves. And to have heard some of the ideas they liked to exchange in order to gain their pleasure refreshed me too, and filled me most of all with a longing that one's behaviour might, if humanly possible, fit into the patterns they had extolled and which had made them what they were. I heard MamSwazi approach through the sitting-room, gaily calling her daughter to come too. The sound of their voices reminded the visitor of the hour, and as they joined us his mood had changed to that of a contented 'Asking for the road'.

Part Two

CONFLUENCE FARM

12

ALTHOUGH my father had studied railway time-tables and mapped out my journey, I felt intimidated by the connections, the tedious waits at junctions, and decided to take the long-distance Native Bus instead from East London to Umtata, the Transkei capital; and from there a local bus to Xhokonxa, the infinitesimally small town nearest my uncle's place in the depths of the country. He asked if I had not forgotten what such a journey could mean. It would be rough, physically trying: I would be squeezed tight among yokels anointed with fat and surrounded by mountains of household goods; would have to pick my way through knobkerries and fighting sticks held upright in the bus by pagan braves; probably sit between squealing piglets and hens strung up and contained in pillow-cases – the sort of journey he had made hundreds of times into parts of the country far more primitive than ours on The Border where we were, so to speak, comparatively refined. I could avoid the inconvenience by travelling 'incapsulated' in a second-class compartment all the way, rubbing shoulders only with those of my own kind. When he had pointed out the hazards and found I did not shrink (actually because I was shrinking from the train journey), my father was delighted.

'Well, you will not be comfortable, Jili. But there is no better way of improving your Xhosa than by taking such a trip. You will be among people who truly speak the language. To keep your ears open will be an education and a pleasure.'

The bus did not carry only Africans, but it was they who mainly used it. It was part of the service run by South African Railways into inaccessible rural districts; cheap fares, spartan accommodation, wooden benches only, no unnecessary luxury of leg room.

The bus had, however, a special compartment sealed off by a glass partition at the front that was different – upholstered, roomier, which cost more. There was a curtain inside it which could be drawn across the partition, but was not always so drawn. That section, however, was labelled 'Europeans Only'. The few whites who travelled in such buses were generally bound for European estates within the Reserve or hamlets where they ran trading stores, the little gold-mines like the one in Alice that sell 'Kaffir Goods'.

At the terminus near East London's railway station, I found a great crowd and thought they must be seeing off friends in the usual gregarious fashion. But I soon realized that practically everyone in sight was clambering on to the bus. Women with babies tied on to their backs with thick woollen shawls, and leading toddlers by the hand; men of all ages, some carrying newly bought portable gramophones, satchels of mechanical tools, knobkerries, fighting sticks, tin trunks, pillow-cases filled like Christmas stockings with personal belongings. The pillow-cases were hand-embroidered with legends in English such as: 'Beloved', 'Persevere', 'The Time is Nigh'.

Some of the girls and women balanced Singer sewing-machines on their heads, or new cooking utensils that gleamed in the morning sunshine. In the bus they piled them on the floor or on their laps. Every kind of 'sophisticated' or 'backward, primitive' seemed to be represented, with the gradations in between. There was the usual uproar, laughter, shouts, outbreaks into song.

The white driver and conductor stood apart with two or three fellow whites who were coming, looking on at us with the familiar expression on their faces which reminded me of how Africans say, 'They have a philosophy of joylessness those people, meet life with clenched jaws, are grim.' None of the Africans paid them much attention and, watching the contrast, I was struck as often before by the ebullience of the blacks which seemed to mesmerize the whites as they stared, chewing, clenching jaws at the scene of irrepressible gaiety, the yells of delight despite the discomfort.

I soon heard (because they yelled it), that many boarding the bus were going home to the Reserves after spells of working in town as house 'girls' or garden or messenger 'boys'. They were going back to the country to attend to their responsibilities, since they were, of course, grown men and women. Their thoughts turned to these home affairs for the shouted conversations were about them as people exchanged greetings; asked after one another's health; into reasons for travelling; and for news of births, marriages, deaths.

The scene seemed exotic even to me because although most of the men were dressed soberly enough in Western clothes (ancient tweeds and flannels, Prince of Wales checks faded by many suns), there were those who draped the ubiquitous toga over their shoulder, on top of shirt and trousers. One such man, wearing a new and wide-brimmed jet-black Stetson hat looked like a Spanish grandee. And his two companions wore earrings and spotted kerchiefs round their heads. They reminded me of storybook pirates. The women wore variegated coloured cotton dresses under home-knitted cardigans or sober-coloured heavy store-bought woollen shawls. I thought how when women have to watch every penny, and skimp and make things do, their clothes look haphazard and sad, not gay despite the bright colours. The more matronly wore black turbans drawn to a knot at the back and thrust through in front with old-fashioned hatpins. The younger ones wore white or coloured berets set at rakish angles, and crocheted cloches – favourite style enduring since the twenties. And as I climbed up the steps in my uncrushable suit of man-made fibre and laden only with a lightweight case because of travelling by air, I realized that other people were examining my get-up as much as I was examining theirs, for they made comments.

I walked down the corridor of the bus between the stark wooden seats, and remembered the remark the passer-by had made to our housemaid about pounding his behind on third-class railway seats to Queenstown, how he had exclaimed, 'But it was travel, nevertheless!'

We set off through the seaside town along metalled roads bordered by European bungalow-houses washed white or cream. Convolvulus, morning glory cascaded over porches; and roofs were painted or tiled red or green. The dwellings looked inviting, cared-for. Soft lawns lay in front of them and black gardeners held hoses, watering before the sun should rise in the sky. In the hedges as we sped by, there were flashes of colour: poinsettia, hibiscus, flamboyants. East London, *eMonti*, is a clean, orderly, bustling port and residential town with a long frontage on to the Indian Ocean, almost all of whose pleasant sandy part beach-line is reserved for 'Europeans Only'. It was not long before the bus was heading out of the town and inland.

We climbed up, then down and round the spreading hills of now rather bare countryside, sometimes dotted with huge granite boulders and stumpy succulents, or with thorn trees short, bent and twisted; or it stretched out smooth and featureless, with isolated houses in the distance protected by windbreaks of tall trees. There were occasional windmills whose shining metal wheels were immobile because the day was windless, although fresh as yet and bathed in that clear light which is a feature of the Eastern Cape; mornings when, after the vivid colours of sunrise, the day settles into tones of silver, and afternoon becomes flat, almost harsh.

We started the journey in the transient, luminous phase which makes one so wish that South Africa had its Vermeer, its Corot – some such miracle painter of light. I noticed my companions on board looking out at the landscape. They sat back when they had loosened shawls and togas, and settled down to what comfort was possible in the restricted space, and prepared to enjoy the spectacle. Their faces, the usual varieties of browns, looked happy and expansive as the sun's rays filtered in through the windows. They gradually assumed the expressions of people 'sitting-in-the-warmth (of sun)'. There is a verb for it, not to be confused with the other that refers to enjoyment of a different source of warmth – fire. Neither of them have English equivalents. Nor do we have an equivalent in our language for 'sun-bathing' because southern Africans never engage in it. You see them sitting in the shade, only watching Noel Coward's 'noon-day sun'. I had been astonished when 'abroad' on the same continent to find not only Englishmen sitting smack in it but blacks too. My fellow southerners in the bus would have been equally taken aback. We were enjoying the sun now in the customary way, *ukugcakamela*, warming you benignly right through your body, not 'broiling your outside like a piece of bacon', as we say.

I had a corner seat. Beside me was a woman who looked in her middle thirties. She had boarded the bus carrying a baby on her back. To sit down, she had unstrapped the shawl tied across her chest, swung it round her body with the child cradled in it still asleep but automatically adjusting its little legs from their clasping position round the mother's hips; and she laid it across her lap.

She wore a neat, spotted knee-high frock, crumpled at the saddle of the back because of the baby. A red scarf was tied round her head, perfunctorily, for it did not quite cover the thick plaits in which she had arranged her hair. She smelt very clean, of carbolic soap; and glanced round, her eyes bright, expectant. She craned her neck to see into the far corners of the bus as if hoping to espy a friend. For a time she fidgeted so much, sizing up all the occupants, that I wondered the child did not wake. But it lay in her arms and breathed deeply, its chubby cherub's cheeks framed by the shawl softly draped about its face. The baby seemed as peaceful as the mother was restless. She lost no time in striking up conversations with those near – with me, then with people in the seats before us; then to her right, to those before them; to say nothing of those in the seats behind us. She found nobody she knew, but those present would do. We were transfixed by quantities of bags and baggage, baskets of provisions to eat on the long journey. In between them inquisitive infant girls attempted perilous steps, clutching some treasured tattered doll made of rags; or mealie-husk doing duty for one and wrapped in cotton scraps; or little boys a battered toy motor car. But mothers would drag them back, straighten out miniature frocks or trousers, and ruthlessly wipe running noses. All of us bobbed up and down as the bus bumped and swayed, and it was difficult to control one's voice. We shouted, answering shouted personal questions about one another.

After a while, personalities began to assert themselves and one of these was a man sitting behind me. He gained the attention of the entire bus-load by launching on a discourse about the locality we were passing through. An authoritative-looking man, in his fifties; obviously a labourer, but dressed as one long accustomed to town life. He wore a blue scarf like a cravat at the neck, a respectable felt hat and underneath the heavy overcoat which he unbuttoned, an exceedingly old suit in clerical grey, chalk-striped. When the bus was outside Potsdam, he called out, '*Heyi!*' Do you people *see* the good country those Germans received here when they were brought to settle? These rolling plains, my friends – land *made* for cattle. *Bafondini!* It is said that of old, this grass was so nutritious, cattle grazed themselves to a standstill, were bewildered by repletion. Then these Germans were allotted the land, dislodging people who already herded here. And, of course, they wanted to remind themselves of their country. Hence "Potsdam" here, "Berlin" there. Little Germany! Yet the Hottentots, *amaLawu*, had already named these places, having been here even before *we* arrived. Or rather, *ama*Xhosa arrived.' It was already clear from some of his phrases that he was not a Xhosa man.

'Now *um*Xhosa lived alongside *i*Lawu, on crossing the Kei River. Hear the *Lawu* names of these local rivers: *Q*welera, *Nx*aruni, which the whites pronounce "*K*welega, *N*ahoon" like infants because defeated by the virile Hottentot sounds. But when *um*Xhosa arrived, *he* pronounced them all right; had already taken over those Hottentot click embellishments into his own language. Why? Because Hottentots were people of our ilk: reared cattle. Did not *um*Xhosa give Hottentots a praise-name, salutation, "Sukwini", referring to the skill of that tribe in tanning hides? Those people lived all right with Xhosa, "side-by-side"; both lived proper *masihlalisane*.' Everybody burst out laughing for he used the word in its new 'town' sense in which it refers to a sociological phenomenon; 'improper temporary sexual partnerships' of men and women working in the urban areas, one spouse absent, looking after the home in the country, relationships for which the pagans use a harsher name. His speech was an elaborate joke. We all knew for instance that Hottentot and Xhosa had recognized each other's societies, had intermarried legally, accepting each other as neighbours. He was playing with words and we joined in his merry mood of comparing the past with modern town life – now that the bus was taking us away from it all. His comments made us all look at the countryside anew. People fired questions at him about it, or contributed from their own knowledge.

Climbing up a gentle incline, one of whose slopes was covered

with rows of pineapples, we met a group of pagans cycling.
Their robes billowed in the air behind them, like red sails.
They free-wheeled, laughing and shouting, teeth flashing in the
sunlight. The speaker half rose as they drew level, and called out
to them through the window, all our heads turning to watch
him and them. Then he said to us, but still – of course – shouting, 'Behold the people of Ndhlambe! Daubed in their special
shade of ochre, the dark red that reminds of dried blood.' It was
different from the one preferred in my Middledrift and Alice
districts. 'These ochred ones are getting civilized – eh? Their
Europeans grow these pineapples, wax fat on the exports. Some
of that fat drips on to us and these cyclists. Now I approve of
that. Why should a pagan bother to *eat* those things that rot
the teeth? *He* has more sense, spends the money earned from
working on them on buying things he wants. In East London
some pagans own cars. Chaps who can't read, would go cross-
eyed if you spelled "a*a, ebe, nci*" on a blackboard for them!'
Roars of laughter, interruptions. 'Why trouble himself? Is he
not doing all right? I tell you people-of-this-bus, you Xhosa-of-
Gcaleka from across-the-Kei, these Xhosa-of-Ndhlambe-on-
this-side of the river are overtaking you. Progress! They aim *to
privately own land!* To be themselves exporters, not for ever
"work like small boys" for the European.' You had to smile.
My father had been right about the idioms. In addition was I
not listening to the things people dreamed about? I was suspicious for example of the cajolery about motor-owning pagans.
Was it a reflection of the man's own secret wishes? Everyone
knew that pagans were not interested in the Westernized life.
They pursued their own alongside ours (whom they call almost
pejoratively 'school' people); and restrict themselves -- when
forced by circumstances into towns for temporary work – to the
acquisition of only such habits or possessions (bicycles, sewing-
machines, ploughs) as did not conflict with membership of
their society. Therefore did the lofty amusement over the Red
people reflect a secret admiration for their serenity, positiveness,
the 'lack of *doubts*' that my father's friend had talked about?
In any case the chatter was different from some I had heard on
country buses in England, my other homeland. Here people
were not avoiding personal matters or universal human themes;

certainly not steering clear of religion, sex. They discussed history, politics, land reform, property, sociology – analphabetic though most of the speakers were. These seemed to be the topics they considered important, which superseded 'small talk' about the weather, wages, or whites. Not that those three were not pressing. One saw that they were, but did not seem to occupy the whole of the bus-load's frontal lobes. The travellers probably did not consciously classify any of these subjects. Conversation hinged on them because as individuals they were preoccupied by the history of 'the migrations' of tribes and the encounters that these had brought; and, naturally, by the structure of society, since that had been the root cause of those movements of populations. The bus was now crossing country that had been migrated into and settled by Chief Ndhlambe; and it was his descendants and followers whose huts we were passing and whom we saw walking and bicycling. Their territory stretched from East London to Idutywa, on the far bank of the historical river that lay ahead of us, *i*Nciba – the Great Kei.

The migrations had been, of course, the only way in which a polygynous nation could solve the political problems that accompanied royal succession; the whole thing an expression of the patriarchal family system, based inflexibly on primogeniture which every one of us clung to; so that history was not dead but alive. It was drilled into us subtly or overtly from the moment we learnt to talk. The authoritative labourer was dealing with subjects close to our hearts in talking about who peopled the land; the particular successions that had brought them; about heirs; about the '*idiocy*, nay backwardness, savagery, of nations such as Boers whose custom allowed *all* of a man's sons to inherit in equal proportions'!

How then was that succession arranged, whose consequences filled our conversation as the bus rolled on? That was what we talked about, and the complex relationships that it involved. People delved into those archives that they carry in their heads. We discussed events like the recurring activities of Regents who tried to usurp the patrimony; a perpetual historical hazard, because the patriarchal system had meant that when the Chief died, the heir was invariably an infant since the 'Great Wife' –

the 'national' wife and mother of the successor – was never the first woman he had married; under polygamy Chiefs were supposed to get into practice, so to speak, in their earlier, 'personal choice' marriages, and only 'marry for the nation' (with cattle contributed by it) in middle life when they were proven sires. This very Ndhlambe had 'usurped', and at the great Battle of Amalinde not far from Middledrift had tried to displace his young nephew Ngqika ('Gaika'), the true Right Hand heir who had removed to what is now called the Ciskei; and whose 'following' my own family belonged to by descent. My male relations came under a further sub-division for the purposes of war. Each was a subject of the subsidiary ruler in whose territory he happened to have been born: my brother's liege lord was Maqoma, as the old man had said when my uncles and I called on him. My grandfather's had been Ntinde, in the King William's Town area; and my father's yet another, in the Peddie district; Yet all 'people of Ngqika'. Thoughts of Ndhlambe and his type stirred one woman passenger to shout in a clear treble, 'Usurpers – true examples of the intransigence of human nature, of individuals who do not *regulate* those emotions that are inimical to the public interest!' Upon which lively rhetoric broke out:

'What medicine ever cures covetousness?'

'Or sinister deeds.'

'Or power madness – *ukukhukhumala!*' (I relished that lovely word.)

'Will society *ever* perfect the devices by which it tries, *tries* to eradicate man's anti-social tendencies?' The bus bumped along while a latter-day aspect of the theme was given an exhaustive airing: 'the enigma of *today's* "Paramount Chief of the Bantu".' For that was how Dr. Verwoerd had recently styled himself, and the bus resounded with jokes, 'Cuckoo in the nest'; 'Anti-social'; 'Wrecker of established order'; 'Usurper, worse, gate-crasher; and *okhukhumeleyo* at that, puffing that chest like a pouter pigeon, in a nest where he had no rights whatsoever, either by blood or cattle'. I could only reflect how differently the countryside must appear, wonder what thoughts it inspired, if like some of the Europeans hygienically sealed off from us by the glass partition you perhaps did not know the language and

could not understand what was being said. You would note the
scenery to be sure, with its roadside advertisements for 'South
African Beers, or 'Cigarettes'. You would note the characteristic
hamlets at which the bus stopped at petrol pumps labelled in
English, 'Pegasus Oil', or in Afrikaans, '*Ry mit die Rooi Perd*';
and see the white-owned stores standing in dust and rubble;
the indigent natives, the sunburnt whites; all features that
created an effect of spiritual barrenness because not apparently integrated. However, I had not much time for these
private thoughts. Indeed, the attitude of society, as exemplified
even by my fellow passengers, towards individual privacy
was one of the undeniable drawbacks in the life at home.
Privacy was 'anti-social, contrary to the public interest'
so that inwardly, chasms yawned before you if your
personal inclinations and habits tended against the principle.
Marvellous, I thought, that people like my father managed
to write and think, always exposed to the public gaze, to
sociability.

The woman beside me asked my clan name, where I was
going, and why. The man behind us heard, having for the time
being finished his speeches, and promptly exclaimed, '*O?* So
we have a Jili in this bus? Do you people *know* Jili?' sweeping the
question right round. Three admitted not knowing, upon which
he cried, '"*Kwek!*" Ignorant people are abroad these days,'
and proceeded to repair their knowledge. Meanwhile the culprits gazed at me good-naturedly. Two of them were the young
men who had put me in mind of pirates when I spotted their
ear-rings and the kerchiefs round their heads, the third wearing
the Stetson hat. 'Country bumpkins,' the man now called them
in Xhosa slang. Immobile and silent, they put me in mind of
yet another imaginary type – my idea of American Indian
braves, for each held between his knees like a tomahawk a
nearly six-foot polished knobkerrie. One of them had an
aquiline profile, the nose almost hooked. And all three looked
at me with bland, dark eyes. I stared back thinking how handsome they were. They smiled faintly now that the older man
twitted them:

'*Kaloku* these are *ama*Mpondo, as you see,' he explained. 'That
is the reason they know nothing. For what is the main pre-

occupation among them and the *ama*Mpondomise, over on that other bank of the *um*Bashe? Beer Feasts and Stock-theft. Is it not so, young men?'

But while they glanced at one another uncertainly, he continued, 'Of course it is. *I know.* I am one of you. My clan name is Jola. I am *m*Mbo. No Xhosa, I, although having lived years on end in Ndhlambe's territory, in East London working for these whites. So handsome ones, I may tell the truth about ourselves, eh?'

They acknowledged his privilege with abashed smiles, not speaking. So he went on, talked about himself in order to 'explain about *ama*Mpondo'. As usual the impression was not of an inordinate egocentricity but that he was using a personal experience to illustrate the variety of life's circumstances. He was 'representing' others like him to show how their ideas were tempered by the changing times.

'Now look at me: *I* am one of those who weaned himself *early* from that life of tranquillity-in-sterility in the Arcadia of Pondoland', and he used a metaphor that made us all laugh, one of those that people loved. When the laughter died down, he went on, 'I left *thirty-five years ago* to work in town – understand?' The warriors gazed at him obediently, since he wished it, had taken charge, and they had no choice because of his seniority, 'You see, our chiefs had long ago sent word to "*abefundisi,* teachers" (missionaries) to *come* to us. It was they who taught me to read and write. Wesleyans. Presbyterians. Church of England. Men of *beautiful* works. Their wives ran little hospitals, and sewing classes and such things. Ah, it was beauty, beauty! Then I wished to go forth, see the world, and work; and did myself a good turn. For as you now see me, I know things that I would never have known – through *work.* Therefore,' he harangued, 'pay attention while I tell you who this person is.' Not only the Pondo braves, the whole bus-load turned to look at me, craning necks to do so. However, before he could launch on my family history, a woman of about his age intervened. She could not see from where she sat exactly what he did as he stretched a hand towards my shoulder, and she cried out, '*Yo!* Is he *pointing* at her?' But everyone hastened to reassure her, and Jola shouted, 'No indeed, mother, I declare I am only tapping her shoulder, certainly not being so savage as to *point*.'

The elderly lady laughed good-naturedly, then *she* now launched on a dissertation; about pagan beliefs in the evils of pointing at people It turned out that she too was a Pondo, a 'converted', of Christian family. Now that the talk was about the life of her tribe she was moved to contribute, for Pondoland was a reservoir of ancient lore.

Presently it was Jola's turn to take up his interrupted tale about my family. The mood was expansive for we had all day in the bus. The woman interjected pieces of her own knowledge about Makiwanes, for it transpired that she came from Umtata where my younger uncle lived and where I was to spend the night in order to catch an early local bus the next day to my uncle at Tsolo.

The bus came to the Great Kei. The river lies in the folds of a breath-taking valley, between hills covered with bush and brown boulders. The road twists back on itself down steep inclines until level with the bridge. From above, the water looked like a great serpent and always reminded me of folk-stories our nursemaids used to tell us surreptitiously – about 'water snakes, people of the river', creatures employed by sorcerers; denizens of dark holes in the reeds who had the power to mesmerize and 'draw you into the deep'.

Excitement mounted, for we were approaching a landmark indeed and the olden migrations rose again in our minds. As we reached the bridge and drove slowly along it, we looked from side to side at the waters spreading on to the dunes on either side. A hush fell on us all. We had now left the territory of *kwa*Ngqika, were now 'in The Great House of Xhosaland – *kwa*Gcaleka'.

My neighbour was moved to cry out, 'O, thus-we-arrive, *komKhulu*!' She became so excited that the infant woke at last, stirred, then struggled out of its nest of the heavy shawl. Its mother now took the stage, started to speak about her life and experiences. The opening sentences marked her out immediately as a species of 'New Woman', partly broken away from the society that bred her; independent, fierce, unabashed. She fumbled quickly – clearly a highly strung person – in a small

134

bundle tied round with a handkerchief, brought out a sandwich, began to stuff pieces of it in the child's mouth. It started to eat contentedly, though still sleepy and dazed. She addressed the passengers.

'This is a child that I have "picked up", an illegitimate treasure. Treasure because this was my *third*, and thank God that I conceived a second girl. And I am bringing her *home*, to Gcaleka-land.'

We were very startled. Everyone looked at her expression-lessly, following the custom of 'hearing the speaker out'. For a moment she was silent, assembling her 'speech'. While we waited only the older, maternal, converted woman made a sound. She moaned, then clucked her tongue in distress. When she did it a second time, the speaker cried, '*Mama*, you would not be shocked if you knew the obstacles that I have overcome in this Vale of Tears.' She must have sensed that the scriptural overtone would not fail to stay the old lady. Then she addressed everyone on board, 'Here is how it all began. I was a young girl; proper; virginal. I was courted. But the suitor "changed his mind – *wandala*".'

There was an outbreak of clucks expressing everybody's shock. Encouraged by the response, she repeated herself for emphasis, raising her voice; a crescendo of pain, 'Rejected me, I say. Even renounced the cattle he had already produced in part towards the contract. *That* was how utterly I was rejected. Found he did not want me after all. Saw another. Oh, the matter was discussed at home and intermediaries hurried to and fro; his father, ashamed, mine insulted. "*Kwakubi* – Things became hideous." But he no longer wanted this MaFaku, this MaNyawuza whose story you are hearing today.'

Again she played on our sympathies by drawing on the clan names for they established her as someone who 'belonged to *people*' – who prized her. The salutations gave the family an identity and at once we felt for them; no need to know who they were.

'From that moment, how could I trust a man? My heart was not broken – it was *rent*. I had loved that suitor. I lay in my hut and sickened. When at last I emerged, *thin, thin*, I "betook myself to the River"; washed; scrubbed; anointed my body.

Then made it known to my father that I had "gathered myself together" and must go forth. For me, the land of my birth, this beautiful Gcaleka had *gone black*. I went.'

'Went? Where?'

'"*Ndaziyel' edolophini* – Took myself to town. Worked". I tried many jobs. First I became a nurse-girl; kept my eyes on the cook as she did her work. And how she helped me to learn, improve myself, that *mama* who cooked for those Europeans. She was a widow, *u*MaNtande by salutation, from Tembuland. Never will I forget her. I got a job as a cook. My Europeans ate well, liked my work for I assure you I have skill for that job. When I cook, I "hit that stove", man, until Europeans lie on their sides replete. And they *pay* their staff, those Europeans of mine, unlike some who squeeze your essence but reckon your body must manufacture it unstoked-up by *them*. Years passed. The heart mended. At last I stopped thinking of that suitor. But also came to *entertain thoughts of no others*. My next step was to provide for my old age, for I had decided to be a *Nongendi* – (a "not-marry" – the term for a nun). I conceived a baby as provision for that future. Yes, just "picked it up". No marriage, cattle, nothing. A little nameless thing. My Europeans let me continue working until almost the birth. And to my joy it was a girl. While I suckled of course I could not work, Europeans not liking the smell of nursing mothers. Yet had to live, had I not? I could not go home, not having told them of the path I had chosen, and fearing their wrath and distress. So I set up with a *masihlalisane*. Yes, took up with *that* life of no life. For more than a year, I was a *kephita* – (kept woman). But guess what happened next. Having weaned, I was about to return to my Europeans. But one-two-three, I had conceived again. Yet no longer wanting to *kephita* with that man because he had begun to want to make a permanency of that no-life arrangement. Huh! A man with wife and children in the country – what would I ever be to him? Did he not merely want a permanent "wife" but without cattle, contract, licence, one denied a place in society? Such was his cheek. Yet my Europeans wanted me back and I too wanted work.'

The elderly woman murmured as if involuntarily, 'Ah, when one gets good employers and *good* work, what else to do but cling to it? *Clutch* such a job, *"dig the digits into it till fingernails sink to the very quicks".'*

That drew groans of assent and the younger woman turned to her, saying, 'That is what I have learnt to do. Yet this fix of another pregnancy was preventing me. Finally I could only send word to my flesh and blood and take my girl-child home to the Transkei, deposit her with my mother to raise up. Painful, but a grandchild is precious. Do not even shameful, nameless ones bring their own load of love and consolation? I am on my way to visit that child.

'But that unwanted pregnancy resulted in a *boy* and, as you can imagine, the father wished to have it because it was a man-child. Produced the necessary cattle to my people for the fine for spoiling me, and therefore took his son.'

'*Kwek!*' cried Jola at last, dejected by every aspect of the case. But she cried sharply, 'No, Jola, *I* did not feel deprived. What use are boys to such as me? It is *girl*-children who support their mother when she grows old and useless. Boys of nowadays have other fish to fry. Now here is my life's plan: *Every time I conceive a boy, I will let the father produce the fine in cattle to my people – which will entitle him to take the child into his lineage group!* But I will conceal each girl, whisk her away to the home of my birth. These are my gold,' she cried, suddenly lifting the infant on high. 'My heart is rent no more when I contemplate them.' She sat back, cuddled her baby and was silent.

But her words[1] describing that life's plan left us dazed. Yet had she not shown that she felt no self-pity? Need we feel it for her? But the cynicism, the anti-social aspect, the amorality of it affected everybody; not so much the personal case but its wide implications. Jola took over. We had to strain our ears to hear him. His voice was low and solemn.

'People-of-ours, a painful thing is taking place in our life.' He paused. The silence was marked only by noises from the baby who seemed to have catarrh, breathing stertorously while munching the bits of sandwich. Jola expressed himself, and I am almost 'defeated', as he would have said, by trying now to put it in English.

'*Kaloku tina esiNtwini sasuka sa PUMA enkonzweni yokuhlonipa*

---

[1] '*Elek'ukuba ndi mit'inkwenkwe, nd'akuyireza, lihlawul'isoka, limtate!*'

intombi; this painful thing of which I speak is that "we-of-our-culture *Bade Farewell* to our former reverence for virginity".' He heightened the key words by adding those catalysts that have no equivalent in English: *Kaloku, ukusuka* – the 'Deficients', technically so-called, that give what the grammarian W. G. Bennie has described as 'a snap to the action', and in prose can shift meanings and thought patterns to the level of intensity that a poet can achieve in English verse. Jola's remark forced you to contemplate the disaster on many levels; to consider the setting we lived in; the vicissitudes that involved all the people; and to ask yourself what could be the outcome of the changes being wrought in the nation. Many of us now looked to him as one whose experience might offer an answer, or at least some consolation. But having thrown the idea among us like a man broadcasting seed he said no more. It was the matron who spoke, her voice as sad as his.

'We mourn the passing of the days when girls behaved nobly because the *community* so behaved,' she said. 'Society was strict with itself, therefore strict with them for they were its symbol of honour. At intervals girls had to be examined lest they had been deflowered despite the vigilance of the chaperone. Present generations feel that this was crude. But we *were* a rough people. Nobility does not presuppose queasy petty sensitivities. *That* attitude belongs to *isiLungu* – Europeanness. It is not related to *the sensibility* which belonged to *isiNtu* – Africanness; which was what we strove after, even if indelicate, crude. The ideal of *nobility-in-living-with-people* was served by, among other things, society's demand that a man who transgressed the code about virgins be disgraced, disgraced! The matter had to do with the symbols of our self-respect. Where now that striving, and what use a community that abandons even the outward *symbols* of its thought?' The Pondo braves shifted their knobkerries uneasily as if the reference to transgressions struck near the bone. I would have liked to say what I thought but didn't. It would have been out of place for me to comment. People began gathering up parcels and belongings. We reached the sleepy-looking town, built on the site of the kraal, or 'Great Place' of the Gcaleka Paramount Chief Hintsa, who had reigned when Europeans first penetrated into Xhosaland. The bus stopped and many disembarked. Those of us who were going on said good-bye and watched the new-comers about to join us. I stepped out with other passengers to stretch my legs. When it was time to climb back into the bus, old Jola followed behind me. As he went to his seat he scrutinized faces; exchanged a word with those who had been with us from the beginning; hailed new-comers. He had to halt when I reached my seat because my neighbour had risen and stepped aside into the corridor, child in arms, in order to let me pass through to my corner. But when she sat down, he still stood looking down at her as if worried about something. I hoped he would not start all over again on the subjects she had raised. When he spoke, it was in stentorian tones, throwing his voice dramatically as everybody did, and demanded:

"*'K'awutsho, MaNyawuza: le bus imile nje kodwa umchamisile umntana, wazithuma?* – Kindly say, I beg, MaNyawuza: this bus having stopped and afforded the opportunity, did you *piss* that child and make sure her bowels moved?'" His labourer's face wore a look of real concern, of a parent, probably grandfather, putting the question to a frank and far from queasy or prettily sensitive audience. They judged it entirely proper, echoed it vigorously, and looked at the mother for assurance.

I was delighted not to have missed that exchange. It seemed to strike a note appropriate to my coming interlude in yet another setting within the society we had talked about throughout the ride. Rough the journey had been in all conscience: bucolic, uncouth, odoriferous, inconvenient; but also lacking none of the elements my father had promised: reciprocity, tough-mindedness, imagination, the irrepressible sense of fun.

13

WHEN I arrived at Confluence Farm, indeed while the household were dashing in all directions making a welcome, a neighbouring farmer called to ask why my uncle had failed to turn up that morning for an appointment that had been fixed to discuss a rural matter. I heard *malume* 'explain the situation that he was in', and say, '*Kaloku* I have been arrived-upon by a niece'. And the caller's response showed that he understood perfectly, and shared the masculine pride that rang in my uncle's voice that a sister should have provided the cause. The exchange reminded me of things my mother had said long ago about his obligations as our permanent 'protector'. I realized more vividly what she and other mothers had meant to convey when speaking to children about mothers' brothers, *omalume*; that if, on growing up, homes-of-marriage or lineal-homes became insupportable, a woman's children could go to *malume*. 'Even if in the wrong, his sister's child, an *umtshana*, would never be driven away. The male-mother's responsibility is to persuade, conciliate, reconcile.'

As I have said, I was apprehensive about that. The ritual is no light matter. But my uncle appeared to be in no haste. As that first day passed bringing its range of intangible impressions, I was comforted to sense his pace and to know from it that the atmosphere was to be the usual one of which people say, 'Let things develop and we shall see how we get on.'

Next morning I lay between the sheets in a single iron bed and hugged my hot-water bottle. I had been assigned the hut I usually occupied, and found myself thinking about those of my generation to the family whom my uncle had sheltered when personal crises had overwhelmed them.

I was not expected to do anything in the household, although everyone else was astir with the dawn. I enjoyed the farm noises – cocks, hens, chickens, ducks, dogs, puppies, turkeys; and the cattle and sheep in their enclosures not many yards from my hut.

I call it a hut; it was really a rondavel, the same shape but bigger and with the door and glazed windows of a modern house. It was made of wattle and daub worked smooth in the usual way; and thatched but without a ceiling, so that you looked up at rough wooden beams below the sheaves of plaited grass and reeds. It was one of several rondavels strung out in a semi-circle from the ends of the central house.

My uncle's farmstead is perched on the top of a ridge commanding the vista of hills, mountains, spacious valleys that are typical of his locality. His 'lands' as the grain fields are called, and grazing grounds are at the junction of two rivers, the Tsitsa and the Nxu, hence the name Confluence Farm. The central house consisted of large rondavels linked by a rectangular passage which was generally used as a day-room. Many black and white South Africans are devoted to this architectural plan and think of it, probably with parochial inexactitude, as an intrinsically 'South African style'.

The connecting passage had been my late Aunt Valetta's room, the nerve-centre of the home. There was a low couch in it, and occasional tables strewn with her favourite supplements from my uncle's farming journals and other magazines; and near the window her treadle sewing-machine, the ubiquitous Singer on which she made all the clothes for the family when they were young. A door at one end led into the rondavel which she and my uncle had used as a double bed-sitting-room-cum-study, a very large room. Under one of its big windows stood my uncle's old roll-top desk, stuffed to overflowing with farming papers, bills, receipts, family records. There were bookshelves, upright chairs and a rocking-chair. Only they used this rondavel, but the outside door that gave on to the drive was always open and people knew that my uncle could be found there when he was home from the fields. The drive passed round a small orchard of peach and fig trees, Cape gooseberry and other bushes; a part of it facing my aunt's day-room was a flower garden where she had grown Barberton Daisies, zinnias, marigolds and other South African favourites. The drive led to the main gate and, beyond, the ridge was edged by great slabs of rock and sloped into the shallow valley of the rivers.

The other door out of my aunt's day-room led into the rondavel dining-room. In there was an old harmonium made in Germany. I understood it to have belonged to my grandfather. We called it rather grandly, 'the organ,' and in Xhosa *uhaadi*; why, I never found out for I invariably forgot to ask. The rooms were hung with portraits of Makiwanes. There were steps down from the dining-room to the kitchen, which was efficiently arranged and fitted with shelves where my aunt had stored home-made pickles, biscuits, bottles of fruit; in her day it had seemed as if they never bought food but produced everything on the farm, even salting bacon in great vats.

The views from the whole homestead were breath-taking. I had long ago given up trying to take photographs of them. You needed what camera-men call a 'zoom lens' for it was giant country, Brobdingnagian sweeps of mountains, valleys, plains and skies. At the back and far across another of these valleys rose the tall conical hill-mountain on its enormous spreading base. That was Tsolo, whose name meant 'pointed'. It was like a splendid phallic symbol, as if a Cyclops had poised and placed it on the landscape. The district was named after it. The formation of hills and ridges seemed of a different kind from that at Middledrift. Here the gargantuan terraces of the rise in altitudes from coast-line to South Africa's famous plateaux, table-lands, were seen from a different angle: features which used to give us moments of torture in geography classes at school at Lovedale. This whole territory of the *Ama*Mpondomise in Eastern Pondoland was now scheduled to become part of the 'separate African ethnic group area, racial paradise, show-place of Bantustan, when, "under real *apartheid*", each race would enjoy self-rule'. Such was Dr. Verwoerd's dream.

Certainly it was a 'green and pleasant land', less drought-stricken than ours farther south – a climate affected by the altitudes, the slant of terraced terrain, trade winds, distribution of grass lands and plains and forests. And its inhabitants seemed, like my uncle, inclined to live high on ridges, a typical southern African characteristic, for we say 'we like to see and be seen, not huddle in declivities'. It would be cosier down there no doubt;

certainly less strenuous when the harvest has to be hauled home. But enemies could take you by surprise, therefore the tradition was to settle where you could 'command a view'. I had heard many rationalizations of this, such as: 'To be at a height, to gaze on scenery so grand, enabled our people to breathe freely and be at peace with themselves and with creation.'

Over the years my uncle had made improvements, built more rondavels standing apart on both sides of the central house. There was one for the three sons, Cobham, Asquith and Kehle. Another was for the women who helped with the house-work. The one I occupied was my cousin Cecilia's, the only daughter, she who had been 'my little tail' when very young; and was now in her middle twenties and away in Natal teaching at a boarding-school. Beyond hers was a general utility room close to the cattle kraal and sheep pens. It was left mud brown, a proper 'native hut' with mere fist-holes for windows, while the main household was colour-washed, usually white, sometimes pink – a pleasing contrast with the tall dark trees of the wind-break behind it. The utility room was where the herd boys kept thongs for lassoing animals, fighting sticks, slept, or hung about by day when on the premises. The women retainers kept their grinding stones in it for processing grain, maize or sorghum, into flour for making bread and porridge. For a fireplace the hut had the perfunctory circle slightly raised in the middle of the earth floor. There the farm hands burned cattle dung, filling the chimney-less structure with acrid smoke.

Away at the back of the main house stood some really enor-mous huts, bigger than any of the rondavels. These were the barns, stacked with farm equipment. The stable was attached to one of them. Others were granaries. Near by was the shack that had housed the Cape and Scotch carts in the old days but was now the garage for 'the wagon, CCY number plate, that had brought my uncle to Middledrift', as our servant at home had put it. Outside the garage walls lay the sledges to which the herd-boys or other farm-hands harnessed oxen to trundle off to the ford to draw water. Drinking water was stored in rain-tanks by the kitchen.

The front doors of the entire household faced east. When the maid brought my coffee and I sat up in bed drinking it and looking out of the doorway I saw day break over the mountains. It set the dew alight near at hand, so that it sparkled fiery white, red, green. I watched the rays flooding my room; and to see them playing on the horizon was like watching the spectrum, for the colours changed as the heat began to build up. Towards noon the sun would beat on the thatch, but the rondavel would remain cool inside. Retainers seldom sat indoors, however. In the heat of the afternoon they preferred the lee of the houses, under the shade of the eaves. And very picturesque they had looked there with their friends when I had arrived, robed pagans draped in dark-ochred togas. The Pondo style was different from ours. They wore theirs as long sarongs, set off by rows of rubber rings round the ankles. I had come when some were sitting about smoking pipes decorated with beads, and puffing away from stems that were as long as their braceleted arms.

And now the boys began to create their morning commotion, the sounds that I remembered, shouting, whistling as they opened the gates of the kraal, and trampling of hooves, a lowing of cattle. They let the sheep out of their pens, upon which there was a rustle of little feet, bleatings, coughings: sheep seemed to be tremendous coughers and clearers of throats of a morning. My uncle's 'stock, *impahla*' (word for property that does duty for clothes, furniture, vehicles, equipment, all of a man's possessions), was being driven past my door, off for the day to the grazing grounds. The cattle stamped and snorted, some straying, stampeding, the boys calling out the names of the recalcitrants, and scolding them.

The maid came again, this time bringing hot water. She put the container down and stayed to chat while I got out of bed. She leaned against the wall, the hem of her skirt hanging unevenly, picked her teeth with a piece of wood while watching me take off my night clothes, even narrowing her eyes to see better; and offering candid comments about what she saw when at last I stood naked. As usual my size and shape did not please. In addition she could compare my body with that of my girl-cousin, evidently especially interested in the texture of our skins. 'Your cousin's is like your late mother's – *beautiful*,' she declared. 'It has the tint of ripe fruit. Yours lacks it.' I did not mind the scrutiny for her age and intimacy with the family gave her certain rights. And after all the rondavel I was using was almost her own. She kept no belongings in it but each night brought a bedding roll on which to sleep on the floor, as she did when my cousin was home, traditionally 'guarding and chaperoning' me likewise during my visit.

This particular servant was something of an eccentric and allowed latitude because of it. She went on to remind me that I need not hurry. 'I will prepare food when you are ready, Nontando. You are to do as you please. The big people will attend to their daily affairs, are now at breakfast.' I was a cross between a big person who is waited on and 'a special child' who is indulged, as the real children of the house would never be.

She had been at my uncle's ever since I could remember and one of her eccentricities was to call me pointblank by my name, unlike the Middledrift servants who for complicated reasons, respectfully avoided it now and labelled me by my daughter's instead, '"'na kaTembi, Tembi's Ma','" or else used my clan name. I had to call her Sis' Nonzondo as we had to 'respect' anybody older than ourselves, if necessary give servants the titles 'Aunt' (the English word) or 'Uncle' (the Afrikaans derivation, ompi) or 'Father So-and-so' (in Xhosa).

Sis' Nonzondo was a local Pondo woman, had joined the household when a young, lame, ochred pagan girl as nursemaid. When my cousins grew up she graduated into a housemaid. And after my Aunt Valetta was stricken by the illness that had paralysed her for many years, she ran the house and became cook as well. She had become a Christian – 'convert, igqoboka'. One forgot that she had ever been otherwise, but this morning I was reminded of it because, when she finished scrutinizing me, she launched out indignantly about a diminutive little herd-boy of her tribe called Mawase whom I had met on arriving when everyone lined up for presentation. He was described as a recent attachment to the household.

'Imagine,' she cried, 'the people of Mawase have sent a Person (emissary) as early as *this* in the day, even before the big people's breakfast, to beg permission for him to go home to *Attend a Beer*. These people are the limit. You don't know. I am telling you. Beer parties all the time. That life of savagery, frivolity, darkness. Well, the Person can wait. I shall not present him yet to ask for the loan of the child. The impudence of coming on such an errand, before the people have even eaten!'

'What can they want with him at a party?' I asked, for he had seemed only about ten years old, light-skinned, sweet-faced, a shy-looking little creature, like a choir-boy, who on being presented to me had drawn a scrap of a toga across almost infant shoulders and cast down his fawn-like eyes. The colour in his cheeks deepened, in agonies of tongue-tied bashfulness. When I dropped his paw and told him he might go, he had shot off like a rabbit and everyone laughed.

'*Shy?* That one?' *Sis'* Nonzondo exclaimed. 'He does not *know* that word. Do not be deceived by the childhood lightness-in-weight like a feather. These parties spoil him.'

'But why do his people want him, having attached him to *malume* for training and the chance to better himself?'

'I tell you, it is the influence of ignorance and backwardness. His people forget those ambitions when they realize he won't be on hand at a Beer to run errands, fetch and carry the drinks for the men. He is a "child-of-the-bowel (last born)", *kaloku*; so the parents keep yielding to the desire to indulge him. Is it not ridiculous?'

'Will *malume* allow it?' She was so outraged that I too had become aghast.

'I am afraid so. Your uncle is not what he was. These days, while he is still strict about some things he suddenly becomes lax about others. Getting old, Nontando. The youngsters began to take advantage when your Aunt Valetta left us; as happens when a home is bereft of the Person who is its foundation stone. Take the older herd-boys, now. Would they have dreamt of being-asked-permission-for when they were Mawase's age and she was alive? Certainly not. The oldest one, Kekane – remember him? He is head farm-boy now; he had to be at the lands yesterday when you arrived. He "became a man" some years ago. When he and I were young, we *feared* your uncle, trembled when he spoke. But I tell you, Gambu treats Mawase with the indulgence of a maternal grandfather, is softer with this whipper-snapper than with his own last born, *u*Kehle.' She limped off, having thrown a flood of new light on my uncle which left me with fresh thoughts about my cousin's awkwardly-timed effort that day at Fort Hare when he had tried to talk about the dispiriting effect on him of his father's sternness. What he had said had clashed with a picture I had cherished in my mind. Years ago I had seen my uncle take him from his attendant and carry him on one arm, walking-stick in the other, and bear the baby off on an inspection of the lands. I had been astonished. But the women only smiled, muttering, 'A man and his last-born.' Yesterday when I met MaDhlomo the new mother, my cousin's ambivalent feelings had filled my mind. I was taken aback for I had not expected them to puzzle me. Yet they had, and had put me in a quandary. For I, too, missed my Aunt Valetta. When the taxi brought me and I saw the homestead again, that had been the moment when she would have run like a girl, petite and muscular, to open the gate; and she and my mother would have fallen into each other's arms. Later she could not; and on my last visit the car had driven to the door before I saw her, tucked among cushions, unable to move, and carried everywhere, laughing, gay. This time 'the new Person' had stood at the door, whom *my* new mother had selected. She was stout, comfortable, walked gravely, and treated everyone with dignity in her present delicate position – under scrutiny, however concealed, her every word, gesture or unguarded expression silently weighed and compared.

In those first minutes I tried to keep my mind open. Would not her generation (and my uncle was standing beside her) expect an older 'sister' of the son of the house to guard against the temptation to fall into attitudes? I noted all that my cousin had conceded about her manner: correctness, the formal precision. Feelers were in the air. But the atmosphere had seemed to me to be in order, proper. In addition I had felt genuine kindness in the welcome she gave the unknown *umtshana*. Or so I had interpreted what I saw when her whole body moved towards me, not only the hand that she put out. She had made to take my things, although servants were standing by waiting to be directed to handle them – as they should, of course, not approach unbidden. When she did that, I saw my uncle's face soften. He smiled. And I could not help responding, for the moment seemed to convey in a flash, that his life too, was complete again. It was an impression that could settle all doubts so far as I was concerned because the preceding circumstances were still vivid in my memory.

During the years of my aunt's illness I had seen him in anguish. Seen him carry her, when she became shrunken and shoulders and limbs huddled, to spots on the farmstead where she could '*gcakamela*' the morning sun, enjoy her flower beds, or talk and be entertained by the people of the house as they worked. One of my relations, lanky 'cousin' Jongilanga Makiwane followed, bringing her special chair, rug, magazines, supplements, knitting or sewing. He had returned to the country from city life as an hotel waiter to help with the farm-work and to look after my aunt. She used to banter:

'Is not Jongi's acquired skill God's work? See how the country boy has learnt to prepare appetizing invalid's trays.' She infected Jongi with her enjoyment of the effect that his actions had on the household's pagan friends. When they saw him bend daintily from his great height to arrange a tiny posy to put on her tray, they cried, '*O?* Are flowers to be eaten, then?'

After she died I had again seen my uncle but at 'the time of my brother' as it was now called, when he was naturally more serious than even he had ever been; and had had to 'speak with' me in person because I was the only representative of the children. His exhortations were attended by all the grown-ups present, and filled me with awe. All those things now left me no way to convey my feelings on becoming aware of his new happiness. I could only think, suffering for my cousin, how can Kehle be tortured with doubts? He must *know* he is loved. But immediately remembered, my mind rushing on, that *he* would not know what *I* had seen when his father used to fondle him.

But I tried to push the thoughts away, turned to wash before the water got cold. It was unnerving to re-live my arrival yesterday, and had been exhausting overnight to wrestle with all these things after *Sis'* Nonzondo had stopped chatting from her bed-roll on the floor and fallen asleep.

I crossed the room and parted curtains to take a quick look at the farm. People were walking about carrying implements, vessels, leather thongs. Back at the wash-stand as I soaped

myself I looked round my cousin's room wondering how to
broach the subject of 'permission for her to come to England'
for hospital nursing. She saw no future in teaching under the
new Bantu Education Act. There was not much more in nursing
either, now that the proposal was being put into effect to stop
African girls from taking the recognized Nursing Council
course and instead make them take a 'Bantu' variant of a lower
standard. My young women relations were in cleft sticks too, 'up
creeks of frustration', not only my menfolk like Mzimkhulu at
Fort Hare.

The interior of her rondavel seemed to express Cecilia's
personality. I liked her little domain; her taste was like that of
both our late mothers who had been greatly attached to each
other. And as I have said, Cecilia lived with us as a child. Her
second name was Nonqaba ('Rare One') but everybody used a
pet name, *'meidtjie'*, Afrikaans for 'little girl' but which had
become transformed into 'Maisie'. The mat I stood on, the rugs
on the floor were among the furnishings she had bought on
becoming 'a world's worker'; thrifty, steady girl, not exactly
like her handsomest brother, who, in the perverse distribution
of family affections, was her father's favourite – or so we firmly
believed.

I could imagine the preparations for my stay that her new
mother would have got under way in Maisie's rondavel. The
floor (of earth, not stained boards as in the main house) had
been freshly smeared with cattle-dung. And whoever had done
it had drawn the popular pattern of chevrons, as at the old
chief's house at Ntselamanzi. When I was young and on
holidays at our farm twelve miles from home, or here at Tsolo, I
too used to smear the floor with dung, *ukusinda*, and once a
week kneel down like the big girls, relations or servants, beside a
bucket filled with it mixed with water to the right consistency.
I had longed to be allowed for the first time; and enjoyed it
afterwards for it was fun, like playing at mud pies. To *sinda* a
room amounted to a regular spring-cleaning, and had clearly
been preceded here by the routine of taking down and launder-
ing the curtains, polishing the windows; dragging the bed and
all movable furniture out to air in the sunshine; and dusting the
beams under the thatch to clear them of hornets' nests and

other creatures. Then the floor was smeared, the effect being to bind the earth so that the dust should not fly; which was not only hygienic but pleasant to look at, the designs in dark green being varied at the whim of the girl doing it. Life at Tsolo was in truer country discipline, less of the mixtures that ours was at Middledrift, or Mrs. Mzamane's at Fort Hare or my Aunt Frieda's at Alice.

When dressed I went over to the main house. MaDhlomo was waiting, and beamed on my walking into the dining-room. She at once invited me to sit at the table, pulled out a chair, then went down the steps to the kitchen to take over from *Sis'* Nonzondo and cook with her own hand the fresh liver of 'my' sheep which *malume* had had ritually slaughtered for my arrival. Useless to protest that I did not normally eat a cooked breakfast, for she sat down to watch me consume the special food for nieces and nephews. And gave me bacon and new-laid eggs to go with it; toast, farm butter, homemade jam, more coffee.

'Your uncle has gone down to the lands. Eat at leisure, MaJili. Do not hurry. This is your home. He will be back before the sun is fully up.' I had forgotten how at the farm nobody referred to the clock, only to the positions of the sun. 'He will take you to lay a stone at your late *malume-kazi's* grave.'

So we talked. I would look up in the act of lifting a mouthful to find penetrating brown eyes studying me. There was the inevitable hair's breadth of constraint between people who do not know each other, and know that they ought to get to know and love; a first contact which under normal conditions would have been eased by the presence of a prescribed companion. But as the Mzamanes had emphasized, the settings of life were changing. Personal relationships had to be worked out in new ways.

For my part, I had become disposed towards MaDhlomo as I have said. But how was she to know? When I answered her formal inquiries about Kehle's health, I felt that she looked at me searchingly, and guessed she must be wondering how much my cousin and I had talked together, blood being thicker than water, about the new mothers in our homes. I longed to reassure her. But it would be the height of unseemliness. The matter was the province of the needed companion. And even so it would have been unthinkable 'haste' for the intermediary to speak as soon as this. My peripatetic tendency to cross t's and dot i's conflicted with the tenet that 'time should be allowed to do its work'.

When I could not eat a mouthful more, MaDhlomo reluctantly called the maid to clear away and I went to my room to fetch the wedding presents I had brought her. She received them with controlled rapture, sedate sunny smiles, and used the terms for thanks that grown-ups traditionally use to children who have 'behaved appropriately'. She had no children but her manner was as maternal as that of my own new mother; and both reminiscent of the motherly woman in the bus when the matter of the voluble, restless, uprooted 'new woman' and her illegitimate babes had cropped up. The bearing of these older women was distinctive indeed. They had 'a presence, cast a shadow'. Those kerchiefs tied round their heads showed their honourable married status. The high-necked blouses and long sleeves imparted an air of remoteness and modesty that compelled in you a respect that was almost paralysing; and you found it impossible to believe that they could have the inclinations that you yourself felt – want to make love, for example. They seemed statuesque, pillars of maturity, with those broad bosoms of their time of life, and in the skirts reaching well below mid-calf. Yet were they not girls once and frivolous? Then young women subject to normal instincts? I greatly admired the status to which they had risen because carefully trained to do so; but could not help thinking, 'I do not want to be elevated yet awhile', or wondering how she and her age-group of 'she-elephants' had felt in transition. While she was speaking my uncle came up the drive, preoccupied, unsmiling, as if this survey of the lands had not fully pleased. Typical farmer, I thought. He was, as he himself would say, 'Not dressed neatly' as when on the holiday visit to us in the Ciskei. He wore rough farm clothes, carried his walking-stick and also a vast black umbrella. His inseparable, shaggy-haired, grey-black dog was at his heels.

MaDhlomo called out, 'Come and see what our niece has brought.' I was very faintly surprised to see him obey, having never seen him commanded, however affectionately. He came in and strode over to where she sat, my gifts spread on her lap. His farm boots resounded on the floor-boards, the expression on his dark face alert, as if wondering why he allowed himself, amid occupations with stock and grain-fields to be drawn into this woman's world. And when he bent down to examine the offerings, his stance was so masculine, incongruous, I had to suppress a smile. He touched the linen as if mystified and murmured 'Household things, eh?' I remembered what Mzamane had said about a man's position in his wife's house. He did not linger over them. When he straightened up, he looked out at the view that the doorway framed, his eyes scanning it as if concentrated on something on those stretches of tough country which engaged a man's proper attention. But when he spoke, he said, 'Well, you have chosen articles that please your aunt. She is pleased.' He did not add, 'And what pleases her pleases me also.' There was a silence, but some such sentiment quivered in the air. Then he and I and his dog went out together, 'To see my late aunt.'

Afterwards we walked along the ridge to the neighbouring household. I was to be presented to another *malume*, his cousin Stewart Makiwane. His farmstead was like Uncle Cecil's only smaller. Here too improvements had been made over the years. Wind-breaks that I remembered seeing planted as a child were now mature trees. We picked our way through building materials scattered in the approach for *malum' u*Stewart was in the process of adding to the house. We came level with him directing the work, he too in rough farm clothes. He welcomed us as if from afar and called to MaXaba. She issued from her kitchen, screwed up her eyes against the light and broke into a ringing greeting, repeating my clan name over and over. She too was dressed in the matronly Victorian manner. She wiped her hands on the apron at her waist then folded me to her bosom. They ushered us indoors, the two men removing their tattered farm hats and turning to scold the dogs of the house which were squabbling with ours.

At last the hounds were quiet and lay at the door rolling yellow eyes, and we sat down. I was asked about my journey, then at great length about how I had left everyone at Middledrift, 'in the Colony'. They used the usual Afrikaans derivation for 'brother-in-law'. After a while a tea-tray was brought by a respectful, very young retainer, a girl of about our own Mawase's age. She laid it before MaXaba and was about to turn and go, but MaXaba halted her so as to 'explain' her to me. The little girl looked on the floor speechless and, finally, dismissed with a chorus of thanks, affection and praises from the three elders, sidled out. The moment she gained the open, we saw her jump and skip as if back at an interrupted solitary game of hop-scotch. The old people smiled. Then I listened while they talked which was for a long time, about farming prospects, the condition of grain and stock, recent events in their territory and especially about the interminable thieving that each homestead had to endure.

They were among the leading farmers in the district and when crops ripened it was their habit to go down to the lands at night and shoot off guns into the air, a method they had resorted to over decades. Everyone including the local rural white police and magistrates had always accepted that they owned these weapons only to flush thieves from among the crops and animals. And it was known that they never handed them to even senior farm-hands, but used them personally, to ensure as Christians, that not even persistent robbers should be wounded or killed.

But shortly after my visit, when they sat chatting in placid accord about this and other local topics, they were to be in terrible trouble with the authorities about their old guns. It was after the famous Sharpeville massacre by armed police of Africans near Johannesburg, women and children among the killed – the event that prompted the Government to impose a military State of Emergency on the whole country.

In that trigger-happy interlude, Pondoland made world news headlines. Its pagans rebelled against the 'chiefs' which the Government appointed over them under Dr. Verwoerd's scheme for '*apartheid* in action' in which South Africa was to be divided into 'self-ruling, independent, separate, ethnic groups'. The scheme did not take into account the fact that the southern system of chiefs is hereditary, chiefs-by-appointment unheard of; an idea that strikes at the roots of life. As a result, social and political upheaval prevailed in my uncles' rural arcadia. And under the Emergency Regulations, no black people might possess arms although they were being issued in haste to all whites, women and boys and girls, included, who were shown in newspapers practising how to use them. My uncles were arrested.

The letters that I received omitted detail, as did those with the news about my other relations accused, and years later acquitted, at the Treason Trial. I could hardly bear to think what that day must have been like on the farms; my aunts MaDhlomo and MaXaba gravely watching; the dependants of the homesteads dumbstruck at the spectacle of the elders being handcuffed and borne off to prison in their farm clothes, carrying walking-sticks, umbrellas; their dogs shooed off as they tried to accompany their masters.

The event coincided with my cousin Mzimkhulu's escape from another part of the district into Basutoland, the British Protectorate; and I and others in whose families similar things were happening, realized that conservative-minded elders were now being picked off too, not only young hot heads. *Apartheid* was becoming 'like a granite wall to defend White Christian Civilisation', because Dr. Verwoerd was at the time urging his followers to make it so. And arrests of people like my uncles showed what was in store under 'true *apartheid*, the policy of good neighbourliness'. The phrase was coined by the doctor, to counteract misunderstandings in the outside world. Tsolo and all the region was sealed off. No travellers, family or other visitors, or newspapermen were allowed. People saw the startling apparition of armoured cars patrolling their lands and grazing grounds.

But the morning I was with them the uncles did not know how their lives would be affected nor that these things were to happen soon. They only knew that the Transkei was seething with discontent like the rest of the country. People were suddenly arriving in every hamlet, 'endorsed out' as the new expression had it, from cities where they had lived for years earning money to send back home. Now there was a law dealing with 'Influx Control'. Those who were forced to return to the Reserves tried to steal back into the cities because there was no work, the countryside in any case overcrowded. My elders talked about such individuals, having met or heard of them in the course of inquiring into neighbours' healths, fortunes, activities. They talked also, since it was a pleasure to have an excuse, of a morning, to sit and sip tea, about the outings they used to enjoy but were now prevented by advancing age, by rheumatism, by that stiffness. My Uncle Stewart declared, chuckling, 'Oh, Gambu, I never imagined what a business this old age would mean. How can one recover stolen cattle and sheep properly when, instead of riding out oneself one has to send these farm-hands of these days, who return empty-handed, tired, wanting only to be fed?'

Uncle Cecil smacked his full lips with evident relish. His kinsman was speaking all too exactly of what he himself experienced, and he could corroborate and say, 'They *tell* you that they "got tired and could track no farther". But how is one to know that they are not in league with the cattle rustlers? We see what people are getting to be, these days.'

Aunt MaXaba echoed and cried, 'Do not speak of it. Me? I trust almost none of these young people of ours lately. They do not look upon us as their fathers and mothers, upon our homes as theirs as their class did formerly. They have been entered into by this new spirit of *ugliness*. They now look on us as Europeans to be milked, as the Europeans milk *them*. Tit for tat, eh? Ever since Verwoerd decreed that black people must be moved from white ethnic areas where they constitute "Black Spots", threats, even these erstwhile tranquil pleasure-loving *ama*Mpondo and Mpondomise are quivering with possessiveness. You hear them cry, "What about the white people making a living in our Reserves, then? Are they not 'White Spots'? Throw them out, if we are being thrown out of our livelihoods in the white areas. Let the Transkei be all black. And let us rule ourselves, not these puppet Chiefs the government wants to introduce who will only obey Pretoria. What *independence* is that?" But meanwhile they vent their spleen on us farmers. O, the restlessness of these times.'

Her menfolk concurred, but presently, their conversation drifted back to the lands, prices to be expected for their bags of grain, the state of the cattle-dips, and such things. At last *malume* reached for his walking-stick, hat, umbrella. MaXaba heaved herself out of her chair to go to the door. She raised her voice to call the little girl then whispered to my uncle, smiling, 'Wait, Gambu, I beg. We have prepared a little something as a welcome for *umtshana*.'

The child ran up carrying a live and plump fowl in her arms. She hugged it as if nursing a doll, and carelessly at that – a Rhode Island Red flapping its wings and squawking angrily because it was held upside-down. It had been captured at dawn, had lain all morning in the kitchen with its claws tied together. It was handed to me with one of the speeches that accompany the ritual gift.

14

About the third or fourth day after I arrived and was reckoned to be settling in, MaDhlomo galvanized the household into action about my laundry. She had pressed me on wash day to throw whatever needed washing into the family pile. But I had had nothing, travelling in quick-drying clothes which I rinsed in moments in my room. But streamlining does not satisfy all householders, as I had already found at home at Middledrift. They were wedded to the Victorian way of life, the kind of 'Westernization' that seemed to have truly penetrated. My aunt was becoming anxious; the household's equipment must be used; I had practically to invent a little mole-hill of soiled things. As at my own home, here at the farmstead you could see a complement of zinc double-handled containers of various sizes in which clothes were put overnight to soak. There were the corrugated boards that were propped up in those vessels in order to rub at obstinate stains; coppers for boiling 'whites', the 'coloureds' washed separately. There were yard-long sticks of 'yellow soap' or 'blue (mottled) soap', and small muslin bags holding cubes of Reckitt's Blue; flat-irons that were warmed on the kitchen range, the sight of which reminded me that my new mother had modernized our own fleet in Middledrift. She had acquired instead a 'Tilly' *spirit* iron. Although I had not given a thought to the old irons since I never had to use one myself, I was shocked, on my tour of inspection of my home, to see a new, sleek, gleaming thing looking like an electric iron stored in the linen closet. It seemed like a reproach on my mother's methods. After the weeks that had passed, and now at this distance, it was disturbing to remember the incident.

Housewives of MaDhlomo's generation seemed to despise new-fangled, labour-saving fabrics labelled 'drip-dry, non-iron'; preferred good old Irish linen, lawn, tobralco, twill; and for grand occasions, alpaca, serge, shantung, silk. As for detergents, 'Could they ever be as satisfying to use as solid soap?' Many older women had learned how to make their own when newly married. It had been a popular course in the women's clubs for home-making and self-improvement, which my mother ran when I was small. I had often watched or 'helped' her and the maids to store billycans of fat to render down for demonstrations later in evening classes. The activities involved in domestic arrangements were part of a way of life that presupposed that you did everything yourself. No sending laundry out to commercial firms, for instance. And because traditionally there would be many pairs of hands in any normal home, Mrs. Beeton's tome on household management was appropriate, and in fact a well-thumbed copy was on the shelves of nearly everybody's kitchen, rubbing shoulders with South African recipe books that set out Boer women's methods for making delicious Fat Cookies (*koekies*), pumpkin fritters, *konfyt*, biltong. And if you had been brought up in this atmosphere, it warmed your heart to see women and older girls working away on baking and washing days, every now and then pausing to wipe the sweat off their foreheads. It was homely to see their back-views as they bent over the zinc containers, when you would catch almost forbidden glimpses of grown-up ankles, even calves, beneath the hems of swinging skirts; and to see the washing afterwards flapping on the line, white and fresh in the sun; and fitting that the background to domesticity was the menfolk out in the lands ox-ploughing – although even more fitting here in the country had they been out hunting as of old.

At the farm they were out grazing the herds and flocks, or pottering about among the grain bags stored in the barns, or repairing equipment in the shed. At midday some of them would eat mealies and brown beans and meat washed down with thick milk. And in the late afternoon those present relaxed under shade-trees or thatched eaves, then started to work again on their evening round. After supper everybody gathered in the dining-room for prayers by the light of oil-lamps. I watched the scenes of farm life, and presently the youth called Ndleb'ende (Long Ear) who was inspanning a pair of oxen to the sledge. His work-mate, a boy named Mangqangqa (Bateleur Eagle, 'Bird of the Warriors, Raiser of the War Cry') had gone on ahead for the day with the herd.

Long Ear was in his late teens, tall, gangling, tending to knock-knees in a pair of khaki trousers handed down to him from my uncle and which someone had cut down into shorts. It would have been impolite to wear them exactly as my uncle had worn them. His leg muscles were thin but looked steel-hard. He affected one of those quiff hair styles that had lately become fashionable, and brushed and plastered what was called 'the front place' to make it stick up. When I exercised my privilege by commenting how stupid it looked especially as the rest of hair was left in snarls, he only laughed and said, 'The mothers and sisters here' (farm servants) 'are always saying that.' I saw that he took no notice, his young man's dandyism not aimed at old women like us.

That morning he had made his journey with the sledge to fetch washing water, and had outspanned and started on other tasks. When I came upon him inspanning anew, the expression on his face suggested that he was not pleased. He was looking towards the trees below the kraal and whistling, drew breath, whistled again. Presently an ox ambled up. He praised it. Then whistled again, and another came, again in a leisurely manner. He praised it too. Finally both stood still, near by but aloof and distant, sometimes turning their faces towards him then away as if looking at the view.

'Does each one know his whistle call?' I asked.

'Oh yes, cattle have brains,' he said proudly. 'You can single one out from the middle of the herd. Of course to teach them you have to persevere. Sometimes they delay coming because they don't feel like being disturbed. But the herd turns to look at the disobedient one, so in the end he thinks: *"Ag!* There'll be no peace until I obey,"* so he pushes his way out of the crowd and comes.' Long Ear gave a demonstration of an ox muscling its way out with head and shoulders. He said a word or two more to them as they stood swishing flies from their hides with their tails, then picked up a yoke, shook and rattled it at the first ox until the animal blinked at him.

'*Dyok, dyok,*' he said (Afrikaans for yoke). '*Dyok!* Come on. man,' and over his shoulder to me, 'You see, he cannot understand why we must go to the river again. We've just come back from there, unloaded the cans and everything. Then *umam'u*-MaDhlomo pipes and says: "Long Ear, my boy, just help, please. More laundry water today. *Kaloku* we have a visitor."' His mimicry made me laugh. Back in his normal voice he addressed his oxen again, 'My friends, it's useless for you to question. We have *got* to go. *Dyok, bafondini!*' And at last the first animal stumbled forward of its own accord and, as if resigned to the caprice of housewives, offered its neck to be yoked. Long Ear repeated the operation with its fellow. As a craftsman he was not displeased that I took an interest in his skill; he was mollified. Nonetheless I heard him confide to his oxen as if to fellow-sufferers, '*Nizakunqina tu! Sifikelwe ngumfazi; amanz' afunwa qho-qho-qho!* You're going to get as thin as rakes; our visitor is a woman, washing water will be wanted all-the-time, all-the-time.' He did not hold it against me personally, however, just against the waisted ones in general; for when he cracked his long whip in the air and trundled off with his equippage he smiled to see me fall in beside him and go along too.

The heavy sledge made a dull sound on the earth and, looking down at the fine sand into which it ground the path, I could appreciate why the method of transport was among the destroyers of top-soil and bringers of erosion all over the Transkei.

'I had no idea cattle were clever,' I said, hoping to start him off again. There was a grain of truth in my remark. A girl can never have first-hand knowledge of their habits. You acquire an attitude of admiration for them because you cannot help yourself. Everyone around you has it. But it is not done for girls and women to be in the vicinity of a cattle enclosure. And to go into a kraal – totally taboo; as it is for girls to milk cows.

I was therefore seizing the chance to talk. Ndleb'ende's face lit up. 'Cattle are clever, all right,' he laughed. 'To teach them tricks when we are out herding, oh, that is real fun!' and began to describe how herdboys spent days which one might think could be so boring, stuck out there in the veld. On the contrary, that life, I now saw, was packed with pleasures, excitements. His usually guarded expression was all animation as he talked of how he and 'the other fellows' conducted ox-races. A surreptitious pastime. He glanced over his shoulder almost as if someone might overhear, for the sport was officially banned decades ago.

Pointing at the animals jogging along before us, he said, 'Some of those chaps are absolutely mad about racing. They know which ox runs fastest and fix their eye on him, not bothering about the rest. Sometimes they try to gore the best challenger; go out of their way to eliminate him, oh, they are too good these fellows,' and he chuckled. Then he talked of the fun of teaching oxen to lie down on a prescribed spot and stay in it unsupervised.

'When you want time off for a bit, say you have "an appointment",' giving a sly look for he meant meeting a sweetheart. 'You can *instruct* an ox to stay put whereas a horse would have to be hobbled. But an ox never lets you down. You can be absent for hours trapping eatables for the pot.' He made the outdoor life sound delectable. I saw how he and his mates supplemented the ration of cold stiff porridge that they took from the farm in billy cans. They broiled rock-rabbits in rusty old herring tins, picked wild fruits and berries; and roasted birds, which he explained had to be trapped in different ways according to the habits of their species. And started to tell me about the birds that 'helped with the herding', especially the fork-tailed shrike. I smiled because Long Ear was unwittingly confirming the old saying: 'The cattle of him who lacks a herdsman are herded by the shrike. *Indoda engena malusi inkomo zayo zaluswa yintengu.*' I tried to think of an English expression carrying the same wry connotation but his enthusiasm rushed him on into more descriptions of his life and I abandoned the effort in the pleasure of listening. I had to tear myself away to get back to the house. When my uncle heard of the lessons the boys were giving me about life at Tsolo, he smiled. He liked to tease my father about our life at Middledrift and say it was suburban, what with the railway and station so near; the road to King William's Town and East London just across the valley; to say nothing of people wearing neckties every day, not only Sundays.

I told my new aunt about how I occupied myself when not with her. My uncle was with us, reading the paper I thought, but when he rustled it to turn another page, he suddenly said

'That is country life, Nontando. You will meet no better teachers than these rascals of ours.'

It was not the first time he had addressed me in that relaxed and companionable manner since I had settled down to my visit. At first I was exceedingly surprised. If all your life you have looked at someone through a ceremonial filter, it comes as a shock when the situation alters and the veil lifts, however gently; and you wonder whether you are imagining things.

Does he really mean it? I asked myself, for he was treating me like a species of adult; and I felt flattered. True, by now I was beginning to get used to it and recovered quickly from the surprise.

Later, trying to find out the reasons for these nuances, I wondered whether it was partly because his manner was so different from my father's. Yet although with him I now felt at ease, I remembered my trepidation when faced with being in his company alone for the first time. I was fourteen, about to travel to England with him, and my mother had had to prepare me for the terrifying contact. There had been no preparation for the closeness to my *malume*; and I found myself noticing how even the way in which he spoke was different from my father's, punctuated by long unsmiling silences. They were alarming, none of my parent's stutters when excited; no mimicry; no great gusts of laughter; no sudden urges to play the piano; no tricks like humming a tune and giving it a simultaneous, whistled accompaniment; no whims to demonstrate how he used to dance the 'cake walk'. Had it not been for my mother trying to 'explain' my uncle, or had I not seen the amazing spectacle of his tenderness with my young cousin when an infant, I would have thought him the epitome of the strong, silent man. Deep down I did think it, and thought him hard too, for I believed my mother only spasmodically.

My reactions to him in the last two years had become confused: his ritual speeches during the family crises had strengthened my awe of him; yet this had been rocked by Mam-Swazi's unwitting revelation of streaks of romance which it had never occurred to me could be in him – in the matter of the rendezvous over silver teapots at the hotel with his prospective fiancée.

And now when he talked about 'No better teachers than these rascals of ours', in a tone of voice that confirmed *Sis'* Non-zondo's strictures about his being 'too tender' and the rascals taking advantage, I hardly knew whether I was coming or going. Was it true that even the herdboys knew him better as a person than I did? On the other hand why should I wonder? They grew up under his eyes, he grew old under theirs. I was beginning to realize that personalities on the farmstead inter-acted; and as he went on talking about them I looked at him astounded that I could have been so blind. He turned over more pages of his newspaper, still not looking at me and said, '*Kaloku* Nontando, these young people may not read or write. But this Transkei countryside is an open book to them. They can tell *you*, from your Ciskei suburbia, things you never knew.' There was a smile in his voice, though not enough to rate an exclamation mark as it would have with my father. 'They read the signs of the veld; have eyes like hawks; can see for huge distances when out on these ridges and hill-tops. They are re-sourceful, know how to maintain farm gear, mechanical things – why, even the entrails of the motor car do not defeat their long fingers. And when on journeys tracking stolen stock, they can live off the country like soldiers on the march, like the *impis* of old.' A speech from him as long as that reduced me to silence. MaDhlomo took over, as if guessing the situation, and teased and argued with him especially about stock-thefts – touching on the possible defections of these paragons that he and his con-temporary had bemoaned at the other Makiwane household. Uncle Cecil now defended them, sitting forward to do so, laying his paper aside, and smiling at his wife, even laughing out loud. The spectacle gave me even more complex sensations. It was as if in his old age and second happiness she was bringing him closer to someone of my generation, into a clearer view, less interfered with by that sense of awe. What had my mother said once? 'Your uncle is a lovely man, do not be excessively afraid.'

One afternoon I was out for a walk and saw something of what he had meant. The sky was overcast, troubled. I liked walking out in cold weather, unlike everybody else at the farm. They had a healthy respect for the coughs and ailments that it brought, and did in fact seem more liable to them than I was. And they would say, as if making allowances for me, 'Oh well, you are used to it, no doubt. "Overseas" you never see the sun, do you?'

But on my way back the weather became unpleasant by any standards. A drizzle set in that drove into the eyes and blinded. The inspiring expanses seemed to foreclose, become grey, dismal, lowering. I began to think about the fires back at the farmstead and decided to take a short cut.

I hit on a faint footpath. It wended its way round boulders, over tussocks and other plants that tripped me up, so that it was while still some way from home I came upon Mawase, herding sheep. My heart went out to the little boy far from any beaten track. The mountains, the ridges, conical Tsolo itself, every landmark was veiled in the drizzle beating against my face. He was a solitary hump huddled on the veld covered, except for his pale face, by the blanket draped from shoulders to the ground. As I came the dogs with him sprang, growling and snapping their teeth. He shouted in his treble voice but they took no notice so he rose to chase them away, the sheep lying on the wet grass and watching him as he scampered about.

To my surprise, puffs of smoke billowed out from where he had been sitting, and seeped out from the folds of his blanket as he controlled the dogs. I walked up and found he had been sitting on his haunches over a fire made of a handful of embers, not more than half a dozen carefully balanced together, and glowing and spluttering as the drizzle fell on them.

'*Yo!* Mawase, hasn't the cold got you?' I cried. But he blushed and muttered something inaudible, too shy to answer properly. I looked at his fire and he too gazed down at it with a frown for the drizzle threatened to put it out now that it was unprotected. He was poised to drop down and huddle over it again, but too polite to move until I should give him permission. I was as awesome and inhibiting to him as my elders were to me so I said, 'All right, sit down.' He dropped on his haunches immediately and rearranged the blanket over himself, then looked up as if wondering how long I would pester him with my presence.

'It is so dark,' I said. 'Why not bring the sheep home?'

He smiled, shook his head, eyes cast down again.

'Because it's not time?' I prompted him.

'Yes, *Sisi*.'

'But you have no watch, how will you know today with no sun to tell you?' At which he looked at me, eyes wide. For the first time since I had known him he smiled and so far forgot himself as to make a speech.

'But at sunset, I shall hear by *udwetya*, shan't I? Meantime I am comfortable with my fire.'

'*Ngo dwetya?* What's that?'

His mouth fell open. He was absolutely incredulous at the question; then hung his head again, relapsed into his usual shy but alert speechlessness. I could not get an anwer out of him. But looking on I could not help admiring the way in which he managed his outdoor life. I said so but he uttered not a word. Even when I gave up and said good-bye and moved on he did not speak, only gave a not unfriendly grunt.

Back into the farm the way I came, I had to pass the utility hut. Through its open doorway I saw *Sis'* Nonzondo and a number of the other retainers congregated there with some friends. Girls and women of the place tended to use the hut as their sitting-room on gloomy or wet days. They ground grain in there, a job they otherwise did under the eaves. *Sis'* Nonzondo alone was grinding, kneeling at her slab near the door. On looking up and seeing me she called me in. Others stood behind her watching corn-cobs roasting on the fire at their feet, while some among them talked and laughed, keeping an eye on the cattle in the kraal a few yards outside the hut.

As I darkened the already gloomy doorway, *Sis'* Nonzondo hailed me again but continued to work. Her body swayed rhythmically while she explained me to the people in the room. There were murmurs of '*Ah! Umtshana* of here-at-home'. In the gloaming I picked out more figures standing against the wall, their blankets pulled up to cover noses and filter the acrid smoke. Brown and black eyes fastened on me. Two youths were perched on their heels on the earth floor, their fighting-sticks beside them. I told *Sis'* Nonzondo about having seen Mawase and asked about his *'udwetya'*. In her unpredictable way she happened to know that 'in the Colony where I came from' the name for it was *itshitshi*, which of course was the Cape grass-bird.

She was not more travelled than other people who passed whole lives in remote rural backwaters, but she stored bits of knowledge in her eccentricity. My father had often explained that such people are held in awe and are said to be 'gifted' in a way that defies analysis. Her explanation caused all in the hut to exclaim and look at her anew as she ground away. One seldom saw her idle. She was always occupied while lost in thought. 'The Devil finds work for idle hands,' she would say. My Aunt Valetta used to wonder whether had she not joined the household, *Sis'* Nonzondo might have become a diviner or 'prophetess' or medicine woman. As a girl she had been subject to those moods of disequilibrium and self-questioning which were known to pave the way, the emotional state known as *ukutwasa*. 'Her people had resigned themselves to it,' Aunt Valetta said. 'They saw she was that kind of "artistic type" who, if men, end up as poets (*imbongi*) or if women, as diviners and so on. Once the red people recognize the symptoms in one of them, they pack her off for training, you know. In Nonzondo's case, she resolved it herself by turning into *'i*convert' and coming to us. But I doubt if her gift has found its outlet. She is often abstracted.'

I saw that the grain she was grinding into paste was millet. It had been preboiled and was damp and warm, giving off steam. As she worked the paste accumulated on the edge of her slab in terraced heaps of brown, *umpotulo*, until it tipped over on to the woven grass mat placed ready to catch it, afterwards to be scooped up and made into bread or porridge. I dropped beside her, snatched some of the paste and ate it, as we used to do when children, unable to resist the taste.

'Nontando look out! Your fingers!' *Sis'* Nonzondo cried out in irritation. She knew that my left hand fourth finger had been crushed in this way when I was young and is flattened across the top, 'Will you never learn? Do you want to bring your *malume's* wrath on me by making me injure you?' Everyone sided with her and shouted, 'Hey! Leave off, MaJili; behave; don't cause

166

this accident – the Makiwanes will be against all of us in this hut, "*baya kuxabana nati*" if you come to harm.' I was terribly touched, and accordingly desisted. Upon which they smiled and breathed again.

15

AMONG them was Kekana, the small boy of years before, and as
Sis' Nonzondo had said, now a responsible circumcised man
and my uncle's head retainer.

I was behaving, doing nothing dangerous any more. But I
began to splutter and cough, eyes streaming because of the
smoke. Kekana turned on me. It occurred to nobody that the
fumes could be the cause, for their eyes were hardened to it, had
first blinked at birth in such atmospheres. They assumed I was
sickening for a cold. He declared as I dabbed at my face, 'It is
this going for walks in all weathers.' His friends all looked at me,
exclamations breaking out:

'Walks? You mean the niece just – walks?'

'Pointlessly? *Yo!* It is not enough to trudge miles every day
to the lands, to the river, to Macdonald's?' The stranger called
the trader's shop *kwaMadondile.*

I realized that people only walked for a purpose: to the
trader's, to Beer Parties, to the cattle dips, or 'work parties' –
the gatherings where people helped one another hoe, reap,
harvest, build, rewarded by the festive beer drink afterwards.

'Does she not know that one uses one's legs until they are
worn to stumps in this countryside?'

'*Kaloku* at overseas, that country is like the island, is it not?'
someone said, pointing in the direction of an eyot not far from
the confluence of the local rivers. 'So they can walk round it,
those people, just for fun.' Laughter.

'For "fun", *I* like a lorry ride. Had one to Xhokonxa, two
months ago come Saturday. It was *good.*'

Kekana was superior. No open lorries for him, with legs
dangling over the side in the dust. He drove often with my uncle
in the motor car and every week rode on errands to the local
town on one of the horses. He scolded me again, 'You will kill
yourself walking about on freezing days. Listen to what happened to me, now,' and told a story of how one winter he had

nearly died of a chill caught from just such carelessness. 'It was only a cold at first, then turned to an illness for the death.' He did not name it but it sounded like pneumonia. 'I was laid up, helpless between the blankets for weeks. At nights, the pain? Imagine, in the end I hid my head under the covers, to "Dip into That Which Pertains to Children", man, that's the truth.' He used another of the euphemisms that I had forgotten, for the "phenomenon of an adult in tears", and it seemed suddenly worthwhile to choke and suffer just to hear it; but the talk was full of such linguistic delights, and we laughed. 'From that day, I swear-by-our-sister, I never go near water in winter time, not me. Don't touch the stuff; don't wash. I wait for the summer.'

Everyone began to rag him until he said in self-defence, 'But am I alone in that? Certainly not —,' and lowered his voice conspiratorially and pointed towards the big house. 'I am not half as bad as your *malume*; now there's one with healthy respect for the cold.'

'Are you saying *malume* does not wash either in this weather?' I asked.

'Oh *well*,' he hastened, recoiling at the bluntness, 'I am not exactly saying so for I would not know the facts, whatever I may, shall we say, suspect. *Kaloku* in the house are there not devices to heat water for *Sis'* Nonzondo here to carry bucketfuls to fill that sitz-bath affair placed by the lighted fire in the room? I am only saying that, not possessing sitz-baths or able to deck my bed with sheets and eitherdowns to curl into afterwards, *I* do not mess with that element called water.'

Later I joined my uncle and aunt in the study-rondavel enjoying their leisure before supper and prayers. He sat in his chair reading a Xhosa weekly, long legs stretched out, his dog at his feet. My aunt and I sat a little away from him and chatted in low voices. When I repeated Kekana's remarks to her I saw his eyebrow lift a little. My aunt threw her head back and began to laugh. I saw a shadow of a smile play on his features. But he went on reading. She said, trying to subdue her laughter, 'What are we coming to? What next will these youngsters say about big people? But there *is* a grain of truth in those innuendoes. Truly, these young people don't miss a thing.' Laughter forced her to break off and she stole a look at him.

'You mean when it's wintry he doesn't—?' I whispered.

'*To!*', she cried. 'Don't you know why they nicknamed him "Fish"?'

I giggled. She repeated the anecdote about his recalcitrance as a schoolboy and added, 'There you are.'

My uncle went on reading but I could swear his eyes were travelling over and over again across one line; and then I saw his cheeks become pointed – he was suppressing smiles. I egged her on, feeling rather daring, and revealed more snatches of the gossip in the utility hut. She leaned over to nudge him. His dog pricked up its ears and watched, face resting on its paws. She said in a penetrating whisper, and shaking in a now not very serious effort not to laugh, 'Shall I – tell *umtshana* how I found you the other night?' Silence. Then he growled, rubbing down the tell-tale cheeks with his finger and thumb:

'What other night?'

'*You* know what night I mean,' and she went off into a peal of laughter. I did not remember ever seeing my uncle teased in this way by a woman, and was all eyes.

'Well, shall I tell her?'

He sighed, then suddenly smiled broadly, a transformation, and said, 'You don't mean me to prevent you, do you?' At which she turned round and tapped me on the knee passing her tongue over her lips in her pleasure.

'It was before you came, Ntando. We were in the grip of a bitter spell of cold. The mountain peaks were white. Water containers iced over at nights, in the mornings the grass hard as iron with frost. Well, girl – listen. Your *malume* went to bed early, as usual of course whatever the weather. I had odds and ends to finish off about the house before turning in. When I joined him, got ready for the night and pulled the blankets back, what did I find? There lay the fine fellow, in his farm overcoat. Under it I spied the old leather windjacket which you know, its revers pulled across his chest. I parted them to see what on earth was going on here. And there were the pyjamas. But underneath again, three lots of thick winter underwear – as true as I am sitting here.' She collapsed back into her chair laughing, the tears rolling down her cheeks, and my uncle put the paper on his lap and started to chuckle; the chuckle developed into sustained laughter and finally he exclaimed, '*Kwek!* Nontando, your MaDhlomo has "made a fool of me – *undiphoxile*". What am I to do about it?' and rose to his feet, took a stride across the room as if in a quandary – but still smiling and stealing looks at her as he moved. His dog jumped up precipitately, slipped on the polished floor, then, righting itself stood looking at him and wagging its tail, a paw lifted towards the door that gave on to the drive.

My uncle took another stride – he had decided what to do – and went to the roll-top desk, the dog following him, claws scratching on the boards, its body bumping against his boots, and whimpering now, disappointed at the vanished hope of a walk. *Malume* rummaged among papers in a drawer and at last pulled out a pile of family photographs – which he had promised days before to show me and so far had not; at the farm you seldom carried out non-farm projects immediately. My aunt and I had begun to wonder when alone whether he had forgotten or changed his mind. But the impulse now seized him – as if to divert my aunt's pleasurable teasing and restore order. Seeing this she winked at me and wiped her eyes, and lifted herself out of her comfortable chair, still giggling and murmured something about going to see about food. As she went I saw him give her a quick parting glance. His smiles had gone but had left an expression that mesmerized me; and I thought, by no means for the first time, how strange it was to see in old people the signs of new affections. It took me back to Middledrift.

He sat down. The dog went back to its place at his feet and I too pulled my chair close to his and settled down to be serious and pay attention.

There were many such moments during my visits, when my uncle would unexpectedly spend time with me and talk about the farm, the family and other topics. Sometimes in the middle of an anecdote he would fall silent, as if it brought back so many memories that he could not decide which to select. And then he would suddenly say, 'Your Aunt Daisy in Johannesburg will tell you more about that' – as if he had talked long enough and either relapsed into a silence or else would fold up his spectacles, put them away and prepare to do something else; usually go out of doors with his companion trotting beside him.

As time passed I felt less frightened, yet my inherited attitude towards him was still powerful. When after some days of not seeing much of him, *Sis'* Nonzondo would seek me out to announce gravely, *'Uyabizwa* – you are wanted', her tone of voice sounded much as if she had said: 'You are bidden to the presence', and all my apprehensions rose again and I would start up and go, not just walking but hurrying, almost running, and on joining him would find it difficult at first to accept that he had sent for me out of companionability. I would listen to the low rumble of his voice but scarcely hear what he was saying, expecting some kind of ritual address; and when it turned out that that was not the reason for my summons, I had to adjust myself to his ordinary human aspect.

On one of these sessions, I came and found he wished me to see what he said was a precious family relic – a faded print whose corners were twisted and dog-eared – photograph of an enormous group; old-fashioned; stiffly posed; all the sons and daughters, daughters-in-law and sons-in-law of my maternal great-grandfather, Makiwane Lujabe, who when he had sensed that death was not far off, had sent for his children to come and 'make this record, this picture'. *Malume* told how they had travelled in rumbling ox-wagons drawn by teams of six or eight pairs. They had to negotiate the ford, and he and other little ones went to watch as to a show. 'No bridges in those days,' he murmured, 'and that ford, how it needed looking after', and he relapsed into a reverie.

Meantime I gazed at my ancestor and his vast progeny. He was the very old man, bent with age although 'In health at the time of the photograph', said my uncle. He was in the centre of the middle row. My ancestress sat beside him wearing a straw boater clamped four-square on her head. She sat upright I noticed, not bent as the old man. I reflected on the carriage of a woman who had brought forth all that multitude. Her striped blouse had a bow across its high neck.

My uncle interrupted his reverie to pick out each of the fourteen other figures in the picture. I thought the men looked almost as ancient as their father. Some wore goatees, others thick spade-shaped beards; and all sported enormous moustaches and whiskers. Like so many black Anthony Trollopes.

'We small children were not included. We stood about behind the photographer watching him manipulate his black cloth, thinking it sinister. Some of us climbed up a tree, here' – he waved a finger in the area where the tree had been – 'to get a better view. But Mother' – picking her out – 'scolded us saying we would tear our trousers. Now that one there' – pointing – 'that is Father – your grandfather Elijah Makiwane.'

I was startled to hear him use for the words 'father, mother' the versions that children use; and I had never thought of him as a small boy in shorts, whose mother would keep an eye on him in case he got up to childish pranks.

'And my aunt who afterwards married and went *Kwa Mzili-kazi* (to Rhodesia). We never saw her again. The opportunity for her to come south never occurred. We have never even seen the family's children by her. 'Here is the father of my cousin Stewart, your *malume* along the ridge.'

'*So,*' I thought, 'Uncle Stewart is my first cousin once removed' . . . and started to work out the Western-style designations of this stoloniferous Makiwane family but was interrupted again in astonishment, to hear that *Malum'u*Stewart, venerable old gentleman greyer than my uncle, had been among the small fry who nipped up the tree and had been ordered down.

'This is the only remaining copy of that group, Nontando. Father lost many family mementoes; manuscripts too; he was a great writer, you know, though only in spare time from other work, not a professional who lived by writing like your Jabavu grandfather. Things were burnt or disappeared, got damaged in the big fire that destroyed the manse.'

I had never heard of it, and so far forgot myself as to cut in on him in mid-sentence, asking to be told what had happened.

'*O?* You do not know about that? Truly? How strange. Oh well, it was arson.'

'*What?* Get away!'

He looked at me. I too had shocked myself. But suddenly he smiled at the near-familiarity; I relaxed.

'Yes indeed,' he said. 'Part of a long story – of fissions in the Church, and jockeyings for power.' His eyes grew dark and for a moment he was silent. I held my breath, afraid he was going to murmur: 'When you get to Jo'burg your Aunt Daisy will tell you about that.' I waited. I had never noticed until then, because you miss detail when in awe, that his eyelids were inclined to hood; yet I am one of those women who usually find that physical characteristic an inexplicably distracting secondary sexual attraction in a man. Now watching him I could imagine how he must have looked in his prime. He sat as if debating whether or not to postpone telling the anecdote. I dearly wanted to hear something of my grandfather's life in that manse long ago. Finally *malume* decided to go on.

'Now of course you know the Mabandla homestead over there,' he said, pointing out of doors in a different direction from Uncle Stewart's. I nodded. Only a day or two before we had talked about the Mabandla family with whose daughters I used to play, so he had no need to establish them. 'Well then, the whole thing began with their ancestor, one Mbovane Mabandla. A queer customer, malevolent; bad; evil, although highly born; Mbovane – a name for Makiwanes to remember.' When he declaimed it like that it became sinister and filled me with alarm for my relations. The name meant 'ant', and I pictured a giant Soldier Ant. 'He was the younger brother of Chief Jamangile Mabandla. Now his people had been placed here as a buffer state between Europeans and BaSutho on the other side of the mountains, at the time your ancestor Lujabe came into possession of these lands here, in this territory of Chief Mditshwa – you know, of course, about the different Houses of the Pondo and Pondomise people.' I did not know accurately, having only heard snatches as a child about those political manœuvres. But I did not want to interrupt. Big mother in Johannesburg would tell me. 'Mbovane was a mortal enemy of Father, your grandparent Elijah, you understand.' He paused.

I was surprised, and longed for more detail; for I had only ever heard of amicable relations between the public and my maternal grandfather – a peaceful man from all accounts. It was my paternal grandfather whose fiery personality either

won him passionate partisans or made him enemies. I made
another mental note to ask my old aunt later to fill in that gap.
'Mbovane sought every means by which to break Father, when
we were children. He tried *this* and failed, tried *that* and failed.
Finally he decided to join the church. He was a pagan, of
course. His plan was to wreck your grandfather from within.
Unscrupulous but clever. Even from a distance and covered in
ochre as he was, he got wind of the power within the churches
that strong individuals could wage – Sectarian leaders;
Separatists.

'In Father's time, able men wanted power for less complicated reasons than now. Men like Lennox Mzimba – you know
that his daughter and your Aunt Daisy were the first African
girls to matriculate? First my sister, then the Mzimba daughter.
Mzimba had one of those personalities that needed to manipulate a following. That is how he led a 'Separatist' faction from
the Presbyterians; broke off and founded *his* church – up on
that hill of his which you know.' I nodded, and he took up his
tale. 'Red-blanketed pagan Mbovane decided to "become converted" so as to get in on these scrimmages, get *inside* Father's
territory. Once there, he immediately looked round for break-
aways in Father's congregation to gather around himself. The
baptismal water was hardly dry on him but he had collected a
following, made himself their deacon. The pagan becomes "a
convert"; then self-made minister, then deacon. One-two-
three; all in five minutes.' My uncle spoke calmly but his face
had grown mobile, eyes flashed almost as my father's would.
However, he did not stammer, or give low whistles of excitement. His was controlled.

'Now we come to this fire at the manse. You young people
should know these things. Our parents brought us up in times of
stress, of struggles about ideas – conservatism against progress,
paganism against Christianity; tussles between strong men.
Because they wanted us to grow up fearing God, they saw to it
that we were *told* these things. Also, loving us, they therefore
brought us up strictly. Your generation do not know what
strictness is. Sometimes I think we have been remiss in not being
as vigilant with you as they were with us.' Another pause and I
was afraid he would go off at a tangent. But no. He told a

stirring tale of how my grandfather, several miles from home one night, with my grandmother, conducting a revival meeting, was gripped by *'uthuku,* a premonition' in the middle of his sermon that all was not well back at the house. He struggled against the feeling, for was he not engaged on God's work which nothing should interrupt? In the end he persuaded himself it was a signal from the Almighty, and slipped out, on foot, breaking into a run dressed as he was in dog collar, pancake hat, black serge suit. He learnt later that in breasting the final hill and seeing the house in the distance, ablaze, he had actually met the destroyer, Mbovane, coming away from his handiwork. My grandfather was in time to raise the alarm and rescue all his dependants, eleven souls, my mother among them.

As usual with family anecdotes, the telling left many things not clear. But my aunt's version later helped to fill out the reasons that he had only touched on for the growth of separatist churches and the machinations within them. I had not realized that the phenomenon had begun so long ago. The personality of each of the big people in the family tended towards details that one or other of them either forgot; or passed over as no longer interesting; or did not know; or missed out accidentally in pressing on to some aspect that specially claimed his or her attention. My uncle was pressing on to something that was on his mind at that moment. He asked, 'Would they be able in England to make copies of this group?' The negative had been lost. I took it from him saying I thought that probably Rhodes Tremeer at Alice could do it. 'I will write to him,' I said. My uncle was surprised. The present generation of South Africans do not meet across the colour lines as his had done at the same age. 'Besides, Rhodes Tremeer is a celebrity in the photographic world,' he said. 'You even read about him in the newspapers.' Nevertheless, Rhodes Tremeer carried out the order so that my uncle's surviving contemporaries each received one to hand down to the offspring who 'should *know* these things about their forbears'.

It was during one such session that I finally screwed up courage to 'ask permission' to arrange for his only daughter, my little tail, to come to London and train as a hospital nurse. I was nervous and despite having rehearsed my speech beforehand

I must have blurted it out precipitately for he started and the immediate reaction was, '*What!* Maisie leave home, leave South Africa for overseas?'

I stammered, 'Only for a few years, *malume*, not for good.'

'*Certainly* not, definitely not for good. I do not like this business of young people leaving our homeland.' Nothing more was said. The matter was left in the air, indeed was not referred to again or even hinted at for days, not until I was about to leave. It made a small cloud.

Meantime life went on as before. I was fed like a horse, treated with care and tenderness until I felt 'baffled with repletion' (as the man in the bus had put it) by the emotions aroused by gazing into the mirror of ancestral conditions and 'umbilical' attitudes. But now because I had dared ask about Maisie and got nowhere, I felt inhibited to broach the other matter – of my youngest cousin's anxiety about his education. I was torn too now, on the further matter of his unease about his new mother. She had been splendid to me. I had no complaint. For me, to be 'at home' here felt as before, in Aunt Valetta's time. All these things made me feel almost relieved that I was not to be delayed over moving on to my next home. I would lay the matters on my Aunt Daisy's lap, *uMam'omKhulu*, as she pedantically insisted that we call her. When I saw her 'at the time of my mother', she had disliked the way in which family relationships were blurred by the slap-happy use of the English and Afrikaans imported nomenclatures, and had said, 'They ignore the exact definitions of kinship.' The older she became, the more particular about these things. And the older I myself grew, the more I found I was beginning to be grateful for her pedantry. It added to one's sense of belonging to define these things. So I thought: 'Let her intercede about Kehle.'

The further thought occurred to me, that should anything I tried to say about his difficulties be considered 'crude and indelicate' (as it probably would be, in my nervous and precipitate state), the blame for my conduct would be laid at the door of my overseas life. For at the farm when local people called – landowners, doctors, teachers, lawyers and other professional men and women – all expressed the opinion one heard elsewhere, that 'overseas people are crippled by their insistence on privacy and individualism and therefore no longer know how to handle delicate human matters properly'. Since I was anxious to help my cousin achieve her aim to get to England I should watch my step, not queer the pitch for her; I must allow 'time to do its work'.

Before I left Tsolo, something happened which moved me, probably out of proportion for it was so slight. Mawase had had time to get used to my being around, and on becoming aware from the preparations that were afoot that I was about to leave, he made an approach. Naturally not directly. *Sis'* Nonzondo limped up to me on his behalf, saying, 'Nontando, you know that neck scarf that you wore in the jacket of your suit when you arrived?'

'What of it, *Sisi?*'

'Well, I've been sent by Mawase. He saw it that day, when he was being presented to you.'

'Saw it? But he was too shy even to look at me.'

'Shy to look?' she retorted. 'Have I not told you that the rascal is as sharp as a tack? So "shy", he now asks if you will make that scarf his parting present.' It was my favourite scarf, a silken one from Liberty's in London. My mother-in-law had given it to me as a token of a reconciliation in an incident in my 'other life overseas'. How could I now give it away? On the other hand, my mind quickly revolving, what was the use of a present that was not really wanted? I thought of Mawase living on at my uncle's after I had gone and remembering 'the time the *umtshana* visited' and thought of him huddling over fires in the veld. I stopped hesitating and saw in my mind the fine figure he would cut in his own eyes at the next 'Beer Party' at home among his relations, how the scarf round his neck would set off the little toga that partly covered the grubby, off-white twill square wound like a baby's napkin round his slender loins. I gave it to *Sis'* Nonzondo for him.

But he did not wait until another party. Within minutes of receiving it, he strutted up to the door of my rondavel smiling to thank me, already wearing it. Not at the neck as intended, however, but tied round the forehead rakishly, giving him the air of a pirate, miniature version of the Pondo braves on the bus in which I had travelled into the Transkei.

The parting gift that I in turn valued came from my uncle when the entire household gathered to wait for the taxi that was to take me away. Long Ear had spotted the car while it was miles up the valley, the sunshine gleaming on its body. Presently he sauntered along the drive, past the orchard and on to the gate to open it, saying he would stand there to be the last to wave good-bye when the car turned. Actually he would have to close the gate, but this was how he put it and I was affected. My aunt and *Sis'* Nonzondo stood by the door, subdued, holding the provision basket they had prepared for my journey; and others stood about sharing the holding of my two pieces of luggage in such a way that that, too, was touching to see.

My uncle spoke out of the blue, while looking down at his dog: 'About this matter of Maisie. I have thought it over. You may make your arrangements. They will take time, so we need not have been startled. Look after her there in England. It would have pleased your late mother that your tail should continue to follow you – although,' and he smiled, 'this "child of yours" is hardly a *little* tail now; taller than you.'

I reeled at his decision, and at his mention of my mother. But he went on to say something that made me speechless. It explained what had seemed his recalcitrance about paying Kehle's college fees and made me ashamed to have been so un-perceptive. Kehle was young but I had no excuse for not having looked at the matter in this light for it was in tradition. He said, 'An act such as this of yours towards your cousin Maisie is not to be discouraged. Sisters and brothers, brothers and brothers should try to assume responsibility for one another as we were taught to do. If in the event you young people can't manage, then of course the big people behind you will step in. But in these days of changes and pressures, it is good when custom survives and is seen to be respected.'

He stopped, MaDhlomo added only, '*u*Malume has spoken.' After that we talked desultorily. Pirate-kerchiefed Mawase had skipped off and clambered on to a near-by boulder to watch the coming taxi as it negotiated the contours. My uncle, Ma-Dhlomo, all of them had overwhelmed me. I was overcome too, now, with thankfulness for the cowardice which for days past had prevented my yielding to the impulse to speak about my youngest cousin.

Mawase's pale little arm suddenly stretched out and he gave a shout. We looked up. He had struck an unconscious pose against the skyline, more than ever like a budding sailor; and excited now, 'The taxi is climbing the final incline,' he said. Conversation tapered into silence under the load of things not said, and I had time only to wonder how my visit might have turned out had my uncle not trusted the policy of 'not rushing matters'; and to wonder too, how one could justify his trust, the companionable talks, the sense of continuity, of belonging.

The bonnet of the taxi appeared at the gate; we saw the glint of chromium in between the fruit trees. Mawase hopped down from his look-out, and the dog leapt and barked – until his master, to reassure him, murmured in a deep, low voice as though to MaDhlomo:

'*Kwek!* What is to be done with this chap? Does he not realize—' and explained, smiling and bending to stroke its back, that the motor was no stranger but that of someone the dog had known all its life. The owner-driver pulled up, calling out greetings, a European neighbour of years from the infinitesimal capital of the district. While my things were being loaded, he and my uncle chatted about the steps of my journey after this first lap by car to Xhokonxa; from there it would be a bus to Umtata, and from there a night and two days by train to Johannesburg.

Part Three

JOHANNESBURG

16

A JOURNEY not unlike other South African train journeys that
I have described elsewhere, and at last we were on the final lap
to the big city, gathering speed across the High Veld – vast,
enormous bareness. The sight of these particular plains did not
reassure. They were not like those of the Transkei when my
long-distance bus had crossed into them over the Kei River.
These seemed of a foreign country; huge stretches inhabited by
total strangers; no locality – as through stretches in Ciskei and
Transkei – where I could think: 'Such and such a family,
friends, live here.' It seemed harsh, hostile, and made you feel
ill at ease. The emptiness began to give way to the occasional
Boer small town, *dorp*: bungalows with verandas crouched on
straggly streets, squat Dutch Reformed Church. The *dorps* in
turn began to run into one another and to spread into suburbs.
Looking out of the window as we raced past I thought them
dreary, featureless. But then a willow tree would stand out
against the skyline, strikingly tall here in the Transvaal, far
bigger than the ones I was accustomed to in the Eastern Cape.
I was filled by a mounting nostalgia for 'the Cape Colony' as
people even in the Transkei called my part of the country, despite their region having for so long been incorporated into the
Cape Province. Northerners here too called it that.

The Border was of course in the front of my mind, the buffer
state with its olden fortifications – Forts: Wellington, Beresford,
Murray, White, to say nothing of Fort Hare or Fort Cox, Fort
Beaufort, our localized stamping-grounds. Their very names
took me back to those conflicts the uncles had talked about in
the car, when black and white 'Cattle-keeping tribes' had
wrestled over pastures and living room; of the equivocal role
that 'the second white tribe' had played when dominant; and
of its policies of expediency. These had doubled back on the
British. Now they were themselves dominated by Transvaal
Boers. Even their splendid English language was demoted to a

secondary status. How any of my relations could bear to live here was a mystery. The more I looked at their adoptive territory the more I missed the kind of veld I was used to – undulating, contoured, not dead flat like the land I was now crossing. I missed my kind of mountains, their folds, the *kloofs* covered with dark green forests, their crowns of majestic granite crags. But I reproached myself for being parochial, for in fact I loved South Africa's variety and vastness.

As the suburbs grew denser, my uneasiness deepened. I had seldom been to Johannesburg and this was the third visit in my whole life. The first had been when I was about nine years old. My mother had brought me and my tiny sister – my brother not quite born – on a prolonged visit to a suburb called West Rand, where she organized some Women's Clubs, and was also visiting her youngest sister, my aunt Linda, whose husband had been drowned when fording a river on horseback and overtaken mid-way by one of those outbreaks of sudden storm and flood during a drought – the sort my Uncle Rosebery had been so wary of. She had a baby girl. We stayed for what seemed years but may have been perhaps three months, with a family into which Aunt Linda afterwards married. Possibly that was the purpose of my mother's trip, I never knew, only that I had never remembered the visit with pleasure but with deep disquiet. For our hosts lived in a house that was on the edge of a native location and I was forbidden to leave their yard and go into the location as I longed to do and play with the children. I could see them swarming in its streets all day, never apparently going to school while I had to submit to morning lessons from my mother. My baby sister's nurse who came with us from the Cape and watched that I should not escape, told me of unnamable terrors that went on inside Jo'burg locations; of dirt, disease, robbers and gangsters, squalor, and of '*the language*' that I would pick up. The grown-ups confirmed her proscription, probably initiated it; it seemed everybody was frightened of the very word 'location, *elokishini*', and I trembled, dreading it yet wanting to go – for I had no playmates. Occasionally the younger children of my eldest aunt (to whom I was now travelling) were brought from Klipspruit near Nancefield where they lived before moving to their present home at Pimville. They came miles in the train, and had to be shepherded home again before dark 'because of the terrors of the location'. When I saw my mother begin to pack and was told we were going home, my relief was immense. The thought of returning home to 'the Colony' was heaven, idyllic – back to grass, veld, mountains. No more dirt, disease, fear of robbers. No more barred windows or locked doors. And I would be allowed to wander about freely again with my friends.

My second trip to Johannesburg had been last year to my Big Mother. I had been unaccompanied, and petrified – this time with cause: those Jo'burg gangsters, of whom everyone had gone in dread, had finally moved into *my* family's life far off in the Cape when they murdered my only brother up here studying at the University. I had had to come to my aunt because she was unable to travel south on that occasion because of her age and health.

The reason I was making this third visit was again because of her – would I *ever* come to this place otherwise? I sat tight in my seat realizing, and admitting, that this time, too, I was scared. My trip had been preceded, like last year's, by an avalanche of letters from my aunt, she and my uncle at Tsolo writing back and forth arranging which train I was to catch, times of connections at junctions, so that I should be met at Park Station by one or other of her daughters and shepherded from the heart of the city to where they lived eighteen miles out. All my cousins worked and were not able to take time off too easily. The arrangements therefore were intricate, everyone wanting to be sure that none of them should miscarry and leave me high and dry, alone and unprotected. In the end letters were followed by telegrams, in turn followed by others confirming and acknowledging. The whole thing was beset with anxieties and they welled up in me now that I was nearly there. Suppose something went wrong at the last moment and nobody came to Park Station, I asked myself gazing at the Rand, the string of towns that make up greater Johannesburg. I looked at the dumps beside the gold mines – those huge hills of white dust dredged up from six thousand feet below and more. I saw cranes and derricks with wheels in the air, gaunt mining machinery, cables, rusty fences plastered with bill boards – all of it a jumble

amid a conglomeration of factories cheek by jowl with bungalows and double-storeyed houses that gave on to tarred roads,
street lamps, blue-gum trees, motor cars, lorries, bicycles,
people of different races hurrying. Where in this hideous mess
would I go if my cousins did not turn up?

Fellow passengers began to stir and walk up and down the
corridor and sort out baggage.

Of course I had the addresses of many families on the Rand;
but I would have to hire a car, not knowing the local trains and
being an absolute fool about arranging any detail in my own
travels. But the thought of a cab was terrifying. We all knew
down in the Cape that for a green-horn to hail an unknown
taxi in Johannesburg was suicide; you would be robbed,
probably knifed, your body abandoned on the veld or in some
location back-yard. I turned the problem over in my mind.
How had my young brother adapted himself and managed to
live, let alone study in such surroundings? He had had difficulty
I knew, and could understand, looking at the metropolitan
spread. Towards the end of his course he had been afflicted by
bouts of what was diagnosed as narcolepsy, a condition of the
nerves of which we had never heard until then. It made him
drop off to sleep anywhere, often during lectures or at sports,
even at times when driving his motor car. In my case just to
sit and look at Johannesburg was making me wish I could fall
asleep, and wake up to see Middledrift again or Tsolo.

Voices around began to rise, swell into a hubbub: Sesutho,
Xhosa, Sechuana, Zulu, and mostly Afrikaans. The people were
becoming excited, the journey almost over. They pointed out
landmarks to one another with animation. I felt out of it, not
interested. The train drew into Park Station. My heart began to
pound. I went into the corridor and leaned out of a window to
scan the faces of the crowd on the platforms, saw scores, black,
white, brown, lifted up, preoccupied, they in turn scanning
ours as the train passed. I noticed that even Africans were unsmiling with dour expressions. They were not passing the time
of day by joking with those standing next to them as people did
at country stations. This was the cold anonymity of the Golden
City, *eGoli, eRautini*; I had arrived. The train slowed right
down. I became absolutely filled with terror. Then I saw a

woman wave to me. She was in a thick belted tweed coat, wore a sports felt hat and under its level brim I saw a preoccupied light brown face break into a rapturous smile when our eyes met and she shouted out my name – it was my cousin *Sis'* Tandiswa and I thanked God.

She stepped forward and walked alongside, her arm lifted to my window to try and hold my hand as I reached down. But she fell behind, having to dodge carrier carts and mounds of luggage. At last the train ground to a standstill. Passengers flung corridor doors open, leapt out shouting, joyful, laughing, and joined their friends. I too grabbed my case and was on the platform embracing my cousin, overwhelmed by the feeling of having been rescued from danger. I flung my arms around her and clung until after a while she held me off and looked down at my face, her brows knitted quizzically. Then she hugged me again and finally said, smiling and pretending to scold, '*Now*, child, are you *reassured*?'

She was the second oldest of my known cousins on both sides, the eldest of my aunt's four daughters, the second born, the *mazibulo* being an only brother. She had been named after my mother. I called her '*Sisi*' rather than '*Sis*' Tandiswa because to pronounce that name made me feel somewhat uncomfortable. But I did sometimes call her '*Sis*' Tandi'. The diminutive did not embarrass. I only realized later that this was because it had never been used for my mother. She was so much my senior that I did not know her exact age, and taller than me, buxom, and unmarried like all this particular family except for one. *Sis'* Tandi taught in a primary school, loved teaching. I knew that it was out of devotion to 'the blood', that she had freed herself to come, instructed of course by 'our' mother who in her old age now stayed in her home, never leaving it; a queen-bee in her hive, arranging, planning. The last time Big Mother had travelled was when my mother died and she was driven down to the Colony by my brother in his little English car. He brought a friend, a fellow medical student, Caleb Mokhesi, who was no relation but whom the big people at home at once treated as one, 'the only way to thank him sufficiently for the service he had rendered us.' He had interrupted his work to act as my brother's co-driver over the huge distance which had to be

covered practically non-stop, my mother's death had been so
unexpected. And I would never forget the picture Big Mother
made when the trio arrived.

Our house was thronged with relations, friends, mourners,
and we all stood and watched the small round bundle of
elderly womanhood, black satin turban wound tightly like a
toque round her head, wearing spectacles, a shawl over her
coat, dressed entirely in black; and absolutely covered with
dust, even to the crow's feet at her eyes. Nor would I forget my
impression of the two young men as they skipped out from the
front of the car to help her out before any of us could move.
She was stiff after the journey, and blinked in the sunlight. My
father, already tense, became excited and shouted with joy, relief 'because the sons of the house had safely delivered their
precious cargo'; while her brothers Cecil and Tennyson murmured '*Wafika uSis*' Daisy'. Her presence comforted the household. She was so much my elders' senior that even *their* generation felt as if a protectress had come. Neither would I forget
how she had afterwards sat, as if on a throne in our sitting-room
or under the wintry leafless vine on the veranda and taken
charge, delegating the duties that had to be performed. The
reunion with *Sis*' Tandi in Johannesburg provoked such thoughts
all over again and they affected me; her mother stood for much
that had gone, was going, for ever. And my cousin was now
teasing me, by way of dispelling some of the tensions. We both
knew that the old lady was going to speak with me about these
matters, about the people we had shared and loved, and of the
diminishing number who were still here -- some of whom (it had
to be faced because of the unique situation of my living so far
away), it was probable that I would not meet again.

'*Kulungile* Jili, let us go,' she said, and added on glancing
down at our feet, 'Where is your luggage?' I pointed at the
suitcase and small hold-all for books and overnight things.

'Is this all? Good gracious! And I ordered the big taxi from
our man at Pimville, imagining you would have so much since
you have travelled so far and for so long.'

We looked at each other and smiled. She had forgotten about
the aeroplane weight limits. We were not very well acquainted
because of the gap in age. My intimates were her two youngest

sisters. They had often stayed with us in the Cape when I was a child: Ntombizodwa ('Daughters Only') she was slightly older than me, and Constance Nontutuzelo ('Comforter'). She was younger and had been born soon after their father died; the reason for her second name. 'Zodwa was a trained nurse and worked in a hospital at Benoni, one of the towns along the Rand. *Sis'* Nora the married one, lived with her husband and children at Pimville not far from home. Their brother was a mine clerk and lived at his work in bachelor quarters. At the house at Pimville my aunt had her eldest and youngest with her, and 'Zodwa' when off duty.

The distance between the eldest and myself was modified by my aunt's industry as a letter writer – Victorian journalist background perhaps transmuting itself in old age, and because she was Big Mother to many scattered nephews and nieces. When each of us had lost one or both parents over the years, she filled their places in our lives at however long range, wrote regular letters to us individually; none of those futile round robin family letters that some overseas dynasties engage in that turn out to have been meaningless when the writers met in the flesh. Her especial 'affection' was my cousin Boniswa, her mother (Aunt Linda whom we had visited at West Rand) having died soon after her second marriage. *Mam'omKhulu* was the anchor of all those linked through the Makiwane navel. She seemed to be with us as my cousin grasped my suitcase and led me through the 'Non-European' Exit from the station and out to the 'Non-European Taxi Rank'.

Sis' Tandi kept looking round over her shoulder to tease me.

'How are the palpitations, Ntando? Still bad? I could feel your heart – my, was it pumping. *Lunjan' uvalo!* You're really scared of Jo'burg, eh? You people from *eKoloni* are all the same, your faces like an open book; you act as though you are at the entrance of a lions' den when you arrive at this poor old city of ours!'

We climbed into the cab, a very elderly American saloon, its driver welcoming her back. He drove us through the city. I had eyes for very little. *Sis'* Tandi pointed out landmarks, historical monuments, read out the names of famous streets. None of them made an impression, they glanced off my closed mind. To this day it is as a clean slate about Johannesburg, as if I have never been there. The atmosphere hampered my re- actions; and my fear of the violence up there blots out memory almost of anything I glimpsed on arriving or leaving. I never wanted to go up to town when my cousins went shopping and offered to take me sightseeing. Only when the cab had driven into their location called Pimville *Township*, and approached her house did my nervousness begin to subside. This was a house I knew, where I had people.

It was in Timana Street. They had lived in it for over twenty years and were themselves something of a landmark; everybody seemed to know them. I saw people on the road or in haggard doorways greet my cousin as we drove by in bottom gear because of the usual un-made up condition of township roads. Voices hailed her and the driver; he too was a local landmark. I began to feel I was among friends.

Yet the sight of the friends did not yet reassure altogether. Their houses looked dreadful from the outside – to me they could be gangsters' and lions' dens, thieves' kitchens. As for the road we were grinding and bumping along on! Potholes, refuse, dirt, disease, squalor – and sure enough, the '*language*' too, for I heard harsh-sounding words above the greetings directed at my companions, and my nurse's warnings of long ago crowded back into my mind. Probably I was only mishearing unfamiliar accents. Later, on going into some of these houses I found I had to amend my first impressions. But for the moment I was wrestling with fears of the unknown. *Sis'* Tandi noticed signs of this and said, while acknowledging greetings, 'Believe me, you would get used to things if you lived here, Nontando.' I shivered with a sudden wave of relief that this visit was to be short and cried, 'Never!' but immediately felt stricken by my disloyalty and could not speak.

'Oh yes, you would,' she said hurriedly leaning forward to look out of the window, adding in a whisper, 'One must be care- ful not to cut people. They know why I am home today and not at school. Greet them Ntando, they are looking out for you.' She was in the act of raising her hand to a woman on the way- side (where there should have been a pavement but I saw only an open drain), so I did the same. The woman smiled, renewed her waving and shouted, '*Teacheress! Uzenaye uMaJili,* you have brought your relation? She is welcome, welcome – yet such a *girl,* where is the grown woman and mother you spoke of? Wonder of wonders' (this with a burst of laughter, her head now at the window for the driver had slowed right down for her). 'Salute MaGambu for us please, Teacheress, on the lovely day of the coming of her late one's children, "*nonwabe torwana,* be happy together!"'

Again I was thankful for the convention that forbids you to attempt an answer. It seemed incredible that in the midst of such squalor, conditions so purgatorial, antipathetic to life, people could be fine. At least at Middledrift and at Tsolo everything was on their side – the peace, the grandeurs of the scene, the environment to which they could feel they belonged. Did not those settings enable people to share their life's sacraments and pleasures? And what in heaven's name, in these other surroundings could prompt the spirit? As the woman's voice rang out, her face alive and glad, I began to look at the location with shifting emotion. 'Began' only; for I was still repelled as last year on arrival; and filled with a disgust of which I was ashamed because I knew well enough that the surroundings were not of my relations' choosing, nor of friends and neighbours such as this woman.

Sis' Tandi went on prompting me as the taxi started up again, 'I tell you, Ntando, you would get used to it. There are *people* living here among thieves and gangsters, *people* like back home in your beloved Colony. Why, before your brother was shot, he once told my mother of something that happened when he was coming down in the train from town one afternoon to visit her. It was what decided her to write and advise your parents, you know, to buy him a car, to use while he was a student up here.' I hadn't known.

'That train was suddenly boarded by robbers, *otsotsi,* as so often of course; one of the facts of life. They held up each passenger with a revolver, made them hand over their wages, wallets. But one of them stopped his mate who was just starting on your brother and shouted in Afrikaans, "*Loes hom! Loes hom, man. Hy es Professor Jabavu's se sien,* Leave him – Professor Jabavu's son".' You see? Even some of the robber savages are people; twisted but not to be dismissed; perhaps even to be for-given for "They know not what they do" – Do not be afraid.'

I admired her serenity but was not yet able to envy it.

So was my aunt serene, watching us arrive and dismount from the taxi when it stopped beyond her fence. She was at the front door, standing on the raised entrance which I noticed with surprise was smeared with cattle dung. She looked smaller than I had remembered from last year; and rounder, compact in warm clothes, knitted jersey, cardigan. And about her head, the tight widow's toque that she always wore. This time she leaned on a man's walking-stick, a new feature and to see it gave me a pang, realizing that the passage of a year at her age was not what it was at mine and my cousin's. I came level with her and she put out both arms, the walking-stick in one hand and now lifted in the air above my shoulder. Her eyes, behind the tortoise-shell rims of her spectacles glistened. The sight unnerved me although I expected it.

She let go in order to fumble and pull out a white handker-chief from an old-fashioned style of pocket at her waist. It had been a tense moment and I looked away and around me. Be-yond the fence in the street, my cousin was paying off the driver. He had climbed out of his cab and now lifted his battered hat to my aunt, burly figure framed by a square building whose plaster was peeling away in patches – a Native Separatist Church of some sort, with the poverty-stricken houses and shacks huddled close to it confronting your eyes on all sides. 'God keep you, Gambu,' the man said and wished us a happy reunion. My aunt finished using her handkerchief and acknow-ledged his words with the grace one was accustomed to hear from old people, and he stepped into the car and started up his engine ready to go on down the street. This too was like the others, unmade up, pot-holed, and bounded by the same appalling squalor; yet men and women were in it, about their business in apparent unconcern; and ragged children were at play, darting out from the low doorways; teeming life – some quite young little girls had tinier tots slung on hips or tied to backs but managed to play hopscotch. To look at my aunt's carefully tended pocket of front garden forced me to more ad-justments. A staggering spectacle in such a scene; the contrast with its surroundings seemed more striking than when I had come before. Presumably I had been numbed because of the reason for that year's visit. When the taxi finally pulled away, I cried out, '*Mam'omkhulu*, how do you *sinda* this entrance, where is the kraal? Who does it for you?' I stopped, surprised to hear my aunt break into a gentle laugh. She said, to herself more than to me, '*Kwek!* this child!' then raised her voice, 'Do you hear, Tandiswa? This person is truly fresh from her father. It is he who greets people, talks to them all the time not missing an item about their condition.' Her face was radiant now as if the pain of the first sight of me was giving way to the pleasures of thinking about those of whom I reminded her.

'"Where's the kraal"? *Kaloku* Ntando, even here *e*Goli, people try to maintain an animal or two to milk for their young children. What I do is to beg them for the dung. This smearing is the work of a girl whose parents send her round from time to time "to beautify their former teacher's home" – mine. Does she not do it exactly like a country girl? Of course we ought not to keep cattle in the location, Verwoerd forbids it. It has always been forbidden; even under sly Smuts. But since the location is uncared for, the municipality surrounding it with the open sewage farms that serve the European suburbs and are disgorged here, since our roads are never made up, what difference in hygiene does the presence of a cow or two make? And people's children must eat. Besides, it is good for these town-bred youngsters to know that milk does not come out of tins only, condensed. And since some of them never *go* to the country, *emaXhoseni*, or Basutoland, Portuguese East or wherever their people came from, would they ever *know* cattle except from hearsay if they did not see them in the location? We are lawbreakers, sinners, and you are looking at your mother who "is an accessory after the fact", I suppose.'

We laughed and moved indoors already launched on talk about the facts of life in urban areas. All the same the house was reminiscent of both my home at Middledrift and my uncle's for intangible reasons, one of them because it felt lived in; the family had been long established. It was well built, as 'our' others were; indeed seemed more so, after the sight of the others around it. My aunt lived in the same style as we in the country.

She liked stained and polished floors, liked covering them with rugs that had been used over the years, liked the same kind of furniture, sofas, rocking-chairs, roll-top desks, things that seemed to have been always with us while other families changed and renewed their possessions every time a catalogue arrived from the stores in the nearest big towns. I was glad now that my elders were the conservative type, although I had not been as a child on seeing other people's houses gleaming with smart new things and chromium fittings. Here at my aunt's too, another link with home and not so good – there was no electricity or running water. Although they were in town, such amenities were lacking for a reason which, as usual, we recapitulated as we ambled through the house – the one about 'Natives' being under the perpetual threat of being 'moved on' as 'white' suburbs spread themselves. With these plans in the air, broadcast, published daily, would it not be 'folly' as the authorities put it, for municipalities to spend money on services to locations that were only temporarily where they were? Government policy being what it was, first to discourage and now to forbid permanent life in towns for the blacks who have to work in them, continued the survival of migratory shacks that people put up, desperate for somewhere to live. It cast a blight on municipalities like Johannesburg, which often wanted to act.

'Jo'burg had a good record, as municipalities go,' I heard my aunt say – and gasped, incredulous after what I had seen outside. But she insisted on being fair, in her elderly way, and on reminding me of the city's industrialists, businessmen, chambers of commerce: that these did not all share the Boer Government's dedication to the idea of migrant labour. Some of them spoke about the *benefit* to the whole country of the existence of a settled working class with roots and belongings in the cities.

We were automatically talking about these things because the noises from the over-crowded location wafted into the house and would not let you forget. Or at any rate, would not so soon let me, I should say. We walked along the passage, my cousin and I regulating our speed to my aunt's steps, her walking-stick punctuating our remarks and interrupting the glances I was casting into the rooms on either side. They, I saw, had not changed since my last visit, and looked orderly, secure, as always, amid the surrounding insecurity. Our conversation was a kind of small talk about familiar things that acted as a tranquillizer, for we were excited; moved by the ritual of being together again, by the different levels on which we were being reunited, to say nothing of the personal reason for my being here.

So we talked about the unrest that had gripped 'the country', meaning our people, the tensions risen higher in the last two years because here in Johannesburg, Sophiatown, the location closest to the city, White 'Western Area' and serviced with water, drainage, electricity, was being demolished and its inhabitants 'moved from the European Ethnic Group Area'. We talked about those belonging to us or close, who were in the front line of this phase of our country's social strife. My brother's digs had been at Sophiatown – after a prolonged effort on his part to get as near to the University in town (at Milner Park) as possible. Sophiatown provided that proximity. I had been taken last year to see where he had lived, in Toby Street, which afterwards made history because its houses were the first to be destroyed. It was on the edge of the 'Buffer Zone', a strip of unoccupied grass thirty yards wide maintained in order to separate whites in their suburb called Westdene from the blacks in theirs called Sophiatown.

Newspapers where I happened to be at the time in Italy showed pictures of the destruction, of the inhabitants watching the bulldozers work while soldiers and Saracen tanks imported from Britain stood by. Armed white policemen scanned the evicted Africans whose belongings were in sad bundles on the ground waiting to be transported by military lorries. In one of his last letters my brother (not a prolific correspondent) had described what he had seen:

'*Sisi*, you should have been here. The Boers' (policemen's) pale blue eyes were glinting steelier than ever that day. Their fingers tickled the triggers of revolvers and the hands clenched and unclenched the handles of those *sjambok* (leather) whips until the knuckles were white.'

And my aunt now murmured of him, 'At the end of that scene our young son was translated, in God's wisdom, to spare his sensitive soul. He did not see the acts that were to follow in this play.' But we had friends who had been settled citizens of 'Sophia' for decades – Dr. Xuma and his American wife; Mrs. Motsieloa; many others, with homes better appointed, more elegant than any of ours. They were among those awaiting their turn in the great 'removal of Natives'. They had become property owners before racial demarcations, and had lived in pleasant spaces; but over the years became crowded by later arrivals who had nowhere to live and therefore put up the shacks, creating slums. Our friends' houses were to be destroyed too, which seemed to us extraordinary. And their titles to free-holds were to be ended – a decree that alarmed the country; for black freehold owners were a tiny number, less than one per cent in all South Africa. You had to use a magnifying-glass to see the statistic on a graph. It was the evolution of these 'property–owning natives' whose existence had provoked the Group Areas Act. Under Verwoerd the Government looked on their enterprise as a threat to white people; and at the new 'Native' Areas on the Rand to which they were being removed, Africans would be offered a thirty-year lease on Government property, on certain conditions. The property consisted of rows of structures recently built, miles from the city. They were small houses, uniform in type, described as 'simple and rec-tangular, self-contained, asbestos roofed, with brick walls, divided inside with rough-plastered partitions; fitted with a front and a back door and windows, a hole in the roof to take a coal-stove chimney; no other fittings; running water outside next to the lavatory; also a drain under the tap.' So ran the official Press hand-out, evidently sincerely calculated to make it sound delightful. It also announced that the Native Areas would be commanded by white superintendents. We all knew that it was no mere slum clearance.

Thoughts about it were therefore constantly in our minds. *Sis'* Tandi showed me the bedroom I was to share with my age-mate, cousin Nontutuzelo. I was impatient for her to come home from her job. She taught in a school too, in the location. I unpacked, washed and changed, hung my things in the ward-robe where she had made room for me. I sorted out the presents and mementoes that I had brought for everyone and for the house. *Sis'* Tandi reappeared, took me to the little sitting-room at the front where my aunt was waiting. I was still feeling un-nerved because of the unfamiliar location sounds beyond the house. As we walked in to my aunt, she looked up at me keenly, and then told my cousin to close the front door.

'This person-of-ours is still half-ears outside,' and they both smiled – which I knew concealed their concern. And to me she said, pointing her stick at an armchair next to hers, 'It is early, but we will sit here in the *voorhuis*.' She did not notice my smile at her Transvaal use of the Afrikaans; in the Cape none of us called the sitting-room that: for some extraordinary reason, when we did borrow a word for it, we young ones said *e*room*ini* and I could never fathom why it was not *e*sitting-room*ini*. And more puzzling still, why did we prefer to 'borrow' a *Xhosa* word (for this particular room) which was simply the locative for 'house'? And why never *e*room*ini* for example for *bed*room but ekamer*ini* from the Afrikaans? I worked out the puzzles later. My aunt was speaking. 'We will sit here in the *voorhuis* while your cousin prepares: for you must give me the news of your Uncle Cecil, of MaDholomo there at home, and of your father.'

We were to sit for many hours talking together in that little *voorhuis* with Makiwane and Majombozi portraits gazing down from its walls; and to the accompaniment of the noises in the street between us and the rickety Separatist Church.

17

BUT now that I had reached Jo'burg, it was harder than at Tsolo to become steeped in a feeling of timelessness; I was conscious of those aeroplane bookings, of the fact that the days would soon pass and my visit end. When my thoughts filled with the intangibles that I was supposed to face and conquer, I almost panicked. Nobody referred to them. When would I be '*thethiswa'd*, exhorted?' I would suddenly long for action; to get it over. At such times my stomach seemed to churn. Once my aunt said, not looking at me but ahead of her thoughtfully, '*Kuyakufuneka ubabhalele ekhaya, ufikile nje.*' It was an eminently gentle sentence using tenses that soothed and soft-pedalled, that only glanced and hinted. But it filled me with alarm for had I not been thinking the same thing too but done nothing? It was as if my aunt knew for certain that I had not been in touch with 'home, *ekhaya*,' since leaving there for my uncle's; as if she knew about the procrastination, when she murmured on another day at breakfast, again more to herself than directly to me, 'Food is *placed* before you; yet you put on no weight, are thin, thin.' I gobbled my plateful of porridge – to the cacophony outside in the street. Eating did not soothe the stomach. Its turmoil continued to rage. And then my mind would take refuge by slipping into a kind of neutral gear.

But in those moments of vacuity I began to be aware of the theme underlying the seeming inaction of my family. I remembered what Mr. Mzamane had said that night at Fort Hare. For some days I had forgotten his comments about the people's sensitivity to 'individuals' psychologies, the technique with regard to them, the state of upheaval that these were in because of the pace of Westernized life; and their conflicts with the tradition of 'avoiding haste'. My aunt arranged my daily programme and at first I did not notice that she was doing so, for her plans seemed to fit in with what would be happening in the house anyway, in the natural order of domesticity.

'Now, Ntutu,' she said, 'when you and Ntando go round to your sister Nora's today and pass that corner shop, you had better get this list of extra things.'

My cousin looked at it and said, 'But they have these at our usual shop.'

'Oh? Anyway they would be pleased to see Ntando at the corner place, and talk about her father. The proprietor is one of his old students but he went into business. Took his Arts degree, then discovered he was a Midas. That one cannot be seen for enterprise. *Spins* money. "*LiJuda, elo, uku*over-charge*a kwake*." What do *you* say overseas – "Armenian", eh? An interesting type all the same; not to be dismissed even if one does have to take one's custom elsewhere to save one's pocket.' We laughed, and put on our coats and obeyed.

The programme was leisurely so that the days seemed to be filled with nothing very much – except the continuous vibration from the location. It seemed not to abate, morning, noon and night. Nevertheless when we carried out one of these plans, I became occupied and for a while was not conscious of being restless.

Like her eldest sister, Ntutu wanted me to see Jo'burg in perspective; when she and I lay in our beds at night talking in the dark, to shouts outside, laughter and the occasional blood-curdling screams and I exclaimed in alarm, she laughed and said, 'I suppose it's because I was born and brought up in Jo'burg that I am not continually conscious of the surroundings of the raw pagans who arrive daily – *Ama*Tshangana and Tonga from Portuguese East, *ama*Ndebele and so on from up north, all sucked into jobs in the metropolis. You just accept the boiling melting-pot and the types it throws up: the women in those tribal costumes that you saw when we were out, with the ox-hair necklets they wear to protect them from goodness knows what: and "Shaka" hair-do's of these Zulus' banked up with fat and clay. Such people are brand-new to town. But they soon copy the established residents, the old hands. In no time they dress normally, to suit city life and get into step with *le*industrialism – oh, people are quick, *Sis'* Ntando, they imitate. "Like looking glasses, they are – *banjenge z'pili*".'

'But what suffering, at what cost,' I said, thinking of people I

had noticed, looking out of place, uprooted, faces lined, for all
that they had laughed and gesticulated as they went about
their business in and out of sordid yards. Some of them had led
by the hand naked tots wrapped in the small sacks, *onompo-
twana*, in which potatoes are delivered to retail shops. I had not
cared at all for these northern pagan mothers' pagan dress. To
me it was not a patch on that of the splendid pagans down
south. But Ntutu only laughed when I said that and went on
talking about the tiny tots.

'And do they adapt *fast*! You saw them at that nursery school
but did not realize that many of those were of the same background as the ones wrapped in *nompotwanas*. When they get
into a school, they wear their first tiny khaki shorts and shirts.
And burst with pride about the belt – if their grown-ups can
afford it and not tie a piece of twine round the waist instead.
Kaloku the leather belt has a shining snake buckle.'

I was amused at this and could not resist reminding her that
when my brother at the same age grew out of cotton tunic
suits and into khaki shorts, he too was inordinately proud of
belt and buckle.

'You heard that class recite its *a b c* and: "two-TY-mes
one-ah TWO-OO-OO". I joined in her imitation of the
children chanting; 'two-TY-mes two-ah FO'—' and so on.
'two-TY-mes sev'n -ah fo'*tiiin*. . . two-Ty-mes TWEL-fah
twenty-FOH!' clapping our hands to the 4/4 rhythm until we
had to leave off for laughing. That was how we ourselves had
learnt arithmetic tables at infant school. I began to identify
myself in a way that I had not done that morning, when Ntutu
had taken me to see government schools, also private schools –
and there were many of those, run by women in the shacks that
they put up or rented. Couples on the Rand mostly both com-
muted to town, on those gangster-ridden crowded trains, to
work. Many of them, some married, others living *masihlalisane*
style, clubbed together and paid someone to teach, feed with a
midday dinner, and care for those of their children for whom
there was no room in the education system – which of course is
not compulsory for Africans.

These illegal impromptu 'schools' were everywhere, and an
acquaintance – I had better call her only M. – who had joined

us on our walk pointed one out to us. Ntutu being at work during school hours did not know any. M. pointed at a 'school' in a
gap between: on one side a prospering grocery shop (run and
owned by BaSutho who, when we had gone in to buy, were
flint-eyed, watchful for shoplifters and gangsters although
laughing, gay and joking), and on the other an undertaker's
business; and next to that a cobbler. Another school was beyond
that, next to a carpenter whose hammers and mallets rent the
air by the hour drowning the children's voices as well as those
in a native medicine man's tiny stuffed-up emporium. It was
festooned with dusty bags containing 'lion's fat', baboon
testicles and other 'cures and strengtheners', and herbs. Schools
were cheek by jowl with all manner of enterprises conducted in
lean-to's. And all around, the din of loudspeakers bellowing
jazz or hymns on 'Native' records. And over the wire fences, the
children – when their attention wandered – could see pedes-
trians hurrying to and fro. Among these I saw two '*skokiaan*
queens' who had stopped to gaze over the fence at the children
in class, crowded together on rough benches with slates on their
knees.

The 'queens' dressed the gaudy part that they played in
urban society as pedlars of prohibited liquor (usually the home-
distilled and virulent *skokiaan*) since Africans were not allowed
to buy wine or spirits except for some 'educated Natives' who,
if they had passed elementary Std. IV, might apply for a special
permit to buy a limited quantity each month. Location life
seemed packed with such recondities and I hardly knew which
item to absorb first as M. and my cousin and I talked.

These were the first 'queens' I had ever seen. Fat and pros-
perous-looking in tight, gleaming dresses, brilliantly coloured
high-heeled shoes, showers of gilt ear-rings, they personified my
idea of harlots. I was mesmerized by the sight; presently
bewildered to see the totally incongruous expression on their
painted faces (hard jet-black pencilled eyebrows) as they
looked at the children in class: the expression was tender,
motherly, smiling – fond approval. I had scarcely assimilated
its import, that these women too were 'people, *abantu*,' as *Sis'*
Tandi would say, taking a harmless stroll from work (even
though that 'work' was running an illicit, probably noisome,

drinking den), when what do I see next but they turn and talk
to two white policemen in their familiar Nazi-style peaked caps,
revolvers in holsters on their hips. They seemed to know one
another, and exchange jokes. I was astounded, and nudged my
cousin and indicated with my elbow. M. took over from her to
explain – for Jo'burg needed much explaining;

'*Tyini*! (Great Scot!) – don't you know that that lot are all
friends together?' I did of course, but not having seen it, had
not fully known. 'Those policemen arrange with the queens to
raid and arrest them only alternately. Then each does not get
hauled up too often to pay the magistrates' fines. And they pay
bribes to their policemen pals, who drop in regularly at the
parlour for their share of the illegal booze. Free for them of
course; and of course, *they* get the whisky, gin, brandy that is
reserved for special customers, not *skokiaan* from methylated
spirits, potatoes, whatnot. You know, at one time the fines were
raised so high, the queens refused to pay, went on strike, and to
jail instead. The police got fed up because they were getting
neither bribes nor free drinks. The fines were reduced, the
queens paid them; no more jail. Life could go on as before. It's
no secret; everybody knows and talks about it. Even now, those
two that you see are from drinking at that other den over there,
opposite that school. Everyday the children see drunkards pass
out under the influence. And being children, they mimic
grown men tottering and staggering, and shout, "Look, this is
how he is 'herding his troublesome goat-kids – *uqhub' amatakane!*"
I bet those police are on their way to raid people's houses;
there's the pick-up van on the corner – see it? And the Non-
European police sitting waiting for the white ones to come?'

I followed the direction of M.'s index finger, not having distinguished the illicit den. To me it looked like any location
shack dwelling. Neither had I seen the van. I was dazed by the
whole melting-pot. But now I was forced to realize, for indeed I
saw the officers of the law give matey farewells to their illicit
friends and stride up to the van and climb in. M. warmed to
her theme throwing in an imprecation. I learned later that she
was a 'good-hearted girl – but brought up in a rough sort of
home'.

'They're off,' she cried, 'Somebody's going to catch it, anybody; I just wonder who. Not the queens, they are safe for today.' We watched the van drive off.

Later, in bed that night, not ashamed to seem a country bumpkin I went back to the subject and asked Ntutu;

'What did she mean, "anybody"? Could they have been coming to our street, have *you* ever been raided?' It seemed incredible that my loved cousins had such experiences. I was curious and fearful all at the same time.

'"*Do* they come down this street – ever been raided?" *Yo*! Are you teasing, *Sis'* Nontando?' It was not altogether dark in our bedroom. There was a glow of moon light, and stars at the window. I watched them as my cousin paused and drew breath.

'You suddenly hear whistles,' she said, 'Rattles, screams. Northern pagan women ululate the alarm, startled dogs bark, all kinds of ear-crashing sounds rise up like a whirlwind; men and boys shout to warn nearby households. The police try to take a house by surprise, but it's difficult because the moment anything happens in the location everybody sees, and anyway the engine of the van accelerates and attracts attention. You hope it will pass your house for somewhere else; but the brakes grind and you see police pour out and leap over your fence like athletes over hurdles. You really should have asked M. about a raid. She is convinced that this hurdle-jumping art is their favourite way of entering, to demonstrate that they are all-powerful and don't need to use your gate like polite natives.' We laughed and agreed that 'that girl was priceless'. She had developed her theory after her own home had been raided.

'She says they rushed in. Pushed the door, *broke* it with axes because it was closed, and ripped up the floor-boards to find the still, the brewing well. Then started digging up the yard.

'But one time, it happened to a neighbour of ours. Police burst in while the family was eating breakfast. And the old lady of that house – I shall never forget her description afterwards when we and other people went to help straighten the house and repair the damage. "My dears," she said. "Would you believe – I couldn't help myself; when this young Boer leapt into the room, face all red, veins on his temples pumping, and stood glaring round, eyes starting from the head, revolver lifted, *so*, nostrils quivering. I found myself offering him my cup, saying,

"*Baas*, would you like some coffee?" Those blue eyes bulged at it like marbles – what a stare a European has. He turned that revolver at *me*, but before I had time to say my last prayer, he suddenly dropped his wrist and snarled "*Sies!*" at *me*; the obscenity of these Boers, to a person old enough to be his mother! Then he crashed the cup to the floor with the gun, turned on his heel, stalked out into the yard. At which I burst out laughing; *ii*nerves, *kaloku*."'

'What happened?' I asked.

'The old lady says people told her that the Boer bent over and was sick.'

I was convulsed, as any but the most fair-minded black (like my aunt) would be, ignoring the streak of decency in the young Boer which drove him to disgust or terror at his own action. Our nightly conversations were full of such things, the hazards of anyone's life in the location; common knowledge but to me revelation. We talked of other things too, however, like: why all but one of my cousins had not married: and about spinsterhood. We talked of her life as a Government servant and of her holidays in Basutoland or by the sea or visiting relations. And of functions that took place in the location – weddings, concerts, about which I asked if my father was right when he declared that choirs attempting gigantic choruses such as Handel's *Hallelujah*, 'sing sharper, off-pitch, till you feel their ambition is slicing your liver, your ear-drums with a razor blade.' She chuckled, 'Oh, Uncle is irrepressible.' We talked too of youth club work, in fact of all of her life's jollities, frustrations, relaxations, duties, restrained pleasures.

'You have to live. You can't be for ever worrying about the risks of being shot, robbed, murdered. You carry on in spite of them – taking care, of course. You become aware of danger by that sixth sense that you develop. Everybody is like that in Jo'burg. And wouldn't swop for the quiet life of any other place. You feel you are in the most significant spot in all South Africa, where things are *happening*. The excitement is not *only* about racial violence or the famous frustrations that make black people into new-style cannibals robbing and killing one another as well as whites. It is in the melting-pot of advance, progress. Usually two steps forward and one step back, of course, but *movement*. As for politicians up here, you should hear how they declare: *they* are not dozing like you people in the Reserves, *emaXhoseni*.' Glimpses of the Rand through the eyes of its partisans were startling.

'And up here,' said *Sis'* Tandi when my aunt had planned that I accompany her on some errand, 'you see resilience, Ntando. People survive and surmount wonders. They are indestructible I tell you. O, the soul-destroying obstacles that they conquer!' She was finishing off a story (familiar to her) that one of my aunt's daily callers had been retelling when we left the house.

We walked out into the garden at the back. Building plots had been reasonable in size when she first came to live at Pimville, and people had been allowed for a time to build to their own design. My aunt had sited her house so that most of her pocket of a garden backed on to other pockets, to give a breathing space of green; and had improved both house and garden after she was widowed and worked as a teacher and brought up her children. We walked past the orange tree that she had planted, past her decorative shrubs, across the little patch of lawn where they liked to sit under the shade-tree of a late afternoon in the blistering high-veld summers.

'You have made it all look like our other homes.' I said, thinking again of Uncle Tennyson's at Umtata, Uncle Cecil's and my own at Middledrift or even our little farm at Rabula.

Sis' Tandi said, 'Well, your Big Mother says "Are not the homes related?" In her travelling days when she went to the Colony now and again, she used to look at her brothers' places and your late mother's and say, "The progenitors would be pleased if they saw their descendants – like peas out of one pod and living with respect for tradition, as *they* did when on earth".' We smiled, for Big Mother's viewpoint ranged backwards in time as well as forward. When with her, you found her habit was catching and began to feel yourself part of the flow.

'But one has to mark time now. It is difficult for people to build or live in a settled state with all this talk of being moved from towns. But they hate to endure the squalor while they wait; so although they know that all will presently be razed to the ground, they try, some of them, to make the so-called houses as presentable as they know how. They say: "We may be here a year, two, five, twenty before these Europeans carry out their threat; so why be on tenterhooks, squatting on haunches? We may as well live decently since we have children to bring up." Let us go this way,' she said as we stepped into the street, 'I will show you what I mean. Big Mother wants you to see *ema*Tank*ini* – the Tanks.'

My aunt had talked one morning in the *voorhuis* about the settlement into which people had overflowed from the unendurable overcrowding in near-by locations, and in a body made a determined movement to 'squat' on empty but forbidden ground. There they had built themselves homes out of *water tanks*. It sounded like a similar phenomenon down in the Eastern Cape, outside Port Elizabeth, the thriving seaside town about two hundred miles from my home. There too a 'Squatters' Movement' had happened, like an explosion from a spontaneous combustion due to congested living conditions. People made themselves a city of 'houses' out of the crates in which Ford motor car bodies had been imported for assembly, a major industry in the region, employing thousands of Africans. When these workers had begun the illegal squatting they had had to be let alone for they had nowhere to live although big business needed them; the settlement was nicknamed *kwa*Ford*i*. As we walked my cousin said, 'The Tanks is not only tanks. Some houses are made of reeds like those in Zululand and Portuguese East. Many of the people come from there who make this influx that industry seems to attract. Work wants them; they want work. But where to live, since they are not supposed to be here? However, necessity is the mother of invention, so houses of discarded water-tanks were invented.'

As we approached the stretch of corrugated-iron erections I saw that the only way to live in a tank was to roll it over on its side, when top and bottom became front and back of the house. Then you cut holes for doorways and windows and fitted them. And you trimmed and straightened the curve that touched the ground. Some people had raised their houses on platforms of mud-brick. Indeed, as you continued to look, you saw that each structure showed its occupants' imagination or lack of it, for they were different despite being of the same shape. The windows on some were well-proportioned, on others haphazard. It was the apotheosis of 'Do It Yourself'. Whatever materials came to hand had been used, collected from every conceivable source my cousin told me. Gazing at the expanse of poverty-stricken improvisation dispirited me; my mind wanted to resist, go into a sulk as it were. Yet when I looked away there was only the heartless Transvaal veld; or further blisters upon it of pitiful dwellings. The lovely southern light was wasted on dusty roads, lorries bowling along them carrying loads and ragged lorry-boys seated on top laughing and waving so that one marvelled at their vitality and cheer; for what was there to look on with pleasure? I was forced back to the detail of the tanks. And it began to force my resistance away.

I now saw that many of the ramshackle 'houses' had been given coats of paint. Some had creepers trained up their curving sides so that leaves waved jauntily above the roof that was a continuation of the curve. There was convolvulus, morning glory, passion fruit. And in some yards I saw wooden trays with seedlings in them and rusty watering-cans alongside. There were earthen pots, big and small, filled with annuals, little labels attached bearing the bright coloured picture of the plant that would bloom. The approaches to one or two front doors, miniscule front-yards, were stamped hard to lay the dust; and swept clean, the edges outlined by bricks stuck in the ground in such a way that their corners formed a line of continuous *w*'s. Others again were fenced with chicken-wire to prevent animals and children from destroying the attempts to establish pocket-handkerchief-size lawns or minute vegetable patches. My cousin said, 'It is useless just to walk past. You see nothing that way.' I protested that I *was* seeing and was amazed.

'*What* are you seeing?' she laughed. 'Your eyes are glazed and you look as though a rest would do you no harm. I am going to take you to visit. You know, even Europeans born and bred here feel as cut off from the people of Jo'burg as you strangers from the Cape. For one thing whites may not go into a native location without a permit. Regulations about race. But in any case, many of them are scared by the ramshackleness. And thinking that people living here must be savages, and about dirt, disease, murder, rape, vice, robbery, they accelerate, get home to spacious Houghton and collapse on to writing-pads. Then we read those letters in the paper about the terrifying influx of natives. Here is Mrs. R.'s house. I teach her youngest. Her others have passed through to older classes.'

We turned into a toy-like home-made wooden gate. As my cousin closed and latched it behind her, a large brown woman peered out from the open doorway where she sat on an upright chair. She looked in her late fifties. She recognized my cousin and cried out in Xhosa, '*Teacheress*, is it you? And whom have you brought? *Awu!* I am being visited.' and drew herself up, very fat, positively obese, and stepped forward from the tank, her hand stretched out in greeting.

We went in. I saw that she had had an enamel basin on her lap and had put it on a bed behind the chair she had sat on, next to a small sack filled with peas. She had been shelling, and now shook off remnants of pods from her apron as she bustled about and got busy and hospitable, drawing up chairs for us in a minute sitting-room area. While she was welcoming us and my cousin 'explaining' me so that both talked at once, I glanced round.

The interior was like a caravan, packed to overflowing with furniture and belongings. At first there seemed not an inch in which to move. I wondered how she negotiated her elephantine proportions. But she did. She talked almost without stopping to begin with, laughing, glad because of our coming. And all the time, I saw how meticulously she picked her way, moving things to one side and replacing them as she went, neat and controlled as very fat people often are; and graceful. She negotiated her-self as one adjusted to her surroundings. After sitting us down she carved herself a path to the other end of the tank, face beaming, teeth very white and even, crying, 'Tea! Cup of tea my dears, let me make you Mazawattee-*teee*. You have caught me without *i*favourite *yam*, *i*Five Roses Brand.'

I found myself warming because she was so cheerful, so large-hearted. When she went to the other end of the room, I saw an arrangement of small primus stoves set on top of a series of soap-boxes. These were lined up side by side to form a kitchen table of convenient height, the top covered with wipeable American cloth. She lit and pumped up one of the stoves, never stopping talking, then reaching up with one arm or the other to some home-made shelves along the wall, took down cups from hooks, saucers from little stacks, tea-pot, milk-jug, sugar basin and so on. What she did was a study in time and motion. It explained the order that prevailed: bedding-rolls stacked underneath each of the two made-up bedsteads that were along either wall; between them halfway down the middle of the room, a folding dining-table with a crocheted doily across it and glass jam-jar doing duty as a vase filled with paper flowers. Close to one end of the table, the front door end and minute sitting-room area, there was an improvised armchair, a motor car bucket seat. Its back was wedged against the back of one of the dining-chairs which were tightly drawn up into the table. To sit down to a meal, you would have to pick these up and temporarily disturb that particular arrangement for on one side of the motor-seat there was an aluminium and canvas folding chair and on the other a proper armchair. I would not have thought it possible to fit in so much into so little space; the backs of both armchairs were tight against the sides of the beds along opposite walls. The beds and the proper armchair were covered with cretonne frilled at the hems. The same material hung as curtains and pelmets at the windows – everybody had cretonne, it seemed, even in a tank. The rather uneven floor was covered with lino at the sitting-room end, of a design that made your eyes a little restless when they travelled from it to the pattern of the cretonnes – but although worn and cracking, it gleamed with polish. Mrs. R. brought the tea-things on a tray, carrying it on one hand raised to shoulder level like a waiter. The other manipulated the pieces of furniture in her way. She would not hear of our getting up to help her; and she seemed to have powerful wrists. Her voice was joyous above the rattle of tea-spoons against china and decorated tins of home-made cookies and biscuits. Putting her load on the table, she sat down and mopped her brow with the edge of her apron then began to pour out, talking – a deep mezzo-soprano torrent of words that vibrated in the crowded room. I felt as if wedged in the prongs of a resonating tuning-fork.

'Ah, MaJili, I see you are taking a good look at this house of ours, you who have surely never seen the like. Wondering how its people manage, eh? Girl, you are welcome to examine. And *tell* those overseas people how we savages live.' Uproarious laughter, while handing the cups. 'As for us, even if we knew how to tell, we have no time. You are noticing those sleeping-rolls tucked under our big people's beds? The children's.

'That is where a woman's time and energy go in places like *ema*Tank*ini*: the daily battle to keep clean, orderly; to train the children likewise. And cook, wash.' She waved her strong arm in each direction indicating the arrangements she had devised, 'Especially cook, Jili, that your man may feel too full to wander off to the brandy parlours, understand?' Her gaiety was gigantic, and catching.

'As for training the children – *yo!* The home-work to be done for school. It is done at this table. So you have to make yourself small, small. Believe me, *I* shrink to the size of a *mouse* to keep out of their way. Yet being young, *ijong* span – lovely alignment of Afrikaans words attached to suitable Xhosa noun-class initial letter – 'needs must pull out that Columbia gramophone tucked at the back of the roll at the wall under *that* bed over there, and play records while they *do* that homework!' and she imitated a sort of arms and shoulders dance where she sat – 'Their beloved *kwela* and penny whistles.' Her eyes twinkled, face beamed all over. She stopped 'dancing'. '*Kaloku* that is *eyona* traditional music and dancing – the *umbhayizelo* of these town youngsters of ours. But better that they *bhayizela* and shake here in the tank, not so, *Teacheress*?' More laughter. 'Otherwise, the *habits* that can be picked up out there in the street —' she shuddered.

My cousin said, at last getting a word in, 'Some of you *ma*-Afrika are never satisfied. First you complain of the children's needs when they are home. Yet when Government relieves you of these very children so that you can be left in peace, again you complain.' But her eyes twinkled too.

Mrs. R. threw back her head, slapped her huge thigh and laughed fit to die, everything about her emphatic, and cried, '*Owu!* Mistress!' put her hand to her chin, supporting that elbow in the palm of the other and turning to me in mock re-proach, 'How this big sister of yours likes her jokes,' then to my cousin and jerking her head in my direction, 'Does this person-of-ours know what you are teasing about now?' When my cousin only shrugged her shoulders and smiled, Mrs. R. explained the joke to me: all about when 'native males' reach the age of eighteen, head-tax (Poll tax) age, they may no longer live as children with their parents, in a town location. One of her sons was in this delicate situation of having to live away from home; also to pay the 'lodger's fees' that become due from 'employed natives' of his kind, which have to be paid to the white Superintendent: he who granted the indispensable Permit to Work, without which a native could not be in town at all. If not employed, that is to say by Europeans, you had to quit, return to the Reserves, even if like many eighteen-year olds you had never in your life lived in one. Her son pretended to live at another location, went there regularly to pay the fee and renew his work-permit, hoodwinking the Boer there. I could not imagine how it was done. Parts of the puzzle were left out in the explanation and I did not like to ask. I could see well enough that it was risky, a matter of time before he and others living surreptitiously in their parental homes would be found out, fined or jailed, and expelled from town, 'Endorsed Out'; and for such reasons I have not brought myself to mention their names. Mrs. R. now got up again and crossed over to the wall. She detached a leaflet that was pinned to a picture-frame and handed it to my cousin who sat back to read it while our hostess tried to talk to us at the same time about different things. She said to my cousin, 'That is the reading matter which that rascal child "Criminal-because-home-dweller" of mine brings back as a trophy from his latest trip to his fee-eating boss-Boer. A Congress leaflet. Oh, red hot African National Congress these boys!' She also kept up a lively conversation with me. Presently my cousin stretched forward and passed the leaflet to me to read, without making comment, not being politically inclined.

But Mrs. R. intervened, saying, 'Take it with you, Jili *omhle*. Study at your leisure, that you may know why our small fry are as they are: on hind legs against the state of the nation, growling. *u*Verwoerd has stirred them up, I tell you. A few of us conservative old ones seek consolation in weekly Mothers' Meetings, *orooibatjie* and such pastimes. In that way we rest our minds occasionally from contemplating the Gadarene rush of here-our-country. We shut our eyes while the *jong span* defy' – and she hid her eyes with her fingers but peeped at me through the gaps – 'Can we blame them? We may not *like* what they do; it may make the back hairs creep, the toes shrink. On the other hand, what did *our* peaceful lawful methods achieve? How can we not be *with* these youngsters and their leaflets? We *are* with them, as we tea-meet away! "Accessories after the fact," we are, making signals in the air like windmills; encouraging if not actually prodding from behind. And you know, youngsters like this boy read and read: books I never heard of, I, brought up on *uHambo lomHambi* (*Pilgrim's Progress*). The other day he said, arguing as usual: "*Mama, uthi u*Edmund Burke" – I ask: "Who is this, now?" He: "No *kaloku mama*, the issue is not a matter of '*who*'; it is this: Burke says, 'There is however, a limit at which forbearance ceases to be a virtue'. That is the point. Don't you understand? Burke has nothing to do with Congress, mother; isn't a South African; isn't even alive. But he shows why the method of the All African Convention and all that 'gradualism and constitutional channels' business is dead, and why we are Congress." So spoke my son, *Teacheress*.'

They looked at each other; for my father had led the All African Convention when Africans were provoked by General Smuts's action in taking away the Native Vote in the Cape, the order of society in those days called in English, 'Segregation Policy' so that it was some time before everybody connected its aims with those of the more forthrightly named 'Apartheid Policy.' Mrs. R. again turned to me; 'Jo'burg is on fire, Jili. You are far from the once-idyllic Native Reserves. Those days are gone. You were brought up as they folded their togas about them to lie down and die. Your kind are among the last to taste those antique feasts of the spirit. Savour them, that your children may know what once was. Here *e*Transvaal we are in the boiling-pot, forced to attend to other business – *sibambene ne BHULU*, at grips, at grips. Am I telling her, Mistress?' My cousin did not interrupt for Mrs. R.'s eyes were bright, as though no longer seeing the jam-packed tank room, the slum beyond her door. She was leaning forward, palms on knees, elbows akimbo, a mountain of vigour. But unremittingly cheerful, surveying facts. I noticed she had scarcely touched her tea or eaten the delicious home-baked cookies she had given us; and clearly did not mean to, now that she had started on that flow of rhetoric, to which it was etiquette for me and my cousin to listen until she finished.

I was sorry when we left. My cousin had made her point, for I stepped out feeling as though I had been in a *salon*, not a tank. Our hostess had spoken magnificent Xhosa; I carried away an impression of grace, of a life lived with style amid the squalor and the din aroused by the political dispensation that engulfed everyone. And I liked to think that her vision was coloured by the traditions, into which she had delved as into the treasure-trove, that others of her generation shared with her.

I was glad I could take away a memento of the encounter, not only my impression of it. Afterwards I had only to look at her son's leaflet, 'the trophy'; then I saw that extraordinary room again, the less than lovely doilies, linoleum, paper flowers; the brave, improvised armchair, the stupendous stacking of belongings; and again I felt the cosiness and heard the laughter.

'People do the best they can, strive to be decent,' my other cousin, Zodwa, had said when off duty and home with us, supporting her two sisters' views of life in town.

I did not get the chance to read the leaflet until some evenings later. As I have said, nothing much seemed to happen, but somehow I had little time for brooding. One evening my aunt had arranged a dinner-party. She wished me to meet some of her friends, people who had been calling regularly at the house throughout my visit and who seemed to me to contribute to its atmosphere. Her married daughter and husband were coming. The occasion was an honour for me since I was strictly speaking only 'a child'. But the life 'between two worlds' in which everybody was caught up was physically dramatized in my case, living in Europe and in Africa; and this was another of the special positions that it put me in – being entertained by my seniors. While my two cousins were preparing the dinner, and a caller was with my aunt in the *voorhuis*, I sat down to read.

The leaflet was issued by an organization called The Transvaal Resist Apartheid Committee, and carried a banner headline in three languages – in order of importance: English, Xhosa, Sesutho. I observed that even here in its 'home-province', Afrikaans was not considered of first rank by Africans.

Yet I heard them speak it all the time, one of the major differences between being 'in the Border' and here. Whenever I commented, they explained: 'You get into the habit. Like using a home dialect. It becomes part of you. But it is not a universal language, now is it? What world power trades in *Die Taal*? And do not the Boers come back from Holland crestfallen on finding that their Afrikaans is scarcely understood there, and is thought low? As for literature, Shakespeare goes better in Xhosa or Sesutho. Besides we have our writing too – "*izi Bhal-*'man' *zetu zi* busy!"' slang quite impossible to render, about the part-time authors busily producing books in Southern Bantu languages. English had priority, even among ardent nationalists; otherwise they would not be able to communicate. So the trilingual headline of the manifesto read: 'WE SHALL NOT MOVE! *ASIHAMBI! HA RENA HO TSAMAEA!*'

The first page was in English, the matter repeated on second and third in Xhosa, Sesutho.

'"VERWOERD says Africans must get out of the Western Areas and go to 'Meadowlands' and Diepkloof.
WE say 'NOTHING DOING!'

WE SHALL NOT MOVE AN INCH!

1. We don't want to be caged in a municipal location with a fence around and a Superintendent to enforce permits and lodgers' fees.
2. Moving means 'screening'! The Native Affairs people will reject thousands as 'not employed in Johannesburg', 'idle Natives', 'passes out of order!, and so on. They will endorse these people out into the wilderness. Our own children will be endorsed out if the N.A.D. says they are old enough to work.
3. Moving means being divided up into tribal areas by the Government – BaSutho here, Xhosa there, Zulu somewhere else. That's *apartheid* in action – dividing the people and setting one group against another!
4. Meadowlands is eleven miles away. The transport is rotten. How shall we get to work?
5. The Government will charge new 'economic rents'. They will find out how much pay you are getting and make you pay higher rates than in Orlando, Jabavu and other towns where the people

have refused to pay the new rates. We must not betray our fellow Africans in these townships.

THE WESTERN AREAS REMOVAL
SCHEME IS LEGALIZED ROBBERY

The Government is taking away the right of the African people to own land and trying to make us propertyless serfs for ever.
The African National Congress warned you that this was only the first step towards the wholesale uprooting of Africans all over the country. Now Dr. Eiselen, Secretary for Native Affairs has said that the Government means to kick 178,000 Africans out of the Western Cape Province.

WAR ON THE AFRICANS

The Government declared war on the African people. Africans in the Western Areas are in the front line of defence. The whole of South Africa is watching and supporting us! The whole world has been shocked by the shocking scandal of the Western Areas Removal. Millions of people overseas have expressed their sympathy.
We shall not surrender! The struggle of the Western Areas is the struggle of the African people and of all freedom-loving people. Anyone who moves willingly is helping the Government to enslave our people. He is acting as a traitor and bringing shame on Africa.
DON'T FILL IN THE FORMS!
DON'T GET IN THE LORRY TO GO TO MEADOW-LANDS!
BE READY TO OBEY CONGRESS CALL!
JOIN THE AFRICAN NATIONAL CONGRESS – ENROL AS A VOLUNTEER!
RESIST *APARTHEID*!
WE ARE NOT GOING TO MOVE"

Bring your forms and report everything to the A.N.C. Office, 120b, Victoria Road, Sophiatown or phone 33–4069.'

My heart bled as I put the leaflet down. In the first round, Verwoerd had sent his Saracens into the arena as my brother had seen. Desperate slum-dwellers had moved voluntarily, to be sure; or had been moved unwillingly; and probably not many of them necessarily 'traitors'; some doubtless among 'the freedom-loving people of the world'. Where would it all end? *'Discipulus est prioris posterior dies'*, I had heard my father say in other contexts and smilingly render a meaning in our language for the rest of us who were absolute non-Latinists: 'The experience of one day is a guide for the conduct of the next.' But I heard my aunt's stick tap the floor, and gentle steps to the front door, farewells between her and the departing neighbour, who was promising to look in tomorrow, the next day and the next. Laughter and bustle in the kitchen at the other end of the house. I had forgotten for a spell, but now again became aware of the location. I jumped up and went forward to my aunt, who I knew would be serene as ever, at peace with herself and imparting self-respect to those around her in the 'boiling-pot'. Friends had called, others were coming; life went on mostly as planned, not disturbed as I expected in my state of apprehension.

18

MEANWHILE, what of these friends who regularly called, promising to look in tomorrow, the next day and the next? What of the mornings I spent with my old aunt when her daughters were at work?

Every day, except of course week-ends, my cousins left for school immediately after breakfast, having made an early start much as people did in rural households. They turned out the kitchen-dining-parlour while I slept; then brought hot water to the bedrooms so that my aunt and I dressed and prepared for the day, while they cooked. The four of us gathered in the parlour to eat, my aunt first conducting morning prayers from the head of the table. Ntutu and I sat on a little settee, *Sis'* Tandi near her mother. The morning routine here and at Tsolo had not changed as it had at my home. Afterwards sitting on in the kitchen-parlour, I kept my aunt company. She talked in the style of a Big Mother. My father's insistence that there was something special about her was emphasized for me by our continued and concentrated companionship. She was in fact much like anybody else's aunt of her age and class, I would think, looking at her again after a year – a frail, yet solid enough figure wrapped in warm shawl because mornings were cold, sharp; and wearing the toque that was almost a widow's uniform. She would stay where she was at the head of the table, push her empty plate and cup away and, with one hand on walking-stick, her eyes travelled round the room peering over the top of her bifocal spectacles until they rested on me. On satisfying herself about what I had eaten she would settle down to talk, unconsciously making one of her preliminary gestures which was to smooth her small mouth with finger and thumb. On our first morning alone, I imagined we were sitting on aimlessly and that we would move to the other room when she had answered a question I had asked about my maternal relations. I was still preoccupied with them; my uncle had so often said, 'Your aunt will tell you more about that.'

But I soon saw that to remain where she was for a time each morning was part of her system; we were waiting for the daily help to arrive to clear the table, wash up, prepare the food for luncheon and take my aunt's orders for the day's housework. We also waited for the friends and neighbours who, as I have said, were accustomed to look in and pass the time of day. The early callers knew that Big Mother would be here in the kitchen-parlour. Those who came later would make for the *voorhuis*. An inflexible routine. I came to find it reassuring against the pulse of location life: women ululating; car engines revving (as if they were possibly dreaded police vans) – all mingling with children's laughter on their way to school; hammers and mallets banging; jazz; spasmodic shouts in languages I did not always understand.

One such morning, the daily woman busy at her work-table cleaning and peeling vegetables, I was asking how the Maki-wanes came by their surname which means 'Figs'. I had discovered the year before how the Jabavus had come by theirs; and on the visit to my uncle, I had noticed he called my ancestor 'Makiwane Lujabe'. But before I had finished speaking there was a sudden whirlwind of alarms right on our street, at the same time a loud knock at the front door. I jumped but my aunt's sixth sense was not disturbed nor our daily woman's. They both said, 'Postman'; and my aunt waved a hand to me to go to the door.

I cried, 'But what is that *other* noise?'

'Nothing,' said Big Mother. 'You will see perhaps, if you go to the front. Anyway there may be something in the post for you from home.' I opened the door to the smiling postman, a grey-haired man who had delivered mail in the township for more than thirty years. But behind him in the street, the uproar was coming from a procession: six manacled young men wearing flashy clothes being marched in twos by an African policeman at their rear, a hostile crowd following, scolding, haranguing; and little children were skipping alongside, excited. A bizarre spectacle. It made me halt in the act of accepting the batch of letters that the postman held out, and ask, 'Father, what is happening?'

He turned round to look as if for the first time giving the matter his full attention. For a moment he watched and listened, then as the tail end of the crowd disappeared round the corner, answered, 'Those young men are *tsotsi* – robbers. You saw the blankets the policeman was carrying? It seems these *tsotsi* have just been robbing a house, its owners at work. Someone raised the alarm. That is why the crowd is accompanying the culprits, to lash them with tongues, as you heard.' I explained that I had not heard, for the haranguing was in Sesutho and Afrikaans. 'Ah well, it's like this,' and he translated. 'And *otsotsi* know that this is not all. When they reach the Charge Office they are "going to be BIRCHED, *bazakuKATSWA*. Although,' and he shrugged his shoulders, 'I fear such types are too far gone; immune; do not mind about public opinion. Not a shred of shame left in them. They get the lash, prison, but can you deter criminals? Criminals? You can only pray for them,' he finished briskly and got ready to continue on his round, saying, 'My greetings, please, to MaGambu, O daughter-who-has-news-from-home in the Colony!' I glanced at the letters and to be sure, one bore a Cape Province postmark and was addressed to me in my father's hand.

Back in the kitchen my aunt took up from where we had left off about Tsolo. While she was answering questions the woman at her work would interject if she missed points in our conversation.

Big Mother explained about the surname and about errors that had arisen when the British had introduced the system in her great-grandfather's day. Many families belonging to the same line had registered differing patronymics as permanent surnames. I had been told of similar accidents in the Jabavu registration; and that that was why some of us were called Somtunzi and Citywa. We had kinsmen who had been recorded as 'Singer-Woody' because the young English ensign who had been detailed to the task invented that spelling when the red-ochred pagan before him growled that he was called 'Singa-wothi', one of our clan names. My aunt spoke of Makiwanes who had been misnamed, saying, 'Know these things, Non-tando, know them, for such people are brothers and sisters,' and the voice from across the room interjected earnestly,

'Indeed know these things, young people, know, know, *know*. Else your children's children, even their children might inter-marry and commit incest in their ignorance.'

It was such matters that were aired during these talks. Or others would come to my aunt's mind by chance. Once I began telling her about Long Ear's trips at the farm to the ford with his soil-eroding sleigh. She interrupted me.

'Ah, that Confluence ford. It was one of your grandfather's pre-occupations, "*elozibuko – ukulilungisa*, to keep it in repair." Mind you, any of the farm hands could have maintained it. But your grandfather spent much time sedentary at his desk writing sermons, pamphlets, books. That,' in a smiling aside, 'is where my brother Tennyson and I contracted the disease. So he welcomed the relaxation of manual work, "In order to think out what he was writing," he used to say. He would either potter about pruning trees in his small orchard, or liked best of all to stride down to the river to put his ford to rights; replace stepping stones when they got swept away; shovel back the silt that our cattle and horses and sheep disturbed when led to drink. And specially after floods. And of course the Scotch carts of those days *ruined* fords. And when the girls of the family married, and at my own wedding, he worried about the state of the ford.'

On such themes she was liable to digress; but I loved to listen – forgot about the location, forgot letters that I had not written, forgot about my nervous stomach.

'You see, child, I had been away working: a town girl, journalist, far from home; at King William's Town for your other grandfather, as you know. And when I went home to be given in marriage, I was struck afresh by traditional customs. They were the usual ones but I saw them with new eyes because I was involved.' For my part I thought also it must have been because she had trained herself to observe, on the weekly journal.

'*Kaloku* Christians, "school" people, mingled pagan and Western tradition. The old ran into the new. Take the seclusion of the bride. Pagans calling at the farm when I was to be married gave their usual reasons why it was observed: "to make her pale and beautiful, to keep her from getting sunburnt, prevent the skin from peeling, to fatten her by preventing her from all exercise, feeding plenty of thick milk." I could hear all the discussion for they were sitting sociably outside my room.' I asked what my grandfather said in reply. She smiled. 'Ah, father said nothing. His attitude was that there is more to these things than is on the surface, especially the ceremonies the people observed to mark the different stages in the evolution of the individual in society. The idea behind them did not conflict, in his view, with a Christian life. The same when the *uduli* came, the Bridegroom's Party or Host; when they come to lay claim to the virgin for whom they have parted with beloved cattle, the girl who it was hoped would bring forth sons and daughters for them.'

'How many cattle in your case, Big Mother?' She did not hear.

'You should have seen your grandfather prepare the ford for that Host. I was the first daughter to go. I was told in my rondavel that he was at it for days, saying the Bridal Claimants should not encounter the ford as an additional obstacle; there were important rituals of "obstruction" to be dramatized and overcome on reaching the house – the host arriving in "aggressive mood", the girl's family in tears, playing out reluctance to give up their treasure, their "Beautiful Dish"; although', and again she smiled, 'although the whole thing had been agreed, contracted for, fixed, *arranged* months before, and in cases where the girl's family had themselves sought the suitor on her behalf. (As you know, girls may propose too, in paganism, not only the young men.)'

I saw Big Mother in my mind's eye in her ankle-length dimity dress, cameo at her throat, leg of mutton sleeves, and asked how she had whiled away the days ritually confined in that rondavel which sounded much like my cousin's that I had been allotted at Tsolo. She had spent them reading editorials, revising articles that she had been working on until the last moment on my other grandfather's paper; and also listening to the long, loud conversations that the pagan women were holding about her just outside. When I asked what they would have expected a more ordinary girl to be doing, since she was unique among women of the time (a comment that I did not add), she said, good-naturedly, 'Sit in the darkened hut and gaze into space.' I was enthralled, and bombarded her with complicated questions, the sort that have to be framed in several parts; which made her laugh and say, 'Really, I am indulging myself, talking about matters of our household. The people of Jili would call it subversive.' But she prepared to answer nevertheless. Always she took her time, did not rush to assemble her ideas. She liked to present them in order – a beginning, a development, a conclusion. She smoothed her lips, about to satisfy my curiosity; but for the moment we were foiled.

'Knock, knock!' a gay voice shouted at the door, its owner opening it and stepping in, and my aunt cried, 'Ah, Nurse!' She came every day, sometimes early into the kitchen-parlour, sometimes late afternoon into the *voorhuis*; and was Nurse Magobiyane, a professional in private practice, I understood, and a married woman living at home. She was a bright-faced woman of somewhere between my age and my cousin *Sis'* Tandi, slim, darker than my cousins, mid-brown like me, and she had a very deep voice indeed. She liked to wear a crocheted beret, a straight-fitting skirt, a woollen twin-set. She came in always with an air that was a delicate combination of respect, familiarity, deference and affection for my aunt. No relation; a very good friend. I did not discover how long ago the neighbourly custom had begun of her 'looking in' to pass the time of day. She had probably nursed my aunt through one of the bouts of high blood pressure or bronchitis that troubled her in late years.

Nurse's habit was to sit down and *ncokola* (converse with, entertain) the old lady; her stories were sometimes about her twin girls whom I did not meet but gathered were about three years old. I think she also had older children. But I afterwards remembered her *ukuncokola* about the twins because they were a breath of another world in my aunt's house where the youngest was of an age with me.

'Oh, what troubles we had yesterday with our European!' she said gaily. The twins had been given a present of a doll 'European style', made of white porcelain with cheeks painted pink; the head was fitted with long flaxen tresses, and the blue eyes had sweeping lashes and so on. They called their doll '*umLungu*, the European', not long having learnt to talk.

'Oh, how troublesome, naughty, this *umLungu*! Will no longer wet her napkin properly; the eyelids refuse to close as they did. Everything worked splendidly at first, when *umLungu* was new. But its twin-mothers are so *rough*, they treat the European as they do the mealie-husk Xhosa dolls; are now furious because European misbehaves, has even given up bleating like a sheep "Ma-ma" when turned over as prescribed. Things became so bad, I had to *hide* European, Gambu! Verily hide her, to restore order, divert attention, rage, frustration: so up on top of the wardrobe she had to go. Things hidden have to climb up there these days, since we learnt to walk and can now look about and see drawers that we can pull open, and poke inquisitive fingers into everything, and became tall enough to see what is on top of the table.'

Throughout she spoke in the entertainment tone of speech, to enliven moments in Big Mother's immobile day, she who had been through everything in life and had practically passed to the other side as she liked to say. On some days the tone and content were different, depending on what kind of topic my aunt had led with. And on other days again, they communed in silence. Nurse was quick to sense what was appropriate. As she announced herself with that 'Knock, knock!' and came in, her eyes already darted affectionately to catch the old lady's mood.

The same air of diversion fanned the household when my aunt's woman doctor, called Mary Malahlela, now Mrs. Xakana, whom I had not seen for years. Before going to Witwatersrand University to read medicine, she had been at Fort Hare when I had come for school holidays from England.

My aunt was not ill; Mary was driving past her house on business and stopped to look in. She talked about her student days, asked me about mine and described her time at 'Wits (Vits)'. We talked in English sprinkled with words in other languages, for Mary was really a Sutho speaker but a Transvaal polyglot like my aunt and cousins.

'You ask what it was like here at Wits? I'll tell you. Sometimes I might imagine it was all a dream. But the present generation of youngsters still breathe the same atmosphere. Your brother did. Fellow white students in the lecture hall, finding themselves sitting next to you, making a grimace and moving to another place.'

Mary had been the first black woman student to qualify as a doctor in South Africa. What she said reminded me of the narcolepsy that had troubled my brother when at Wits. She went on in her special 'entertainment' voice, 'Man, this thing disturbed you at the time. You were stupid, for honestly, you had not realized what a sensitive flower you were.' We could all laugh. Everyone could swop similar experiences. 'If before going to Wits you had been treated like a leper, you would have known what to expect, not so? Professor X, for instance: *he* did not even *want* Non-European students to take their *viva-voce* with him.' She named a medical man whose specialist writings are studied in English-speaking countries. 'He made no secret of it, and *ya* accept*a i*Wits University.'

'What of the professors who did take you?' I asked. Mary laughed again.

'As I say, if you hadn't been young and starry-eyed about your vocation you would have reacted more interestingly to the irrelevant questions they put to you. Some of these professors appeared to be beside themselves when confronted with "a native girl", yet who was a student like a daughter of their own and not a housemaid or the "black seductress" that they have nightmares about. The situation confused them, man! One of them stammered out: "Where did you manage to learn English? You even write it, I see." I just said, "Yes sir, I learnt to write."' Her laughing mood was infectious. Big Mother evidently knew these anecdotes. Mary had been her doctor for a long time. I laughed, for what else could one do? But wondered inwardly whether one of the reasons for the separate courses in higher education that were being devised for the starry-eyed youth of different 'ethnic groups' was to eliminate the chance of their realizing that they were alike anatomically, chemically, orthopaedically, physiologically. It was dangerous to have them studying together as at present. My aunt said, smiling and twinkling, 'And tell my niece what that examiner asked de Wet at *his* oral finals.'

Mary indulged the old lady. She knew that I knew de Wet Maqanda who had been her contemporary at university. He now practised in the Transkei, not far from my uncle's, and I had met him again there.

'The professor looked for a long time at de Wet,' she said, 'looked again at the papers, then back at him; and naturally Maqanda braces himself for a really searching, tough question – career at stake; those years of swot, sweat, sacrifice; his future. At last the professor clears his throat and begins: 'I see that you were christened *de Wet* . . . How on earth did *you* come to be given that name?''

'De Wet was stunned, but breathed again, gathered his wits and focused them on this red herring. He said, truthfully, "My father's European; he was a Boer, sir." De Wet was naughty, you know.' We all smiled because in his shoes we too would probably not have bothered to explain what did not seem to have crossed the mind of our eminent compatriot: that people did not christen their infants with the names that white employers give their servants – 'Sixpence' and the like; or that some of these 'Sixpences' might be putting sons through university to whom many of them had, unracialistically, given the names that spangle South Africa's history – like Rhodes, Schreiner, Jabavu, Palo, Rose Innes, Hofmeyer, Viljoen, Villiers, even Kruger, Cronje, de Wet.

Every day also, there would be a gentler knock on the door and a younger voice would announce the arrival of a young girl. 'Grandmother, it is me.'

She was no relation. When she came on the first day after I was established in the house, my aunt touched my arm and pretended to let me into a secret while the well-brought-up girl looked on, waited and had to listen.

'You will see that I hold court here, so to speak, Ntando. People make it their business to look in on the old who can no longer get about. Not even location life changes that. It is still guided by *la*reciprocity *nala*interdependence of life in the countryside. Now this young person is my *aide-de-camp*; (she used the Xhosa term *umphakati* but humorously adding a feminine suffix for an unremittingly masculine office), who visits regularly to see if she is needed "for sending on errands", household shopping, messages and so on, which my working daughters have not always the opportunity to carry out.'

The young girl smiled shyly. She was about fourteen, I guessed, wearing an overcoat and the then ubiquitous 'stylish' African teenage girls' white beret, and carrying, on a long strap over her wrist, a shiny plastic handbag – also probably 'sharp-stuff', smart in town circles. She stood stock-still while my aunt explained about her, did not appear to dream of interrupting any more than a country child, until my aunt asked: 'All dressed up for a journey, eh? – *kuyiwa phi?*' Deferentially she cast down her eyes and whispered, 'Ah, yes-no, Grandmother; I was really going to town for my mother's errands. I had planned to do yours in the afternoon. But at the station, that ticket-selling Boer clerk was in one of his moods when he pre-fers to sit and read a newspaper instead of selling tickets to the people. I joined the long queue waiting for him to finish reading and start selling. He reads slowly, and of course the people became angry and taunted him, calling out in Afrikaans: "Slow because he *can't* read. Does he look as if he has even passed that Std. IV of theirs?" They knew he could hear, but knew too that they were going to miss the train anyhow now because of this wretch.'

She began to forget about having to seem bashful; her eyes brightened and she could not repress a giggle. 'And sure enough, he went on reading until the train came into the plat-form. Only then did he fold up his paper, *leisurely*, Grand-mother, glaring at us through the window, and begin, slow like a chameleon, to serve the customers. "They are all Kaffirs anyway at these township stations", the railway Boers say, "What does a Kaffir's business matter if he misses a train?" So my plan has changed. I missed the train. However, I can now use up the time until the next one in doing your jobs, and do mother's later. That Boer has put paid to her schedule for the day. She will be inconvenienced and vexed, but there it is.' She shrugged her slight shoulders. My aunt fumbled at her old-fashioned waist pocket for a list she had prepared.

'Then I must not delay you, grandchild. If you are first in the queue you might win, the Boer might serve you in time –

eh?' My aunt was slow to find the opening at her waist. The girl
laughed with her but, I thought, less gaily than a moment ago;
her eyes were glued on the elderly hand, which continued to
fumble.

'*LamaBhulu* are like that.' my aunt went on, 'And of course
it is Boers on the railways now. Jobs for these "Poor Whites"
who cannot pass beyond Std. IV. They can thank Smuts for
that "Civilized Labour Policy" of his in the early thirties that
flattered them. He dislodged *amaAfrika* from work to install
these fellows however incompetent; and at inflated "White"
wages. Smuts? A sly racialist, first deserting his own camp to
side with the English, next currying favour with his fellow
Boers at our expense. The reason for these acts of malice of this
ticket fellow of yours at the station is only this: Boers resent
anything resembling services to Natives. Civic services, mind
you; no charity. We pay, pay. Yet on Sundays for instance,
when people come from down the line to visit us, one of these
same ticket clerks will pretend he has got only through tickets to
Town and none for stations in between. So friends arrive at this
house having paid a return all the way to Jo'burg, which they
did not want. *iApartheid* opens up opportunities of that sort for
those with propensities to goad, bait, provoke. They can "perse-
cute *to a fine art*".'

The aide-de-camp was becoming restless, as if saying to herself, 'Surely Grandmother could *ncokola* afterwards.' At last the
fumbling produced the list. The girl stepped forward to take it,
cupping both hands and genuflecting. My eye went to the shiny
handbag that hung over her arm for, when you are properly
brought up and perform the gestures of good manners that are
expected, you are sometimes in difficulties. And to be sure, the
bag did get in the way of her cupped hands and bent knee. She
twitched its strap back towards the wrist as she straightened
herself, rearranging it without apparently thinking of it. It was
one of those body movements you cannot help noticing, ingrained in people as they grow up. Like the way in which both
'red' and 'school' women and girls unconsciously clasp the skirt
on stooping, a movement women must *never* make as men make
it; and were trained traditionally in feminine deportment
before knickers were heard of. The custom influences the

moderns, to whom missionaries introduced, among other things, the none too ubiquitously worn *i*bloomers*i*.

She turned to leave, treading softly, almost on tip-toe. But the moment she gained the passage and was 'beyond the range of the big people' she fled, even inadvertently slamming the kitchen door in hurrying out. I stole a glance at my aunt but she was not put out, only shook her head absently and smiled, murmuring to herself, 'Ah, these poor children: *i*youthful energy *yale*jong-span, *ezo*high spirits, *betu*. How it *tries* to control itself and behave in seemly manner, *ibe*polite; *kodwa ezi*worry *eziziswa ngalama-Bhulu walapha e*Transvaal; *ezi*anxieties *nezo*-needless daily vexations —' She stopped for I simply had to laugh: the mixture, delivered, if you please, in the voice that constantly reproved the young for mangling language! She looked up, then laughed too and cried, "*Kwowu*, Nontando, you too, *u*naughty!' but pronounced it "*no-TI*", Xhosa style, which sent me into further fits. In the end she gave up, went back into proper language and pleaded that she had '*only* been going to tell me about the pleasures that these encounters with the young were bringing to her old age.'

19

THE dinner-party brought me comparable pleasures in reverse. My cousin prepared it on getting back from work. The ingredients had been assembled beforehand by various hands, the daily help, the young aide, or myself accompanying one or other of the cousins. When finally ready it was an elaborate affair. The arrangement of flowers and covers gave a festive air to the lamp-lit kitchen-dining-parlour. The table was laid with the best white linen, a sight that took my mind almost wholly off the threats that wafted in unceasingly from the location. But even on this night, things were happening out there. The guests had arrived, we had taken our seats, my aunt said grace, and we were about to start on the soup. At that moment the throb out of doors whipped up – '*Ku! Ku! Ku!*' ululations, revving of motor engines, shouts, screeches, laughter. I clutched my napkin. But the whirlwind diminished as suddenly as it began, passed along the street. Our party was unperturbed. 'Not for this block' and the big people continued to eat and talk 'unhastily', setting the tone for their evening's reaffirmation of old-established friendships.

In a few moments however came another disturbance, as we were about to start the next course. This for some reason made me indignant – perhaps because for the first time in days I was beginning to enjoy eating. The main item was a roast that looked tempting and smelt good. *Sis'* Tandi was a beautiful cook. The new clamour was terribly close to the house, men's voices pitched high uttering coarse words, more of those bursts of raucous laughter, this time seemingly at the door. I found myself on my feet – '*Yo!* Mam'omkhulu,' but again everyone knew that there was no cause for alarm and said so, but murmuring the assurance in chorus so that I did not know which to turn to first. My oldest cousin who sat next to me went into a paroxysm of laughter and squeezed my arm: '*Lunjan'uvalo*, the palpitations, Ntando?' Somebody else saying, 'It's only a gang of mine-boys out on night passes from their Compounds, *impi yenKomponi*. They have probably hired the hall opposite, next to "The Separatist".' I sat down and tried not to listen to the imprecations I distinguished when in Xhosa or Zulu. The big people's conversation was under way again but I failed as yet to pay it full attention; the shouts were dying down to a mumble as if they might cease altogether, which made me prick up my ears. Sure enough, the night was suddenly rent. A falsetto rang out at top voice, again precipitating me to my feet. Before anyone could speak it gave out a tune. A man was 'piercing' (leading a chorus) with the word *TSHO-O-O TSHO-LOZA!*' in deliberate ¾ time, a melody on a dominant note, median, dominant, and key note, a ground bass of harmonies being hummed under it by the other men – the opening strain of a road-menders' ditty or work-song, a popular 'train song' of which there is a whole repertoire based on the theme of railway travel. It imitated the sound of a steam engine pulling out of a station: '*SU-KA!*' and as it gathers speed and settled into a regular rhythm, the voices combine in four parts accompanied by tremendous thumps of feet stressing the beat: '*STIMela si phum' eRHODe-zhIYA!*' I knew the song, one about the train from Rhodesia to the Cape, and felt the wave of relief that recognition brings – had not the passer-by at home at Middle-drift said lyrically, 'We are a nation of travellers, else would we have *migrated* to this South Africa of ours?' The idea that the railway conquers Africa's vast distances fires the people's imagination – did it not take our forbears hundreds of years on foot? I was flabbergasted to hear it in the location. The voices blended together exhorting the engine in the vocative, '*WEN' uya baLEka,*' inflections that praised the locomotive's magnificent performance on that two-thousand-mile journey across tawny veld, through *mopani* forest, gradations of plateaux, karoo, mountains, valleys, until the coast is reached. The choir rendered it in that most mellow noise that only male voices can produce, music depicting scenes that I was home-sick for when abroad; rhythm, gaiety, sunshine. It stirred in me all kinds of emotions aroused by South Africa's natural beauty, and, still standing, knife and fork in hand, I begged my aunt for permission to go and watch the unexpected cause of it. Only then did I realize that my relations and their friends had stopped eating and were watching my reactions with amusement. When my aunt waved a hand and gave me leave, they joined in her gentle laughter. '*Kaloku* this person of ours is excited by Jo'burg,' she said. 'Accompany her, girls, and explain what is taking place out there. Though do not stay too long.' But we missed some of the talk at dinner as a result and our food grew cold.

The passage was dark but when I opened the door, all outside was bathed in moonlight. It softened the skimpy lines of the Separatist Church spire of zinc, of the ugly little hall beside it, and of the shacks. We gazed on a party of working men shuffling rhythmically in the potholed streets; they looked like figures in a painting, the colours muted, silver greys on velvety browns. They wore the proletarian trousers of drab khaki that are patched dandiacally on thigh and foreleg in contrasting colours, some with the Union Jack. Many had flung blankets or travel rugs round their shirts or jackets, as they would ochred togas across bare shoulders for the night was cold. They concentrated on their singing as if nothing in the world mattered, as if 'all losses restored and sorrows ended', stamping the beat, clapping it with their hands; some, crouching, spun round in private pirouettes of joy. The spectacle of the group losing itself in artistic achievement was deeply moving, one of my most enduring memories.

'You are enchanted?' *Sis*' Tandi murmured, smiling. The song changed, without jarring or effort, the falsetto leader merely announcing above the harmony that he was about to strike up a different one; and accordingly his fellows slid into a chant that was new to me. Ntutu explained, 'They are starting up "*Fikile*, we've arrived," the song which announces that people are waiting and getting impatient, what with the doors being locked and the caretaker nowhere in sight.'

She was right. A baritone detached itself from the music-making and bellowed in Xhosa, 'Hey, men, should we not send someone to *fetch* that bastard messenger and his bastard quarry of a caretaker? Are we to wait all night?'

'I'll go' volunteered several. But one voice cried out in disgust, the singing continuing, 'What a *useless* ** messenger to have sent in the first place, why did we pick that idiot to look for

that other **?' Since the irritated man was a Xhosa, we were
not surprised though we winced, that the filthiest imprecations
he could think of referred to incest, endogamy. There were
Sutho and other voices among them but happily, I at least, was
ignorant of their swear words. The music disintegrated, collapsed in disorder, conflicting shouts, vilification. The rapt
artists who had created beauty changed before our eyes,
became a mob of rowdies. Yet I was still mesmerized, although
my cousin now plucked my arm. The silvery figures started to
lope off in different directions waving arms to adjust togas,
swearing; but some also, irrepressibly, laughing at their own dis-
comfiture and frustration. The movement of the scattering
group was exceedingly pictorial, reminiscent of a seventeenth-
century composition of crowds on a winter night, a Pieter
Breughel. But they were suddenly lit by the headlights of an
approaching motor. The shaft of brightness momentarily
caught individuals in rigid attitudes, eyes white, apprehensive;
and a voice hissed, '*Police*?' upon which they broke and ran.

'Come, let's go in,' *Sis'* Tandi insisted. The motor car passed
and was not the police. The people could be pounced upon and
arrested for standing about waiting to enter their hall. We
turned away, the enchantment over. After the heightened
feelings it had brought, I was deflated. The changes of mood
were trying and I had to adjust myself to the idea of going back
to my food.

Back at table we found the big people serene. The dinner-
party atmosphere had built up and they had become welded
together and paid no attention as we crept into our places.
Listening to their talk I underwent still further sensations. With
us were my aunt's married daughter *Sis'* Nora and her husband.
Hers seemed a more retiring personality than her sisters'. He
was a good deal older, seemed almost to belong to my aunt's
generation so that I hesitated to call him '*Bhuti*', the Afrikaans
complement for the title I was bound to use for my cousin, and
I compromised with a makeshift – the English title 'Mr.' and
his surname. This was more or less in order because I hardly
knew him, having met him only once or twice. His big face had
an expression of the greatest possible kindness. Big Mother and
her other daughters had spoken repeatedly of this quality and

were attached to him. He was a very portly man indeed and very dark. He had run an undertaker's business for as long as I had known of him, though he might, like so many people, have originally been a teacher. He died not long after that meeting. He was a MoSutho, and because I did not speak that language, unlike everyone else present, we fell back on English but inevitably leavened with Xhosa, Afrikaans and SeSutho.

Then there was bright-faced, charming, self-possessed Nurse who called every day. The only other man in the gathering was a quiet, refined neighbour who had worked for something like forty years for the same firm in Johannesburg, watching it grow from a kind of Wild West shack in a dusty horse and wagon town into a huge skyscraper emporium with glass-plated front, tiled storeys. Next to him was his wife, who, as my cousins and I rejoined them, was shaking with amusement at a joke against herself. In our absence, talk had evidently come round to 'Verwoerd and *amaBhulu*.' It seemed that her grand-child, six year old Diliza, had been 'cheeky' to the European Superintendent who ruled the township from the spacious Government residence sited on a strategic edge of the location, and who had descended on their house to inspect a garage that they proposed to erect. The Superintendent was a tall Boer and had bumped his head against the barbed wire fence above the gate, grazed himself and involuntarily cried out, whereupon little Diliza had piped up, 'He bleeds, the Boer, *Lahlatywa*, – serve him right!' and the old lady was murmuring about the shocking manners of even the tiniest tots nowadays. Ntutu and I stole looks at each other but could not laugh for the other old people exclaimed, agreeing concertedly, that 'although it was only a Boer, it was nevertheless a *grown-up*'. The old lady had found herself apologizing to the European, trying to make amends for the child's discourtesy. I giggled, but checked myself for my aunt and big people were not laughing – the upbringing of the young was an important matter, no joke.

Sis' Nora's husband said, 'Doubtless that dunderhead flattered himself that you were paying homage to his whiteness. He would not appreciate that you were worried about the *tsotsim* that arises out of the disrespect for elders that is now rampant among the young.' And they echoed him like a chorus. 'Just so. Rampant.'

I looked from one to the other and became aware that my aunt was alive to my reactions, for our eyes would meet when I studiously avoided those of my age-mate, Ntutu. The big people's points of view, formed during lifetimes or scores of years in the Transvaal, seemed sometimes bizarre even to her tonight; although my ideas also often 'needed refocusing,' as she would say when we were alone. She too looked startled when we heard *Sis*' Nora's husband exclaim with passion, 'Talking of manners I will never forget what the Boers did to their *own* old man, Hertzog, who built them up into the power that they are today. I am talking about the disrespect that they showed to him at their Party Conference. Such a gathering should be a scene of courtesy, dignity, should it not – where young men would honour their political mentors, eh? Yet some younger politicians who have been brought forward in the Party by Hertzog and trained by him despite the party caucus not liking them at all, at all, these men having gained power shouted at Hertzog: "You're no longer necessary, get out, get out!" Yes, *that* – to their political father, as if to a dog. I tell you, I suffered for old Hertzog when I read of it – the young men's treatment of their venerable elder.'

Somehow it had not crossed my mind that Boer *leaders* were human beings subject to personal strains as our own were. One never bracketed them with the warmhearted civilized Afrikaners whom we knew at home at Alice as individuals. But the evening was a big people's occasion and therefore studded with these unexpected thoughts. We listened to fair and just statements about white people, as well as sweeping ones about the characteristics of English or Boer.

'Cowards, first-class cheats!' declared an elderly voice at one point. 'Was not their method of war that of hiding behind a boulder and with a gun pick out the distant foe before he could *see*, let alone prepare to fight back? We Africans fought in the open, like men, not uncircumcised boys. O, those poor English grenadiers in red trousers gleaming on the veld – a gift to the killers-by-stealth in the Boer War!'

'Yes, and what do Boer police do today? Follow their tradition, invade these locations to shoot, arrest, all the time hiding behind the boulder of the unarmed Non-European police-eh?' Again the chorus chanted: 'Hiding; taking pot shots.' 'In concealment.' 'Without the honour that we blacks have.' Ntutu and I looked at each other in spite of ourselves, for we had discussed our propensity to generalize in this way once we indulge in 'race talk'; and she had commented, 'Yet all of us are South Africans but we see each group from a distance, and through lenses that produce distorted types instead of reality. Is it not pitiable?' She had more compassion than I would have had living in similar circumstances on the daily battleground of Johannesburg.

But we had to disengage our private exchange of glances because my cousin's husband turned to me as if suddenly remembering that the dinner was in my honour, also that I was in a special situation not only as one of two worlds because of my marriage, but because I was brought up in 'the Colony'. There, historically, as I knew he was thinking, our views had been liable to waver between attitudes of fellow-feeling for the Boers because they were pastoralists, cattle people; therefore upright, admirable; for was their way of life not like ours despite their being in competition with us? The British on the other hand seemed 'fraudulent'. Their experiments in political expediency made them look to us like 'a nation of improvisers, not straight'. In the northern republics the Boers were an inflexible nation, therefore the Africans they encountered had been in no doubts or uncertainties about their intentions; and initial impact between the races had been softened by no experimental 'buffer states'.

'You should understand, Nontando,' he said, 'here in this Transvaal the Kaffir has always aroused *fear* in the heart of the Boer. *Johannesburg se kaffers*,' dropping into Afrikaans but recovering himself and translating back into English in order to continue. He illustrated with racy anecdotes from his own life as a businessman. When he finished there was the usual hush after a monologue, to let it be absorbed, not expose it to discourtesy by commenting too quickly. Then my aunt said, finishing her pudding and drawing her warm evening shawl round her and eyeing the plates of her guests, 'Do you think

235

there is not going to be a "Mau Mau" one of these days in this South Africa of ours? Are people not declaring, "Let each grab a knobkerrie and fight for his rights?"'

They laughed and her son-in-law answered. In doing so he changed the direction of the conversation by reverting to the stabilizing, tension-reducing tones of cajolery; and for a moment I was almost in doubt as to what he actually believed about the future. He said, '"Fight with knobkerries, sticks, while the enemy lurks behind his boulder?"' And that boulder now is the support that Britain and America give the South African Government at United Nations, isn't it? Ah England, why hast thou forsaken thy Queen Victoria's children?' The big people were laughing heartily now so we too could discreetly join in. The occasion was drawing to a close, therefore the entertainment tone was prescribed whatever it was intended to convey or conceal. They gave a collective sigh as if resigned about the larger issues, contented about the evening's jollity.'"We are dead anyway.' Is that not the people's war cry for these "defying" politics of today? Destruction there will be in the end, but, and this is the point: *amaAfrika wona* will not be destroyed, for are we not indestructible? Listen as we survive,' and my cousin's husband raised a hand to direct attention to the location. We listened. There, life was going on as always. Even I had at last forgotten where we were in listening to the all too human, wild conclusions drawn from particulars about nations, races, ethics, historical events; irrational but comforting.

'Yes, hark, Ntando,' my aunt teased me, smiling, 'For what is it we hear but that *amaAfrika* love life? We are conservatives, we; and cling to custom; but at the same time learn and adapt. No longer do we *cling like a grasshopper to the barbed wire fence on which it is impaled in flight, and remaining static only because dead!*' She looked round for the ironic applause that would greet this, and it came, for she had trotted out the well-known figurative chestnut that illustrates the difference between constructive tenacity on the one hand and sterile ossification on the other. The party broke up to comfortable elderly laughter.

Afterwards in bed I lay searching in my mind for another word to describe the condition of our country, some companion term to my cousin Ntutu's charitable 'pitiable'. Epithets suggested themselves: ominous? 'sick?' tragic? Others seemed still more fitting. But I was tired, the day had been packed with events; I did indeed feel in Johannesburg that one was in a 'boiling-pot'; and gave up the search, turned over to sleep thinking only that South Africa was probably all those things, but also droll, droll – what else, if you thought of its cheeky six-year-old Dilizas?

20

Now that I was about to leave, my aunt began to organize. For me departure seemed almost as fearful as arrival in Johannesburg. She sent her young *aide de camp* in good time to book her favourite taxi; and to post my letter to the airways agent in Fox Street. Satisfying herself beforehand that I wrote 'well in advance', she sent her with messages to relations, friends and well-wishers that I was going. A moment came when she was put off her stroke and blinked; the discovery that I would not need the hamper of provisions one always takes on long South African journeys because of the racial difficulties about using available restaurants or hotels. In trains you may only buy food from the dining-car attendant and have it brought to your compartment, so people prefer to eat their own. On the eve of travel, houses are full of bustle, redolent with the smells of roast chicken; home-made sausages; bread being baked; frying cookies. Bottles of soft drinks clink as they are wedged between cutlery, plates, tumblers wrapped in napkins. 'Fixing the hamper, *umpako*' is one of life's pleasures.

The daily visitors came and went. In the atmosphere they created I felt increasingly at home, gay, scarcely listening now to the location; no doubt developing that sixth sense. And all the time while the daily help cleaned and prepared and errands were being run, my Big Mother 'spoke with me' and reminisced. 'You are my captive audience,' she said wistfully, but smiling. Her voice flowed, a gentle *continuo* like a harpsichord, performing endless variations and turns. I did not mind, for I wanted to hear her account of when she was a fresh young woman living as one of the family in my other grandfather's household; and to hear what went on in his office where she canalized her original yearning to pursue mathematics as a career; and how she watched my father grow from a small boy into a slightly bigger boy in his teens. She would call him '*uyihlo* thy father,' using the elders' term. At other times she would refer to him by his name, *u*Don, which for me played on all kinds of 'received' sensitivities connected with ideas about seniority, hierarchies. The unconscious way in which she seemed to observe the conventions threw into relief that link which is felt to exist between the very old and the very young: the 'world of ancestors' to which the old are about to depart, having worked their way up the social hierarchy; and from which the young have newly come, to be trained upwards in order eventually to re-enter that 'ideal state'; life on earth being, as it were, temporal and therefore arranged so that those 'ancestors, *amawetu*' should approve – a less stuffy aim than it sounds when experts speak of it as ancestor worship. It was on such delicacies of speech that my aunt spun her family reminiscences and created a pattern of the framework to which individuals and families and groups contribute. If they do so badly or well, it is according to how the links join them together. Ideally they should function so as to express the theme of 'interdependence'. The opposite of individualism, caprice.

I knew that her view was representative, but that some shared it only out of habit, their perception dim. I was one of those. She saw the pattern clearly, steadily. I would have been an odd creature had I not felt myself drawn in. Before, I had seen sections of it from other angles; as when my father spoke of *Sis'* Daisy and showed us pictures of her among his family at King William's Town, dressed in those Edwardian clothes that seemed to us so quaint. I had tried to imagine the place she must have filled as 'borrowed' elder sister to a quiverful of sons. My father and his brothers had once had a sister, one of the children who had lived only a few months. The infant death-rate in the family seemed to have been terrific. Only four out of ten children survived to manhood.

'These boys spent much time at their maternal home, of course,' my aunt said, sitting upright among the cushions of her armchair, her hand on the knob of her stout man's walking-stick. We were in the little sitting-room. I could see those country-life chevrons smeared in dark green at the entrance to the house. Reassuring, they were. Shafts of sunlight from the window behind fell on her permanent, tiny, black satin turban and on her shawled shoulders, and on her spectacles and the lines on her dark brown face when she turned her head. Some days I noticed the lines more than usual. I had become more conscious of them, or of their absence, in old people after what my doctor Uncle Rosebery had said; and my aunt did indeed seem frail nowadays; and sometimes forgetful that I must already know some of the things she was telling me. For instance, she emphasized the point about my father and his small brothers being with their maternals, saying, 'That is the custom. And your father, as the first child of the marriage-contract had had to be born at the umbilical home under the eye of his mother's mother.' And told me again that her people lived in the country near Peddie, in the Border, nearly forty miles from King.

'A huge distance in those ox-wagon days. At the speed of twelve miles a day, it took two and a half days to get there. Life in town at King was in any case not suitable for children. For one thing "thy fathers" got up to mischief in the traffic: a complication of buggies, Cape carts, to say nothing of the transport wagons drawn by spans of fourteen, sixteen, even eighteen oxen, wheeling in the town square delivering merchandise; and raising clouds of dust. Traffic seemed teeming in those days,' she said, smiling, 'and your grandmother Ma-Biyashe was eaten up with anxiety when her boys ran out into the street; she would clutch her Victorian skirts and start to run after them, crying, "Oh, my children!" and of course have to give up. Married women must not run, even if skirts do not impede. So MaBiyashe would be forced to send one of the servants. Actually, Nontando, between you and me,' and her voice dropped to a whisper, 'she was *over*-anxious about those country bumpkins of hers. After all, if they *did* run out it was only on the impulse to watch their father on horseback. You see, when men like your grandfather had urgent appointments, they used to ride. Well-kept horses too. He would gallop up that wide and dusty street, a large man, over six feet and a splendid horseman. Played to the gallery; your father takes after him, you know. On a horse Jili senior was the envy of onlookers and his sons swelled with pride for they adored horses, Don especially. You should have seen their delight, cuffing one another and boasting to their gang of black and white cronies: "There goes our father, the *best* rider in the world!"'

She described a happy household, the children playing with neighbours of both races in days when there was no colour bar. But life was not altogether suitable for them there because of my grandfather's work as a writer. 'They had to be restrained,' she said, 'even more than by the fact of its being the lineal home, in which children have to be trained to fear the male parent. They could be free only with their mother's people in the country. And there could roam and come to no harm. Trap small wild animals, rock-rabbits and the like. Shoot pigeons with slings and stones, roast them in the woods. Peddie district was wooded country. And herd cattle, which was very important; be real rural urchins.' I found it difficult to imagine my father in that guise, perhaps like Mawase at Tsolo. I had once suddenly visualized him at another stage, as a baby, because of a story he told us one day when my brother was about two and a half; and like all infants who happened to be in the house, used to be taken after his morning bath wrapped in a cot blanket, to my father in his study to play with. 'I love babies!' he would say. We older children would troop in with the nurse to watch; and he had described his own first recollection of life, an incident when exactly my brother's age. I told the anecdote. It had made us laugh; and my aunt laughed, but I realized it was at the faces I was making. She murmured an untranslatable phrase about my father's infectious mannerisms and added, 'Why, you are even mimicking his mimicry!' I retorted by pointing out how vivid she had made his love of the pastoral life at Peddie, telling me stories that I had not heard before.

'One time he came back from Peddie,' she began, bubbling with a very involved story indeed. Somebody's ox had died of gall-sickness. 'The carcass was skinned and the hide cut up into long strips to be processed into the leather thongs that cattle-keeping people can't do without. Now of course they are bought ready-made but in those days to prepare them was a rural industry, a jolly pastime. The men would all stop whatever they were doing to take part in it, and your father watched. It seems they picked out a tall tree and from one of its branches suspended the strips of hide, first winding the ends round a

huge stone of a certain shape, which they had indented so that
the strips would stay in place. Poor Don stammered more than
ever when he tried to explain these details. He thought Ma-
Biyashe and I were not following, was suspicious and afraid that
we were not paying attention. When she moved to see to some
household matter, her bombazine dress rustling, Don scuttled
behind her clutching it and limping, accusing, "Mama, you're
not *listening!*""

But I interrupted to ask why my father was limping.
'Ah'; my aunt appeared to hesitate about lingering over something to her so insignificant, but chuckled and decided to
'indulge' me after all because the reason would help me to
imagine how my father was treated by his maternals. She said,
'I mentioned it I suppose because suddenly seeing him as he
was on that day. What had happened was that about a week
before he was brought to town a big thorn pierced him in the
heel while running about the forest. *Kaloku* children were all
barefoot. In the country shoes were almost unheard of and there
the boys did not wear them even to Sunday School, whereas in
town they were forced against their wish; they attended the
European Sunday School: higher sartorial standard naturally.
And no colour bar even in church those days . . .' She saw my
look and cut the threatened digression. 'Well, Don confessed
that at the time he concealed the mishap from his grandmother.
When MaBiyashe asks why, he says, wriggling: "I was afraid of
the needle, mama. It is more than painful, it is *dreadful* when
grandmother extracts your thorns with it. She uses a great
darning needle, is for ever operating on Dick with it because he is
always getting thorns." But Don's foot became septic. In the
end his walk betrayed him; evasions became useless; and, he
told his mother, getting excited all over again as if it was happening right there at Alexandra Road: "I tried to hobble
away when grandmother beckoned, crying 'Come' and going
for her needle. But I was *captured*," he cried, "by two pitiless
men, hauled and held down for that merciless operator. And
afterwards she put me *in shoes*, there where everybody stared and
laughed."'' My aunt smiled. 'Anyway from that time, the boys
were at King more or less permanently because they had to go
to school. It was 1896 and they were excited over newspaper

pictures of the Jameson Raid against the Transvaal Boers; your father demanded: "Who *is* this Dr. Leander Starr Jameson who invades people who have done him no harm?" In the Cape everybody sympathized with the Boers, even little boys. The next year was the holocaust of the Great Rinderpest Plague. The boys were *shocked*, Nontando, to see thousands of cattle dying everywhere like flies and being dragged through the town to be buried on the commonage. As for when a messenger galloped from Peddie to report the deaths of *all* the home cattle there, animals they had herded and knew by name, the boys were almost prostrated. Lost their appetites completely. You cannot believe how it affected them. They made their "acquaintance with tragedy". Their only consolation was that the two milking cows that happened to be at the King household – they used to be brought in turns – survived. Your grandfather had had them vaccinated in the nick of time.'

These and other things were told me over days, interrupted by the household routine, and by callers when they dropped in, some old enough to corroborate what she was saying; and being of her generation approved and smiled when she remarked, '*Kaloku* these gaps in the young people's knowledge have to be filled. Also it is good exercise for one's rusty old brain. The more you talk, the more you re-live the incidents that marked the way in which individual characters in the families were developed.' But to me her brain seemed far from rusty; most orderly, methodical. I saw why she had been a mathematician.

Often we would find that time had flown and my cousins were back. Then my aunt would send us on one of her 'errands'. She seemed always to have a plan afoot, even if sometimes only to send to someone who was ill or out of work. Her life was sedentary but seemed filled with 'things to do' which reached out from the house into the terrible location, to households in other townships. Down in the Colony we imagined life was 'all anonymity in Jo'burg'. I was having to revise that notion.

But I would persuade her to pick up again from where she had left off and she would laugh and say, 'You want to hear more of *those* news? Well then, where was I?' I reminded her, about having got to the year of the cattle tragedy. After the preliminary gestures, sighing, clearing her throat, smoothing lips with finger and thumb, she continued, '1897 for instance. Memorable for your father and his brothers for a happier reason, the Queen's Diamond Jubilee. The boys made their first acquaintance with the outside world. It was like this. A colossal picnic was held for the whole town on the outskirts of King. Children were presented with a "Farthing Memento". They came back to MaBiyashe full of the delights – buns had been given out; ginger beer drawn from giant casks. And at the beginning of the feasting their eyes popped because cables were read out, greetings from the British Government in London to leading citizens of the Border; and the boys (they had not been listening), suddenly heard one addressed to "*John Tengo Jabavu*: in his capacity as editor of the *Imvo*", to the effect that Queen Victoria conveyed good wishes to all her African subjects. What a bombshell, to discover that their father was important, not only the best rider in the whole world. They bombarded MaBiyashe with questions: "How did Queen Vitoliya *know* him?" When she explained that it was through his newspaper they were dumbfounded. All *they* knew about that enterprise was to fold it up each week as it came out of the printing press and trot off with other urchins to sell it on street corners. The job earned Don the princely sum of eighteen pence per month, which his mother trained him to divide carefully: deposit twelve pence in The Shilling Savings Bank; use the remainder to pay Church Dues – collections, Sunday School contributions. Otherwise he and his brothers lived mostly for cricket and soccer.'

The next big moment in my father's life, in 1898, was of a sort I did not in the least expect. He turned thirteen and 'Signed The Pledge'. Telling me how it happened, my aunt said, 'One of your other "grandfathers", the composer John Knox Bokwe, was a strong campaigner against Demon Drink.' The dated nonconformisms came to her so naturally that I was not even tempted to smile. 'He was a great friend of Jili senior, what with their being both writers and sharing a passion for music. Bokwe enrolled his friend's son in The Independent Order of True Templars.' This was news to me, although I had seen the order a hundred times; on regional or national occasions when 'Decorations had to be worn' as it were, my father and his friends sported it with solemnity. I could not resist commenting on enrolling a child who could not possibly know what it meant. 'My brother was never made to sign,' I said. But my aunt reminded me how in his case, on becoming perplexed by the world's troubles, he and his band of adolescent friends had elected to be puritans, abstainers from tea and coffee. She was right; I had forgotten. Their resolve had endured. 'Why, were they not for ever coming to this house when at Wits University,' she said, 'and accepting Hot Water only as refreshment? If pressed they sometimes added milk and sugar to it,' she laughed, but turning serious, added, 'It was a big thing to Sign the Pledge. Drink was destroying good people, Ntando, as now. I maintain that father John Knox bestowed a benefit on young Don, who was impressionable, easily led. Perhaps you don't realize.' I certainly had not and was much surprised. 'Oddly enough,' she continued, 'your grandfather thought as you do about this business of an age of reason. Otherwise he might have made your Uncle Dick sign when *he* turned thirteen; but did not; and drink was the end of him as a man.' Big Mother paused. But I was too astonished to speak, not having known this about my Uncle Dick. When I recovered, she was already talking again and I lost my chance, could only speculate on the intense pain that must have prevented anyone in the family from ever mentioning it. She was now saying, 'John Knox Bokwe could not guess that afterwards through his second wife, Don would become related to him by marriage; to your mother.' At this point my aunt went by chance into one of her digressions. These chances made me quite thoughtful at times, wondering what pieces of knowledge one missed because big people happened not to seize them, perhaps too busy pursuing some other thought. I now learnt that my Bokwe 'grandmother' (whose grave I visited with Uncles Cecil and Rosebery) was not related to her. Big Mother had had her own mother, the first wife; who had died when her children were infants. *My* grandmother was *second* Mrs. Makiwane, Aunt Daisy's *step*mother. I nearly fell off my chair. The matter had never been mentioned; never a sign. Only now did I understand how we 'were related' to a family, Dhlamini by clan, who lived near our farm twelve miles from Middledrift, and who had always behaved and been treated by us linguistically and in other ways as if closely connected. I now heard that it was because they were Big Mother's maternals, therefore linked with us through the navel. And saw in that instant where she inherited that tiny mouth; the Dhlaminis had thin lips, hooked noses. When she had repeated the fact, she said, 'Your grandmother, MaBamba, was a true mother; never distinguished even minutely between her children and stepchildren. Hence the dreadfulness after her death, of the situation that was created by the third Mrs. Makiwane, the grandmother whom *you* knew at Tsolo; who nearly disrupted the family after our father died in 1928; disputed Cecil's inheritance as the heir; the wrangles, court-cases . . .'

Again I can only say I was staggered. I remembered that old lady as someone respected, treated with deference by all grown-ups. Not a shred of strife percolated to us children when dispatched to those family pastures. She lived in a homestead along the ridge. And when we were taken to see her, she 'presented a fowl', to the usual ritual observances. I now caught a glimpse below the surface of ceremonious attitudes. When I paid attention I found that Big Mother had set those 'maternal family' events aside and was again talking about my lineal home, continuing to spin threads that were startling as well as reassuring.

'Your grandfather's next step was that Don should learn SeSutho. Your ancestor was a planner, Nontando. Marvellous to look back on it, because Don was not a promising child, you know. Cheerful; but volatile, impetuous, temperamental. Far more complicated than his brothers. The clever one was Dick – Richard Rose Innes, *u*Dick*e*, who was also the handsomest; *beautiful* boy!'

'What, handsomer than my . . .?' But she waved a hand for silence. Quite peremptory with me at times. 'Now the other two, Mac and Wilson: sunny creatures, plodders; content with their lot as younger brothers. See how they plodded and succeeded as newspaper-men without the benefits of foreign travel that your father had. Big people often used to say: "Pity Dick is only second-born; has more personality, brains than your *izibulo*." But our law of primogeniture dictates that the *zibulo*, first-born, be prepared for future position. You know,' she said in wistful parenthesis, 'it is seldom easy to be second-born.' I could not help reflecting how different my life would have been if my sister had lived, I too being only second-born. As if reading my thoughts, my aunt digressed to remind me how she had approved when my parents had 'prepared', sent me abroad, in the shoes that were rightly my late sister's; and reminded me that my loved Aunt Valetta too had been 'moved up into her eldest sister's place', to whom Uncle Cecil was engaged, but who died; upon which her parents offered the younger, as consolation wife. My mind wandered, however; it was unbearable to learn about my frustrated Uncle Dick's sticky end. But on hearing what she said next, I sat up, she said.

'Don had a temper, that was another thing; such a temper; truly vile.'

Was there no end to these revelations? Never in my life had I seen my father angry. I had once seen him leave the room in silence when my mother had become indignant about something – what, I had no idea. I found myself telling my aunt that *I did not believe her*. A pause. Then she answered, firm to the point of severity, 'There you are, dear child. MaBiyashe worked to instil self-control into your father. She used to go down on her knees and pray; which infuriated him the more, naturally, being a child. And when he was sent away first to Basutoland to learn SeSutho as I was about to tell you, and later to England, she prayed God to give her son strength to conquer his many failings. As your father grew older and reached his twenties, when thousands of miles from home – Wales and London – he began to mention incidents in letters home which showed he had controlled that temper. By the time *you*-people appeared, you never saw him angry. Was that not prayer? His mother had *interceded* for him.' She tapped the floor with her stick and was silent for some time, as if her heart was too full to allow her to go on. And I too was silent. It had not occurred to me how different a man my father might have been at phases in his life, or our other big people in the family. It was altogether sobering to discover that those whom you most revere are perhaps necessarily those most wrapped in mystery. It was a greater shock than my recent introduction to the warmth and gentleness of my maternal uncle at Tsolo. What were these failings in my father? Did he still have them? There were so many things I did not know; skeletons in cupboards, as in those of other families and groups around us. My aunt got the better of the emotion the memories had aroused and took up her tale again.

'When he went to Basutoland and "life in foreign parts" and wrote home, your grandfather read the first two or three letters aloud at breakfast. The servants used to stay on in the room after prayers to listen, and you know, they made difficulties sometimes for MaBiyashe, approaching her with the request to "whisper privily" their view that *u*Jili was cruel to send the son of the house to those incestuous *be*Sutho who marry first-cousins together. In the train Don was joined by another little boy also being "dispatched to they knew not where", and both sat glum, fighting back tears, too unhappy even to undo their provisions. Apparently a woman passed along the corridor and looked in at them, then went into their compartment and asked their where-from. It seems that the moment they were exposed to sympathy they broke down, as children do. The woman comforted them, unpacked their hampers saying: "Eat, splendid men of the future. You are being wrenched from home for a great purpose. Strengthen yourselves. Courage!" They obeyed and started munching, still desperate. You could tell that from the inarticulate little note. Until finally this unknown Christian exclaimed: "Goodness, how is one to deal with this?" and announced that she would sing for them, and there and then burst into song; and Don wrote of it and moved us beyond words, saying, "She had a beautiful soprano, almost as beautiful as mama's, and sang at the top of her voice. So we sang too, alto and descant. After she left the train we were not too unhappy any more. We promised to be strong until we arrived here."'

My grandfather sent him to Morija College in Basutoland, then a secondary school. He had often told us at home of its picturesque setting amid mountains and steep valleys, the country described as the Switzerland of South Africa; a place with natural springs, waterfalls, gigantic rocks, winding paths along which its inhabitants rode on sure-footed ponies. My aunt now recounted his first description of the new school.

'Don said, "We are by the village of The Paramount Chief, a big polygamist, *one hundred wives* and *ever* so many children! We hunt wild bees. The teachers are kind and do not beat us. They are missionaries, some are English. But the French and German ones speak SeSutho and people think them marvellous linguists for they preach without interpreters." News was doled out in that piece-meal, boy's fashion,' and she smiled. 'But it was charming to see how so sketchy a letter would please your grandfather.' I myself thought it wonderful that she should remember so clearly. When I commented, saying the facility must be due to her mathematical brain, she did not laugh as I expected but put me in my place by replying, 'No, do not invent complications. Children's first letters are short and to the point. If at all you recollect them you do so vividly. You ought to know that, being yourself a mother.' I was subdued, for it was true.

'Well then,' she went on, 'the Boer War broke out. Down in the Colony people sided with the Boers, especially households like your grandfather's. How times change! We did not then concentrate on the cowardice of the Boers in fighting from a shelter behind rocks. What seemed shocking was the English outnumbering the poor Boers and boasting in the Press that the regiments they could draw on back in England were countless. Their bombast was truly uncivilized. When Don came home for the holidays he had to travel over the battlefields. He had grown and could now relate things in a more orderly manner; and describing what he had seen crossing the Orange Free State, he spoke with real passion. "Farm after farm," he cried, "was wrecked, Boer homesteads looted, burning, going up in smoke. There were heaps of feathers of geese and fowls, and bones or sheep where the greedy English red-jacket soldiers pillaged. They stole, helped themselves to Boers' belongings or broke up what they didn't take, oh, it was senseless, ugly! And at night there were searchlight balloons so that even in the train you were afraid to sleep. In the daytime you were frightened by the boom of the cannons, those Long Toms." Your father was quite a hero for having been in the firing lines and seen the whites at war. And what with your grandfather's political sympathies being with that Boer friend of his, Jan Hendrick Hofmeyer, *onze Jan* as they called him, and his Bond Party, in opposition to the imperialist English Progressive Party, Don was soon strutting about among his playmates criticizing "the Jingoes". *Kaloku* the Progressives kept boasting with that popular tag of the time: *"We don't want to fight . . . but by jingo, if we do . . ."'*

She told how the following holidays the railways became impassable because of the war and my father had to stay in Basutoland with people he had come to know up there. 'Even at that age, Don was a great maker-of-friends,' she said, 'and people were attracted to him. He wrote about adventures he had with these hosts when they took him along on an expedition to the Natal border, riding Basutoland ponies. Romantic but dangerous; an experience for the boy. He didn't say this, of course. It was another of his short and to-the-point letters,' tapping my knee as if to show she had not been cross at my earlier comment. 'His description of the journey is easy to recollect, I assure you. All he wrote,' and she counted the points off on her fingers, was that, one: they rode for five days; two: saw no human habitations in the precipices of the Drakensburg Mountains; three: slept in the open, sheltered by upturned saddles; and lastly and most important – "We absolutely *must* have a Basuto pony at home at King!" We laughed at that. I longed to mutter that she was indeed mathematical, making that mental list. But she reverted to the theme that seemed to be of paramount importance to her: that MaBiyashe's prayers for my father were being answered throughout his absence from home. 'God looked after her son,' she said, 'and her ancestors were watching over him because listen now to what happened the next holidays. It was June. This time Jili decided that war or no war the child had been too long away and must come home. It was a bitter winter. Don and his group of "Colony" schoolfellows had first to travel eighty miles from school to Aliwal North to catch the train. They got a lift on a team of wagons transporting wheat to the rail-head. That took *two weeks*. When your father reached home, I tell you he was lean, Nontando, like one who had been through privations. Think of those boys perched without protection on top of the oiled sailcloth that covered the cargo of grain. They froze up to the hips, biceps stiff every night. Each evening the crews outspanned, built camp-fires to cook their miserable *umpako* of mealie pap. Even so he was seeing things he had not known before. I never forget how full he was, for instance, of a degrading event that took place at these outspans. "While the food was cooking," he said, by now telling stories the way he does nowadays, "one of the drivers got busy digging a small furrow; constructed it with great care to hold a long thin pipe made of earthenware. And charged this pipe with a special tobacco and then bent down to smoke. But it made him cough and *cough*. Terrible. We could not think what it meant at first. It was as if his *lights* and bowels would come out. We were frightened; but the other men just laughed and said: '*Dagga*, hemp.' When he finished smoking he got up absolutely intoxicated. Reeled and staggered. Then *talked* without stopping until he got tired and dropped down anywhere, sometimes in the open in that cold; and slept it off." The horror made a deep impression on him; and I am sure,' she added, laughing, 'he would have "Signed The Pledge" then, but that he had already done so! All the same he and his fellows enjoyed that trip. Perhaps his love of "Spartan training" dates from then, who knows? Anyway after supper they would sit round the camp fire and settle down to discuss and solve problems of the world, starting with ghosts, superstition, witch-craft, and end up with politics and war. He chatted away about these talks and said, "We analysed the characteristics of black and white races, compared the various tribes and came to the conclusion: Zulus are good at war, experts at medical herbs, but not dependable at all, incalculable people, too swift-tempered and reckless. And then the Xhosa"', all these Colony school-boys were Xhosa, "'we are far too fond of this stick-fighting; too haughty and defiant of authority. We'll come to no good because of this. Then we discussed the Basutho. More than any race in the world, they love *arguing*, *arguing*: never stop. But we agreed they are buoyant, humorous; and for that we liked them. On the other hand they are hard-hearted, steely-eyed, calculating even while smiling. Extraordinary for that. And as for that cousin-marriage system of theirs – brothers and sisters being married, oh, it made our flesh creep to think of living like that. But still, I pointed out that for horse-management and knowledge, you can't beat the Basutho. Such equestrians – you should see a MuSutho sit a pony; too splendid!"' Big Mother laughed and digressed. 'You see, your father loved horses from childhood, as I have been telling you. I do believe one of the things that helped this arranged marriage with your mother was when he was told what an expert rider she was. They used to ride and ride, together, Nontando; your mother side-saddle of course in those days. A horse-back romance. Your father blossomed into a suitor under our eyes. And some people began to wonder how he had come safely through his young manhood in England without marrying some English girl since those people too are horse-worshippers. Part of your mother's *Lobola*, bride-wealth, was a first-class saddle thrown in with the cattle.'

Again my eyes opened. Not because of the 'arranged' marriage or the bride-price, which I knew about. I had never thought of my father *as a suitor*, pursuing a young lady. It gave me the strangest sensations to do so now. And forced me to look back on my recent time at Middledrift and admit, at last, what it was that had hurt most. Yet had I not been moved as well, at Tsolo, not only startled, by the romantic looks I had seen exchanged by that other set of parents? The whole thing was inexplicable. Was that why my young cousin and I were in difficulties? Like me, he had probably never thought for an instant of a romance, pursuit, on his father's part. Those things never crossed one's mind. In my eyes, my mother had been my father's companion. Had I not heard them discussing things, sharing triumphs and vicissitudes? They had not shared a bedroom, a fact that had only struck us when young, on visiting the homes of our other parents and seeing that they did differently. But it was explained, and we accepted it immediately for we were aware, that my father worked through much of the night writing; and was up first thing in the morning, long before we children were, for he took classes up at the college before breakfast. And my mother had her numerous responsibilities. I had taken it for granted that that was 'being married', that I would be like that one day. Work would be more important than anything else; and to do it well one would live as my mother did beside a man as handsome, entertaining as my father, whom everyone would admire, almost worship. But things at Middledrift had changed. My father worked, to be sure; but was it 'important', as before? Was it not nowadays more to pass old age? And then those jests about my uncle's 'romance'; and a double bed now in my father's room. The atmosphere was not so much of endeavour as of affections. I was wrestling with these blinding enlightenments, which were cripp'ing, when I realized that my aunt had gone on and I had missed much of what she was saying; 'But finally, Don said something that made your grandfather sit up. I saw his eyes brighten attentively, the thick moustache quiver. The reaction was such that I have never forgotten the remark that provoked it. What your father said was this: "We chaps agreed that black people are jolly good imitators; can do anything that white people can do. But too *lazy*. We dislike hard work or anything sustained. We don't concentrate – that is the only difference between white and black. We shall have to overcome this if we are to get anywhere as people." Your grandfather smiled, rose and left the room. I can see his exit now, that deliberate step and expression on his face as if thinking: "This boy will justify what is being done to mould him, the suffering he has endured and homesickness".'

My father was not sent back to Basutoland. The disrupted travel conditions put an end to that. But apparently his SeSutho was established during the three years at Morija. He was now sent to Lovedale. 'At that time,' my aunt said, 'nobody imagined he would end up master of seven of our languages, Latin besides. He insisted on Xhosa all the time, wallowed in it now that he was not forced to speak a strange tongue.' Her comment was that his development showed how his and other young people's inclinations had been transposed and transformed as a result of the earnest and inflexible purpose of the preceding generation. She felt this very strongly. It was the reason she had told me the story in detail. Through it she could point to men and women in our society who had had similar careers, if not as spectacular as my father's. They were the same breed, in her view, and produced by the same influences, the amalgam of old and new.

'Left to himself,' she said, 'I am certain that Don would have been a horse-breeder, and first-rate at it. Instead he became one of the leading linguists in this country, the inspiration behind the Chairs of Bantu Studies in the universities, pivoted round Bantu languages. And this love of people and customs, it started at Peddie, *I* believe; then was expressed in his *Social Anthropology*. And all of it thanks to the *concentration* he had talked about as a growing boy and later put into his work at Fort Hare on these languages. He advanced their exploration when they had not even been considered, except by a few out-standing early missionaries; and had been despised as a subject for higher studies. On finishing his secondary schooling, your grandfather applied for him to attend the European High School at King, Dale College, walking distance from Alexandra Road. No African had sought this before. Your grandfather was a ratepayer like the fathers of Don's white friends with whom he had always run about and still played cricket and soccer during the holidays. *Kaloku* King was a small town, only eight thousand people. Citizens knew one another and your grand-father was one of its most esteemed. No ethnic group areas acts. *u*Verwoerd was not yet heard of.'

'Must still have been in Rhodesia, with his immigrant parents from Holland,' I said. When she realized that I knew the episode she was about to relate, about my father being re-jected by the European High School on grounds of colour, and the controversy his application had aroused in the press of all four provinces, and my grandfather's sending him to England, she confined herself to describing the heartbreaking parting when his father took him to Cape Town to catch the boat.

'Tengo Jabavu felt deeply the necessity to consign his eldest, once again, to no one knew what; and from which he was not to return for ten years. In which time he had absolutely his own way to make in the world. I now left my journalism to be married, but MaBiyashe, who had become my other true mother, wrote to me about him; while she lived, that is to say. She died within two years of his going but had done her work, laid his foundations. That life in the countryside to which she had sent your father as a child was valid indeed. Now, Ntando, do not make me gloss over this part in your impatience; you people should know these things. That life had the simplicity which has enriched Don's life right through to his old age. You Jili people "sojourn only briefly in this eternity". So say your own clan praises. As it is your father had lived longer than your grandfather; he died at sixty-two; and longer than his younger brothers. God must be thanked for having let him remain and we ought not to be greedy, not to take it for granted.' She paused and looked at me. Her face bore the expression one sometimes sees in elderly people when they become wrapped in thoughts of *amawetu*; not sorrowful but ineffable. She uttered those phrases about her time not being far off that were familiar. I therefore missed the full significance of what she was saying and recalled it only afterwards. At that moment all I wanted was that she should clear up a point raised when talking about my father's mother. I asked, 'Why did you keep saying "poor MaBiyashe", Big Mother?'

She stared at the little glass-fronted book case with the portraits of her husband above it, and was silent for some time; then said, 'No, in many ways it was *not* "poor" MaBiyashe. She was a gay woman, vibrant, beautiful. Dick inherited her looks as I said. She had firm beliefs. Jili was in accord with them. And her life was full of variety because of the kind of people who came to the house of the editor, Liberal politician, leader of voters. A writer was respected in that town of white businessmen, and Tengo Jabavu was "an intellectual", accorded the same place in the community as his friends, these Rose Inneses, and Weirs, and other King William's Town notables. Interesting men and women consulted Jili at home at Alexandra Road as well as at the office. I remember Rudyard Kipling calling, visiting South Africa from overseas. Your grandmother's education was elementary. But she was the kind of woman who rises to circumstances. Ran the household as such a household should be run; and was a support to her husband. Yet, yes: I say "poor MaBiyashe" because on top of all that, it was constant childbirth for her, *constant* childbirth; as Olive Schreiner commented when *she* called, that feminist. Said it to your grandfather's face – imagine! She had discussed my job with me at the office (*kaloku* I "made history"!) then went to meet *u*mam'-*u*MaBiyashe and found her surrounded by small children. Christian husbands were not able, like polygamists, to give their wives the proper three years' rest from intercourse after the birth of a baby. Women increased the family too often. That is the main reason for your succession of grandmothers. They were worn out. Then apart from these everlasting babies, your grandfather was not the easiest man on earth to live with. He seemed to be unaware of his exacting temperament, preoccupied with politics, controversies. His life was one rage of red-hot issues and causes; a fire-eater, that one. And of course, writers are a selfish tribe. This grandfather of yours confirmed what I had secretly observed of my own father. But he was a kind, unselfish man by nature, who instinctively controlled the inclination to be inconsiderate when he wanted to write sermons, pamphlets and so on. But Tengo Jabavu was haughty, not by nature kind. Your clan are noted for those characteristics. The kindness was all on MaBiyashe's side, and it was her son Mac who inherited it. Your grandfather had to pray, and *train* himself to it and did not always succeed. And then, see how he spreads himself as his career goes forward: takes on this other house at Breidbach, "a country retreat where I can get away from the office," he said. But "retreat" for MaBiyashe? Nothing of the kind. All work for her there. The elaborate style of the town house had to be maintained. So, in the manner of women in her position, she died young, before Don was twenty years old over there in England. But she had imparted to him her love of people. She was a true product of those Sakubas at Peddie, genuine people; real. That was what my father noted, and why he and my mother – what you call my "step" – arranged that Florence should marry Don after he came home from overseas. *Kaloku* people say: "Sons who are men are made by mothers".' The sentence tapered off. My aunt seemed lost in remembrance. But I now felt that my father's maternals were an ingredient I knew least about in our section of the social organism, as she called it; whereas she had isolated the others and made me feel glad but also alarmed that I was of their blood. What had I inherited from the Sakuba group?

'Your ancestor on that side, the Reverend James Bashe Sakuba, a Baca clansman, was a convert of English Methodist missionaries. We of course were Presbyterians. But even your Jabavu ancestors were Methodists. However, both sects were energetic to a degree in *living* their religion. At the time, Christianity was a fascinating innovation. For those who took to it, it had to be literally "a way of life" as paganism is. The red ochred man's every act is carried out and *felt*, in reference to the beliefs that are his religion. The Reverend James began each day by conducting five o'clock prayers for his band of followers. Flung himself into holding classes and meetings, Sunday Schools, revival services, Bible study, every kind of devotional. And his wife had enthusiasm to match. MaBiyashe's family had become Christian a generation later than Makiwanes and Jabavus, and were still filled with the idea carried over from paganism, that professed beliefs should be demonstrated at every moment. MaBiyashe inherited that. Your grandfather shared it, used to like the quotation: "In Stoicism every Stoic was a stoic, but in Christendom where is the Christian?" Nevertheless, she was more ardent than he; she the woman, who trained and "made" her sons; copied her father who had "acted out his credo" even in mundane matters. For instance, while ploughing his lands he used to pray over the ploughshares. When he had reaped he would make ritual gifts to strangers from his harvest of maize, beans, peas and so on because the Bible said so; always emphasizing that religion was not a thing apart from what one did or thought. All those aspects of his personality influenced his daughter.'

My aunt tapped the floor with the stick again but otherwise sat motionless.

'For instance at King on fine mornings, when your father was home from Peddie, she used to go for walks to collect faggots of firewood so that her son should accompany her. Normally this was one of the younger servants' jobs. She took Don along the old country road to East London. Sometimes I went with them. She was always overjoyed when he was back, laughed to see him scamper about from bush to bush. *He* was only picking berries and eating them! Then, when she had gathered her wood, she would call him to kneel on the ground beside her and join in a prayer. *u*Jili did the same too sometimes, if back from the office; would take his sons for a "constitutional" as he called it, and pray with them out of doors: "*Al fresco*" he said in his deep voice.'

'Oh heavens,' I let out.

Big Mother turned round, the nearest I had seen her in anger;

'That wholesome outlook embarrasses your generation, you wriggle in your chairs – eh? Because you young people take for granted beliefs that were hard fought for, which you are fortunate to inherit. *"Inenenkaz' enkulu"* you are our generation's scourge *that is the big truth*! For we fell short of the endeavour of our predecessors. One wonders just where this fading away of disciplines will lead to.'

I felt ashamed. She noticed and went on in a rather more conciliatory tone, 'For instance, take this as an example of how things have deteriorated. Youngsters nowadays know hardly any sacred music, whereas we learnt it by rote, were compelled to; and in that way assimilated Scriptural passages until we *understood what they meant*. That was how Don and your other fathers were taught, because MaBiyashe used to declare: "The Bible is so vast a treasure of literature, how can anyone absorb it by merely reading it? Do we not so read this weekly journal of ours here-at-home from cover to cover, articles, even advertisements? Yet do we remember the contents? My children will know the Scriptures effectively only if they learn choral music, the words that go with it until they are in the blood; psalmody, hymnology; anthems; oratorios. Those will reveal the Bible to them". Well, she gave her sons that grounding, brought them up to sing and to know goodness by what she called "feeling it". She was a person with a streak of poetry battling inside with the strict discipline that she imposed on herself. At any rate that was my private assessment of her character; the kind of person who is fired by the idea: "O, *ukuvisisisa: okungacingicingiyo*!" although of course she was not to know that.'

I had never before heard 'sensations rather than thoughts' rendered in our language and was momentarily swept off my feet by the morphology: that use of one verb in its 'extensive form' balanced against another verb in its 'repetitive-reduplicative form'; to say nothing of the balanced penultimate syllabic emphasis on each; it was an electrifying cast of phrase and the essence could not be clearer or more concise in the English original. I gasped. My aunt was full of surprises. How, I wondered, had she reconciled this theme, which must mean a great deal to her else she would not have so vividly expressed it, with the other that had fired the imagination of our forbears

258

when they decided to become Westernized? For had she herself
not told me that they became convinced that 'thought and
action must control emotion and instinct'? Big Mother and her
age-group had passed it on to me and mine, for all that we
failed to live up to it. I began to see what I thought was a
qualitative difference between her and my two new step-
mothers. Could their kind of woman, I wondered, examine
concepts as she did? Were they 'statuesque' by virtue of accepting the framework without questioning? She on the other hand,
seemed to represent a stage farther in the status of women in
the patriarchal society by virtue of the training to which she
had submitted her mind. I longed to cry out: 'Mam'omKhulu
you are a realist, more – an Apollonian!', for I so admired
the way she seemed to have resolved the conflicts that these
assumptions arouse; for although she recognized the rightful
status of the male element in our social fabric, nevertheless her
right hand continually gripped, as it were, the pommel of her
fighting-stick. But I had no chance to say anything for she had
gone on speaking:

'Perhaps what I saw when living in your father's family was
God's Will at work. Your grandmother's approach to life com-
plemented your grandfather's. He was all for applying thought
even to faith and intuitions; always planning, as I have told
you. You-children received an inheritance from the groups who
produced Jili and MaBiyashe, on which you must steadily fix
your sights. It is God's gift, along with His other gift of the
ancestors who watch over you.' She surveyed the framework we
belonged to, and what ideally it should contain; talked about
the linking of the parts which ought to hold it together – for in
her lifetime, had she not seen it bend and sway before the driving force of changing conditions and yet remain firm?

Then what was there for me to say? As usual, since we spoke
in Xhosa, she had expressed her ideas in forms of speech whose
inflexions are difficult to convey in another language; and had
illustrated the pattern, which concerned her most, by isolating
pictures from it that even I could test from my own experience.
Those I had not known about she had seen for herself, and shown
me. Fresh designs were being worked out under her eyes now
that she was old – as in the dilemmas that were hampering the

offspring of people bound to her by the umbilical cord, like myself and my young cousin.

But I noticed that her mention of these particular examples did not now fling me into a morbid state. Perhaps the revelations of emotional maladjustments in preceding generations had helped put matters in perspective. Everything she had been, done, and said, gave me a view I had not had before, of underlying loyalties. And to see through her eyes as well as through those of my father and my uncle and the other people I have mentioned, was to accept society's assumptions and aims.

But to accept and even be glad of your background or to realize it had enriched you is one thing. To act accordingly, another. The end would be symmetrical indeed if I could say that from here on all was plain sailing. But I cannot quite. The human beings in the case were all too human. While emotions continue to tug against the desired pattern, the picture that emerges remains out of focus and awry. I would distort it still more for example by glossing over the fact that it was some time before I 'regulated' that tendency to procrastinate about writing home. The pressures exerted by the framework at its various levels and angles succeeded partly; so that when my father died not long after, at a time when I was in Europe and had not yet revisited South Africa and therefore had not communed with him again, my new mother wrote to me because I had been writing to her. She described how it had happened; and in such a way that I could appropriately 'partake' although far away, in the event which marked his change of status, as we called it. And for that moment could salute what it was in her as 'the Person whom we had been sent' that had enriched his last couple of years.

But in spite of the 'devices that society employs in trying to conquer the difficulties', as the passengers on the rural bus had said, the situation in which my cousin and I found ourselves was not yet resolved. This does not dismay the intermediaries who tried (and are trying) to regulate it through what Big Mother kept calling the 'amalgam of new and traditional processes'. In their view, the factors that are now involved in the condition of all families and groups, not only ours, impose a greater need than in the olden days for 'time to do its work'. On personal levels, hearts are now bewildered by a variety of affections as the result of individualism. The group used not to be divided; its loyalties were hierarchical; 'constancy' was its praise name. Choices and caprices that destroy were not tolerated.

Should one admit personal defeat? Yet what answer can you give, faced by change – by uncertainties? Perhaps the consolation is to contemplate the ideal. What would be opposed to nature would be to give up striving, even if the desired equilibrium is probably unattainable.

Absence, as in my case, does not detach one from scenes that preoccupy my aunt and the big people – those repositories of the aims to which tradition is trimmed. Nor does my distance from the smaller issues, such as contiguity of personalities: those parts of the whole that happened to be 'imperfectly articulated' and thus gave rise to the survey I have written about, of factors that must seem almost too mechanical, seen from the viewpoint of different societies. It would be tempting to plead that 'that overseas life' was an excuse. It cannot be; for is it not a home-of-marriage only, whereas the paternal and lineal is one's real home? Or was, in the Eastern Cape, until it ended, as all things must. I have mentioned the chasms that yawn at your feet even while you rejoice in the framework that produced you. Their influence abides whatever happens. My cousins and I and all those who make up that life pattern share certain denominators: hesitations, prevarications, obduracies, steps forward, steps backwards. One hacks a path out of the wood and considers alternative routes within the systems that now exist. For the moment, all that members of our generation can say to one another is what everyone said when my father and his contemporaries took their leave of us: '*Ndlela ntle, Fare Well*' – and that from the bottom of our hearts.